THE
PACIFIC CREST TRAIL

THE
PACIFIC CREST TRAIL
A HIKER'S COMPANION

KAREN BERGER & DANIEL R. SMITH

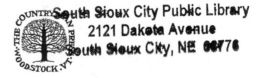
THE COUNTRYMAN PRESS

WOODSTOCK, VERMONT

Library of Congress Cataloging-in-Publication Data
Berger, Karen, 1959–
The Pacific Crest Trail : a hiker's companion / Karen Berger and Daniel R. Smith.
    p.   cm.
Includes index.

1. Hiking—Pacific Crest Trail—Guidebooks. 2. Pacific Crest Trail—Guidebooks. I. Smith, Daniel R. (Daniel Richard) II. Title.
GV199.42.P3 B47 2000
917.9—dc21   00-031476

ISBN-13: 978-0-88150-431-6
ISBN-10: 0-88150-431-9

Maps by Paul Woodward and Steven Hilton,
    © 2000 The Countryman Press
Illustrations by Phyllis Evenden
Interior and cover photographs by Karen Berger and Daniel R. Smith
Interior and cover design by Julie Duquet

Published by The Countryman Press
P.O. Box 748
Woodstock, VT 05091

Distributed by W. W. Norton & Company, Inc.
500 Fifth Avenue
New York, NY 10110

Printed in the United States of America

10 9 8 7 6

Contents

Acknowledgments

Many thanks to Cameron Billeci for letting us rummage through his library and borrow his books for months on end. To Bob Ballou and Joe Sobinovsky at the Pacific Crest Trail Association for answering questions and checking details. To Jeff Commander, for compiling the agencies and permits section. To Helen Whybrow at The Countryman Press for her guidance, support, and good humor. To Don Graydon, whose work on our manuscript reinforced our awe of a copyeditor's skill. To cartographers Paul Woodward and Steven Hilton. To Jennifer Goneau, for pulling all of the pieces together. And, as always, thanks to the library staff at Iona College's Ryan Library for their endless help and patience.

We would also like to acknowledge our debt to the authors of the Wilderness Press guidebooks, *The Pacific Crest Trail* and the *Pacific Crest Trail Data Book*, which we used on our many hikes of the Pacific Crest Trail, and have since used as a reference source. Most of the mileages given in our book are derived from their measurements.

Introduction

Welcome to the Pacific Crest Trail!

The Pacific Crest National Scenic Trail runs 2,650 miles from Mexico to Canada, through desert valleys, atop snowy alpine peaks, along windswept ridges, over lava fields, and into the lush and ancient forests of the Pacific Northwest. As it crosses some of the most spectacular landscapes in California, Oregon, and Washington, the PCT climbs over 57 major mountain passes, plunges into 19 major canyons, and meanders along the shores of more than 1,000 lakes and tarns.

Increasingly popular as a backpacking destination, the PCT offers some of the finest hiking in the United States—indeed, in the world. The High Sierra. Mount Rainier. The North Cascades. Yosemite National Park. Crater Lake. The Columbia River Gorge. Mount Shasta. The Mojave Desert. Mount Hood. These legendary landscapes of the American wilderness are only some of the dramatic, beautiful, and scenic places near and along the trail.

In the words of Clinton Clarke, one of the trail's early visionaries:

In few places in the world—certainly nowhere else in the United States—are found such a varied and priceless collection of sculptured masterpieces of Nature as adorn, strung like pearls, the mountain ranges of Washington, Oregon, and California. The Pacific Crest Trailway is the cord that binds the necklace, each gem encased in a permanent wilderness protected from all mechanization and commercialization.

The Pacific Crest Trail was established as a national scenic trail in 1968, when Congress passed the National Trail Systems Act. It is one of only two national scenic trails to be complete from border to border. Like its more famous sibling, the Appalachian Trail, the PCT offers a hiking experience of mythic proportions, a chance for ordinary people to do something extraordinary—hike from Mexico to Canada through some of the most beautiful terrain in the United States. But it also calls to those who can hike only for a week, or a weekend, or a few hours on a sunny day. Located an easy drive from such metropolitan centers as San Diego, Los Angeles, San Francisco, Sacramento, Portland, and Seattle, the PCT is one of the preeminent recreational opportunities in the West.

TRAIL HISTORY

The idea of long-distance hiking was one of those concepts that seemed to germinate all over the country in the 1920s and 1930s as people like Bob Marshall, Gifford Pinchot, Aldo Leopold, and others began to formulate and implement the ideas that would shape how we use land—and how we preserve it. In 1921, on the East Coast, regional planner Benton MacKaye wrote an article in an architectural magazine proposing a trail to link the peaks of the Appalachian Mountains. A few years later, in the West, a chance conversation between trail enthusiasts Joseph Hazard and Catherine Montgomery brought the idea of a Pacific Crest Trail to the attention of trail managers and hiking club leaders. The idea fell on fertile ground: Construction was already underway on several trails that would ultimately become the backbone of the Pacific Crest Trail—the Cascade Crest Trail (in Washington), the Skyline Trail (in Oregon), and the John Muir Trail (in California).

But it wasn't until the 1930s, when Clinton Clarke, a hiker, Boy Scout leader, and chairman of the Mountain League of L.A., got hold of the idea, that work seriously began on a trail that would link Mexico with Canada.

You can't fault early PCT pioneers for thinking small: Clarke's original idea was for the PCT to have a 10-mile-wide wilderness corridor for its entire length. The 10-mile-wide corridor, of course, proved to be far too ambitious and impractical, not to mention prohibitively expensive. But the idea of a PCT took hold, and in 1932, Clinton Clarke and his younger assistant and colleague, Warren Rogers, formed the Pacific Crest Trail System Conference. In the following years, key elements of the system were completed, including the John Muir Trail, Oregon's Skyline Trail, and Washington's Cascade Crest Trail. California Conservation Corps workers put in connector trails, and in the summers of 1935–1948, Clarke organized a team of YMCA hikers who, in relay style, walked every mile of the trail from Mexico to Canada.

Although the trail could be—and had been—hiked in its entirety, the PCT in many places existed in primitive conditions, followed paved roads, crossed private property with the informal (and revokable) permission of landowners. Much more work needed to be done to secure a permanent, high-quality route. But interest in the trail waned with the onset of World War II. It wasn't until the 1960s that momentum began to build. Warren Rogers, who had been keeper of the flame for almost 30 years, continued to lobby on behalf of the best routing possible for the border-to-border foot and bridle path.

Finally, in 1968, with the passage of the National Trails Systems Act, the Appalachian Trail and the Pacific Crest Trail were designated as the first two designated national scenic trails. Nationwide, there was a new surge of interest in hiking in the late 1960s and in the 1970s. Interest in the PCT also grew as the first border-to-border hikers announced completion of their journeys. Relocations of the route from roads to trails were completed, and negotiations with landowners gave the trail a permanent right-of-way when it crossed private property. The trail was officially considered completed in 1993, when the last section of trail found a home in the Tejon Pass area of southern California. A golden spike in Soledad Canyon marks completion of the nation's longest continuous footpath.

THE PACIFIC CREST TRAIL ASSOCIATION

Today, the Pacific Crest Trail Association is the organization that works to protect and manage the trail, coordinate the efforts of hundreds of volunteers, respond to questions from the public, and advocate for greater protection of the trail where it is threatened by development and commercial activity. We strongly recommend joining the association. In return, you'll benefit from the following services—in addition to knowing that you've helped to support the organization that keeps the footway open.

The Pacific Crest Trail Association:

- Arranges permits for long-distance hikers and thru-hikers, which eliminates the need to contact many national forests and parks individually.
- Works with Forest Service, Park Service, and other land managers regarding trail-related environmental concerns.
- Runs a toll-free hot line giving current trail condition reports (1-888-PCTRAIL).
- Publishes a bimonthly magazine.
- Organizes an annual trail festival, Crest Fest.
- Coordinates the efforts of volunteers.
- Sells trail-related resources such as books and videos.
- Maintains a web site (www.pcta.org).

Membership supports protection and maintenance of the trail. For more information: Pacific Crest Trail Association, 5324 Elkhorn Boulevard, #256, Sacramento, CA 95842; 1-888-PCTRAIL; www.pcta.org.

ABOUT THIS BOOK

Dan hiked the entire PCT in sections from 1984 to 1986. Our joint introduction to the PCT took place on our honeymoon in 1987, when we completed a 200-mile hike in the High Sierra. Since then we have returned to the PCT many times, and we thru-hiked it in 1997. All told, on trips ranging from our 200-mile honeymoon to our 2,658-mile thru-hike, we have together logged more than 12,000 miles on the PCT.

Why do we keep coming back? For the same reason we wanted to write this book: to explore and learn about the many wonders of this endlessly challenging, interesting, and absorbing national resource.

This book is not intended to be a substitute for maps and guidebooks, and it does not give step-by-step trail directions. That information is already available in Wilderness Press's two-volume set, *The Pacific Crest Trail (Volume 1: California,* and *Volume 2: Oregon & Washington).* If you intend to hike any section of the PCT, these guidebooks, which contain adequate maps and detailed step-by-step instructions, are highly recommended. We also recommend that you acquire the U.S. Forest Service (or, in a few cases, the National Park Service) maps for each area in which you plan to hike. These maps will identify more trailheads than we can include and will give you bail-out routes (in case of accident, inclement weather, or impassable snow conditions).

What this book does provide is information not readily available in other sources. While hiking, we became convinced that there was a need for a book that could act as a hiker's companion to the PCT. As we walked along, we wanted to read a book that went beyond the details of where to turn left or right at a trail junction. We wanted a book that would help us to understand what we were seeing as we passed through the land. We were looking for interpretive information about local history, environmental issues, animals, and plants—the things we had come to see. Our interest led to personal research, which led to excitement over what we had learned and the desire to share it. To that end, we offer a book that we hope will act as an introduction and a companion as you make your own forays through the variety of ecosystems and landscapes that make up the PCT.

We envision this book as the well-informed companion or trip leader who can give the information you need to go for a hike of any length on the PCT. Each chapter describes a trail segment of between 75 and 220 miles, with most of the segments averaging about 150 miles. Each chapter begins with a few introductory remarks describing the general character of the terrain.

THE ROUTE

Following the introductory remarks is a summary description under the heading "The Route," designed to help you decide whether that section of trail is one you might like to hike. For those readers who don't have time or inclination to do a 150-mile hike, we recommend some shorter hikes within each chapter. We've also included descriptive material to help you choose the particular sections of trail that would interest you. Woven into the text, and summarized at the end of each chapter, is information about seasonal considerations and gear recommendations. We also include information about road crossings and trailheads, resupply stations, agencies, and permits. Please note that many of the national forests, wildernesses, and parks along the PCT require permits, especially for overnight camping.

What You'll See

After the route description, interpretive information is contained under the heading "What You'll See." This section includes both human and natural history. We selectively examine some of the great variety of species and ecological communities along the PCT. We introduce the early explorers and settlers and cover some of the environmental issues that have affected the area through which the trail passes. And we pay special attention to how some of the trail's residents, from cacti to lichens to bears to rattlesnakes, have adapted to the dramatically varied conditions along the trail—conditions to which the hiker must also adapt.

No book (and no two authors) can answer every question about every plant and animal and historic site along a trail that is nearly 2,700 miles long. We cheerfully admit that many of our decisions to include some nugget of information were arbitrarily based on how fascinating we found it. But we have done our best to consider not only our interests, but yours—and to write about those plants, animals, sites, and issues most likely to shape your experience and pique your curiosity.

A note on the organization of interpretive information: Some animals, plants, and geological formations occur frequently along the trail. Examples include rattlesnakes, bears, and chaparral, each of which is encountered in many of the trail segments. Rather than repeat ourselves, we include information about these subjects either where they first appear, where they are most prevalent, or where they seem to fit the best. Thus we discuss rattlesnakes when they are first seen (chapter 1), but bears where they are most likely to be encountered (the High Sierra). And although chaparral is found throughout southern California, it is not discussed in detail until we reach Cajon Pass (chapter 3) and wander through a chaparral garden where each species is identified. The table of contents, index, and cross-references will help you find what you're looking for.

HIKING INFORMATION

Each chapter concludes with a section entitled "Hiking Information," which covers practical material, including seasonal information, gear tips, thru-hikers' concerns, best short hikes, trailheads, and resupplies. A list of agencies and permit information is included at the back of the book in an appendix.

Throughout the text, we make reference to thru-hikers, section hikers, long-distance hikers, short-distance hikers, and day hikers. The reason for this isn't to stick people in categories, but rather to steer you to information that will best meet your needs.

Most thru-hikers are attempting a single season, one-direction, border-to-border hike of the entire trail. That puts them smack in the middle of some situations other hikers would quite sensibly avoid—like the Sierra snowmelt (for northbounders) and the North Cascades snowmelt (for south-bounders). To deal with these conditions, thru-hikers have special gear needs. They also require more information about resupply options.

Some of the information found in the thru-hikers' corner will be valuable to section hikers (who are attempting to hike the entire trail over a period of several years) and long-distance hikers (who are traveling a distance that requires them to resupply, but not necessarily during the typical thru-hiking "season").

Short-distance hikers—by far the majority of hikers—are those whose backpacking trips don't require them to resupply. They may live locally, or they may be out-of-staters using vacation time to hike one of the PCT's many scenic highlights. Because they are not trying to hike the entire PCT, we give some suggestions for outstanding hikes. We also suggest which sections to skip.

Finally, day hikers have their own questions regarding which sections of trail are accessible by vehicle, and of these, which are recommended.

The mileages given are based on those in the *Pacific Crest Trail Data Book* (published by the Pacific Crest Trail Association), and those mileages in turn are derived from the guidebooks *The Pacific Crest Trail, Volumes 1 and 2* (Wilderness Press). Although some of these mileages are out of date (pending the much-needed revision of the Oregon-Washington volume), we decided to use them in order to make life easier for readers using those definitive sources for planning.

One final note pertains to the compass directions used in this book: As any hiker who has ever trod a trail well knows, footpaths do not run in a straight line. Northbound hikers on the PCT even occasionally find themselves going in a southerly direction as the trail meanders and swings and switchbacks. The straight-line distance between Mexico and Canada is only a little more than 1,000 miles; the PCT is two and a half times as long. In this book, we follow the guidebook convention of referring to directions as if the trail truly did run in a straight line, from south to north. So when a northbound hiker arrives at a road, we assume that the trail is indeed lying on a north-south line, and we would say that the road to the right leads east—even if the true compass bearing is something entirely different. Using *east* and *west* instead of *right* and *left* eliminates confusion among northbounders and southbounders. Also, simplifying the directions by using the trail as a reference, instead of the compass, eliminates the need to pull out a compass and a map each time there is a road or a junction.

At the back of this book is an extensive bibliography of sources on the PCT and its environs. Information about the trail includes several narratives about PCT treks, including Cindy Ross's classic *Journey on the Crest* (The Mountaineers, 1987) and our own *Along the Pacific Crest Trail* (Westcliffe, 1998), written in collaboration with Washington photographer and PCT hiker Bart Smith.

HIKING ON THE PACIFIC CREST TRAIL

This is not a backpacking primer. Many excellent how-to texts are available, and we recommend some in the bibliography. In addition, each chapter has specific information on gear and other considerations that pertain to the conditions and terrain you're likely to encounter.

However, a few introductory words of advice are in order:

- Before you set out, be sure that you have the right gear for the right season and that you have up-to-date information about weather, trail conditions, and terrain—and the skills and equipment to meet them. The Pacific Crest Trail ranges in elevation from near sea level to above 13,000 feet. Conditions, therefore, range from the broiling hot deserts of southern California's valleys to the frigid nighttime temperatures of the High Sierra to the misty rain-drenched forests of the Pacific Northwest.

- Always carry the 10 essentials:
  Map and compass
  Extra clothing
  Raingear
  Firestarter and matches
  Sunglasses and sunscreen
  Extra food
  Water and a way to purify it
  Army knife
  First-aid kit
  Flashlight
- Do not rely on cell phones for emergencies: In many areas, the trail is too remote for cell phones to work.
- Always tell someone where you will be hiking and on which route, and when you expect to be back.

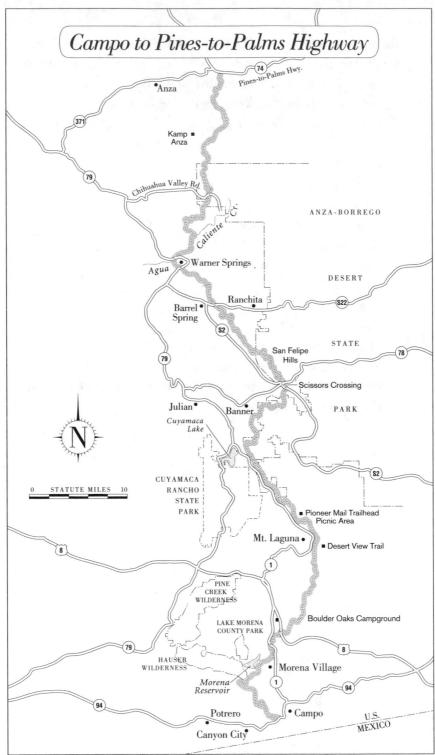

Campo to Pines-to-Palms Highway

74

Pines-to-Palms Hwy.

•Anza

371

Kamp ■
Anza

79

Chihuahua Valley Rd.

Caliente Cr.

ANZA-BORREGO

Agua •Warner Springs

DESERT

Ranchita
•

S22

Barrel • •
Spring

S2

San Felipe
Hills

STATE

78

Scissors Crossing

Julian •   •Banner

PARK

Cuyamaca
Lake

S2

CUYAMACA
RANCHO
STATE
PARK

■ Pioneer Mail Trailhead
Picnic Area

Mt. Laguna •   ■ Desert View Trail

8

1

PINE
CREEK
WILDERNESS

LAKE MORENA
COUNTY PARK

■ Boulder Oaks Campground

79

8

HAUSER
WILDERNESS

79

Morena Village
•

1

94

Morena
Reservoir

94

•Potrero   • Campo

U.S.
MEXICO

Canyon City•

N

0   STATUTE MILES   10

Paul Woodward, © 2000 The Countryman Press

1

Campo to Pines-to-Palms Highway

153.7 miles

The border between the United States and Mexico runs through parched drylands and desert scrub for 2,000 miles along the southern borders of Texas, New Mexico, Arizona, and California. Some 50 miles east of San Diego, the monotony of chaparral-covered hillsides and dry dun earth is momentarily broken by a small wooden monument that announces the beginning of the Pacific Crest Trail. If you turn onto the trail, and if you walk steadily for the next five months, you will reach another marker along a clear-cut swath that marks the U.S.-Canadian border and the trail's northern terminus in Manning Provincial Park, British Columbia.

It is hard to imagine one trail spanning two more different environments. The southern terminus is all big empty space and sagebrush scrub. At the northern terminus, the lush Cascadian forest whispers its windsong to the accompanying babble of a snow-fed stream. But it is appropriate that these two similar terminus monuments are found in such different places: Diversity is one of the defining characteristics of the Pacific Crest Trail. The PCT ranges in elevation from near sea level at the Columbia River Gorge to above 13,000 feet in the Sierra Nevada. On its way it passes through low desert and alpine tundra, sagebrush scrub and old growth forest, mountain meadow and grassland savanna. Hikers who walk the entire trail will have hiked through six of North America's seven eco-zones and seen a variety of wildlife, ecosystems, and historical sites found on no other trail in America.

The monuments, too, are well-chosen—simple, like a walking path; unobtrusive, like a good hiker; hardy, like the volunteers who make the

Border monument near Campo

trail possible in the first place. Trail managers chose a simple design that would blend in with the environment, avoid attracting the attention of vandals wielding shotguns, and survive without constant maintenance in both the desiccating heat of southern California and the soggy winters of the North Cascades. One nice touch: Built intoboth monuments is a little niche for a notebook where hikers record their thoughts, whether their destination is but a day's hike down the trail or the other end of the trail in Canada or Mexico—by current calculations, a distance of 2,650 miles. (As a result of trail relocations, the distance inscribed into the monuments is already out of date. Also note that if you're going all the way, your journey will be 8 miles longer, because from the monument on the Canadian border it's 8 miles by trail to the nearest road.)

THE ROUTE

The first 40 miles of the PCT, from the border monument (elevation 2,915 feet) to the small settlement of Mount Laguna (elevation 5,980 feet), offer a pretty good idea of what much of southern California's 650 miles have to offer. The landscape is dominated by hardy, ubiquitous chaparral, a community of drought-tolerant plants that cover the southern California hillsides like a 10-foot-thick blanket. Like the Appalachian Trail's "long green tunnel" of temperate forest canopy, the PCT's chaparral is a constant companion in southern California. With the exception of the crests of the high ridges and the troughs of the lowest desert valleys, chaparral is found almost continuously from the Mexican border to the High Sierra. North of the High Sierra, it reappears like a trusty old friend whenever the trail drops into low and dry country.

This 40-mile stretch also introduces another hallmark of the PCT: multi-thousand-foot climbs that switchback for many miles, ascending only a couple of hundred feet per mile, but always, relentlessly, ascending. The footway is gentle and well-graded, but in hot weather, the gains and losses in elevation can seem endless, especially to those whose muscles are still city-soft. Neither steep nor difficult, these climbs are merely—sometimes memorably—long.

But what has the most immediate and salient effect is the trail's habit of meandering for many miles without passing a reliable source of water. From the border, it is 20 miles to the first permanent water, at Lake Morena County Park. This means that unless you have reliable current information confirming the presence of water in the two seasonal sources

along the trail, you must be prepared to carry enough water for 20 miles. For most people, a 20-mile hike will include an overnight stop.

Warning: The combination of long climbs, unexpected heat, and the distance between water sources can be difficult. More than one prospective thru-hiker has dropped off the trail at Mount Laguna, defeated by sore muscles, heat, dehydration, blisters, and bugs. For some hikers these first 40 miles teach a harsh but necessary lesson: Never underestimate the power of the southern California sun.

But the sun isn't the only   *Getting water near Pioneer Mail Trailhead*

challenge in southern California. In the Laguna Mountains, a mere 40 miles from the sun-drenched Mexican border, early-season hikers may well be mired in snow. Here, elevations rise above 6,000 feet, snow sometimes lingers well into May, and even in late spring, nighttime temperatures can dip well below freezing. If you're continuing on, you'll want to stop at Mount Laguna for refreshments and to resupply. The small community-store-restaurant-post-office is located 0.4 miles from the trail on Sunrise Highway.

The walk along the crest of the Lagunas offers a stunning view into the Anza-Borrego Desert, a vertical mile below. You will be glad to know that the trail doesn't go straight through the middle of this dry, dusty, dun-colored tangle of highly eroded badlands, steep canyons, and blazing heat—but it does skirt its edges. Leaving the Lagunas, the PCT descends, if not into the inferno, then close enough to feel its breath. The trail passes through several stretches of true desert, including two waterless segments.

The first of these begins at Pioneer Mail Trailhead Picnic Area, where a trough of water—marked FOR HORSES ONLY, but which you might be

Anza-Borrego Desert from Mount Laguna

thankful to drink after filtering—is kept full during the late spring and summer. The trail winds its way along the side of Granite Mountain, where you can look down into canyons that still contain the remains of old gold mines—and sometimes water (an essential ingredient for mining gold). Finally, 25 miles after leaving the picnic area, the trail reaches water at often-polluted San Felipe Creek at Scissors Crossing at California Highway 78. (*Note:* This creek can be dry by late spring or early summer.

Claret cup cactus

Other options: About 5 miles east on Highway 78 is a store; about 1 mile west on 78 is a marsh that usually has water through spring.)

North of San Felipe Creek, the trail heads uphill into the San Felipe Hills for a 24-mile waterless stretch. The decision to put the route here was hotly debated among trail managers, hikers, landowners, and government agencies. Trail managers originally proposed a route through the cooler Volcan Mountains on the western side of the San Felipe Valley. Not much rain falls in any part of this region, and the little precipitation that does fall lands across the valley on the western side. From dun and dusty cactus-covered Grapevine Mountain, the Volcan Mountains look positively Amazonian. Unfortunately for thirsty hikers, a route through the Volcan Mountains was successfully opposed by local landowners. This waterless stretch ends at Barrel Spring.

Continuing north, the trail passes through an unusual arid grassland, looking as wild and wide-open as the African savanna. A carpet of gently waving brown grasses covers rolling hills, dotted with clumps of rock from which you might imagine a pride of lions appearing at any moment. In years of high vegetation growth and poor trail maintenance, the footway can be difficult to see, but it is marked by posts and usually not difficult to navigate.

Shortly after, the trail arrives at the small community of Warner Springs, which has a resort, a restaurant, and—most importantly, if you're continuing on and needing to resupply—a post office. North of Warner Springs, the trail again climbs, and you again experience the environmental and climate changes that accompany changes in elevation. The PCT continues to skirt the border of the Anza-Borrego Desert, but as it climbs, the grasses give way to chaparral interspersed with a southern oak woodland that provides some shade—even if it's not always cool. At the higher elevations, you'll walk through forests of Coulter pines. Views of the surrounding area extend north to San Jacinto and east to the Salton Sea.

This section ends at the Pines-to-Palms Highway (Highway 74) near the town of Anza.

WHAT YOU'LL SEE

Border Region

Technically the border region is not desert, although after that first 20-mile waterless stretch, you may well come to the conclusion that the difference between arid lands and desert is merely academic. (For the academically minded, the traditionally accepted definition of desert is a land that receives nine or fewer inches of annual precipitation. Most ecologists consider additional factors, such as the rate of evaporation and the types of vegetation.) For its first 40 or so miles, the PCT passes through a fairly

San Felipe Hills from the ridge above Cottonwood Canyon

homogeneous chaparral and oak ecosystem of drought-tolerant plants and animals. The region was for centuries home to the Digueño Indians, who migrated between the cool uplands, where they lived in summer, to these warmer lowlands, which were their winter home. As barren and hostile as this land looks to unacclimated hikers, it provided food and even water to the indigenous peoples, who used wooden sticks to dig shallow wells. You'll see their food supply in abundance: cacti, yucca root, and—in autumn—acorns.

There is a store and a small railroad museum at Campo, the town just 0.3 mile from the border monument.

Border Patrol

PCT hikers are asked to check in at the Immigration and Naturalization Service office in Campo. You need not oblige, but if you don't, you may find yourself being buzzed by INS helicopters checking out activity on the trail. In recent years, increased enforcement of immigration laws in the San Diego area has pushed would-be immigrants to try to cross the remote drylands around Campo. Inevitably the trail has been discovered as a convenient route of travel; as evidence you'll see discarded food containers labeled in Spanish.

Between Campo and Interstate 8 (which crosses the PCT about 30 miles from the Mexican border) many PCT hikers encounter illegal aliens. Local residents describe encounters with illegal aliens throughout the border area from Campo to Mount Laguna. There have been rare incidents of theft, usually of water and food. For this reason, hikers are advised not to camp right at the border, and to avoid the Hauser Creek area, 16 miles north of Campo. Hauser Creek would be a logical first-day destination because it is a reasonable distance from the border and has the only significant seasonal water source in the trail's first 20 miles. But the combination of water and a nearby road makes it a magnet for illegal immigrants, too. It's safer to camp out of sight in the bush on Hauser Mountain or, if you are able, to go all the way to Lake Morena in one day.

Laguna Mountains: Rain Catchers and Shadow Makers

Nowhere is the PCT's variety of elevations and ecosystems better demonstrated than in southern California, where elevations range from 1,200 feet to more than 9,000 feet. These swings in elevation have a profound effect on the environment and ecology of the areas the trail traverses—and especially upon temperature and water supply.

After the trail's dry and dusty start, it seems almost unbelievable that a mere 20 miles past Lake Morena County Park, the trail can be snow-covered until well into May when it climbs into the Laguna Mountains. (*Laguna* is Spanish for *lake;* there are two small ponds on the summit of the range.)

The effect of elevation on environment follows a simple equation. Going 1,000 feet uphill is the ecological equivalent of going 170 miles north. Another figure: For every 1,000 feet you climb, the temperature—depending on prevailing winds and precipitation—drops between 3 and 5.5 degrees. All of which explains why the 6,000-foot Laguna Mountains can feel like a refrigerator while the Hauser Creek area (which, at 2,400 feet, has thus far been the trail's lowest point) can feel more like an oven. The 3,600-foot difference in elevation is the ecological equivalent of going about 600 miles north. In other words, climbing from Hauser Creek to the crest of the Laguna Mountains has the same ecological effect as walking north (assuming you were to stay at the same elevation and walk in a straight line) nearly to Oregon.

These differences create different ecological zones. In North America, there are seven eco-zones: tropical, lower Sonoran, upper Sonoran, transition, Canadian, Hudsonian, and arctic-alpine. Each zone can support a variety of plants and animals, depending on factors such as moisture, evaporation, soil content, and climate. These zones generally correspond to latitude, but they also correspond to elevation. The PCT goes through six of these seven zones—all except the tropical. As you proceed farther and farther north, you'll notice that each zone occurs at a lower elevation.

Hikers usually think of tree line as a place too cold and high to support trees—and it is. But in hot, arid lands, there is another tree

EVENDEN '00

Ponderosa Pine

line, *below* which most trees cannot grow because of heat and lack of moisture. Until this point, the PCT has been entirely below this lower tree line. But just before Mount Laguna, the PCT reaches elevations of nearly 6,000 feet and enters the transition zone, which occupies the middle ground between the chaparral and the higher boreal, or northern, zones. The transition zone is

Jeffrey Pine

cooled by the shade of live and deciduous oaks, incense cedars, yellow and sugar pines, and, perhaps most notably, by the sky-spearing Jeffrey pines. Like ponderosa pines, the bark of Jeffrey pines smells sweet, like butterscotch pudding. You can tell the two species apart by looking at the bark and the cones: The bark of the Jeffrey pine is redder; its cones are larger and less prickly. Also, you're more likely to find Jeffrey pines on the eastern side of California's mountains.

Higher also means wetter. Lower temperatures at higher elevations force air to cool; the resulting cold air forces moisture to condense and precipitate. All mountains are to some extent rain catchers, but California's mountains are especially dramatic examples for two reasons. First, the prevailing weather pattern moves moisture-laden oceanic air from the Pacific Ocean eastward to the mountains. And second, many of California's ranges have great differences in elevation (and thus temperature) between base and summit. The San Jacintos, San Bernardinos, and San Gabriels (all on southern California's PCT) reach elevations in excess of 9,000 feet; the high peaks of the Sierra Nevada top 14,000 feet. At 6,000 feet, the Lagunas are not as high as the ranges to the north, but they are high enough to snatch the ocean-moistened water out of the air and cast a rain shadow to the east.

Much of the precipitation falls as snow, and snow accumulations vary drastically from year to year. Depending on the depth of the winter snowfall and the speed of the spring thaw, you can expect it to linger until April in most years. Even in May, nighttime temperatures frequently drop below freezing, and late-season storms can fly in with little warning. Don't under-

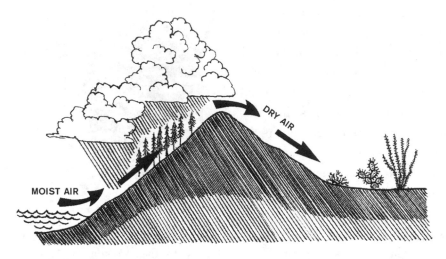

Rain-shadow effect

estimate the danger: Each year, unprepared illegal immigrants are found dead of hypothermia in this region.

Along the crest of the Laguna Mountains, you can see firsthand how the rain-shadow effect of a mountain range changes microclimates for miles around. On the eastern side, any rain that does fall passes quickly through the poor soil, which is composed mostly of fast-draining rock, sand, and gravel. (Good soil requires humus, made from decomposed vegetation. Rotting, of course, requires water and organic matter. In desiccating climates like this one, dead plants don't rot; they shrivel and dry.) Without soil to slow down the flow of water, plants don't have much chance to capture water around their roots. To compound the problem, the rushing water erodes the slopes and carries away the small amount of organic matter that does manage to accumulate. The only plants that manage to survive must be highly drought tolerant, like cactus and yucca. But on the western side, forests flourish. Just past the turnoff for Mount Laguna, the view opens to the west and reveals a canopy of oaks and pines. You don't need a compass to figure out which way is the well-watered west and which way is the rain-shadowed east.

Cuyamaca Rancho State Park

The trail only enters this state park briefly. If you're out of water, you can detour to the park's reservoir (located 1.7 miles from the trail). Parchedthroated hikers might note the irony of the park's name, which derives from the language of the Kumeya'ay people: *Ah-ha-Kwe-ah-mac,* meaning *the place where it rains.* And indeed this region—north and west of the Lagunas—is not rain-shadowed by the mountains.

If you have time for a side trip, the park boasts some of California's largest canyon live oaks and unusually rich (for dry southern California) coniferous forests of incense cedar, white fir, and sugar, ponderosa, Coulter, and Jeffrey pine. Along the riparian corridors are found willow, alder, and sycamore. This wide variety of plants supports an equally wide variety of animal life, including mountain lions, bobcats, badgers, and foxes, as well as a large population of birds including some—like gulls, ducks, and the occasional disoriented pelican—that are more usually seen along the coast. Thirteen thousand of the park's 25,000 acres are classified as wilderness.

A hundred years ago, you would have heard different sounds than the calling of coyotes and the squawking of the sporadic lost waterfowl. Instead, the air would have been filled with the sounds of machinery clanking, digging, and washing. The now defunct town of Cuyamaca was the center of a gold rush in this area. The town grew up around the Stonewall Mine, which was the most extensively developed mine in the region, employing about 200 men. A notable nearby toponym makes reference to the thirst for gold that lured dreamers into the slapdash mining camps and inhospitable canyons. Oriflamme—or *burning gold*—Mountain owes its name to nocturnal sightings of golden flames on the mountain's flanks. Geologists believe that the sparks are caused when wind-driven grains of hot desert sand are blown into quartz on the mountain, which causes static electricity.

The state park has several exhibits worth a visit. The Stonewall Mine site features an exhibition on the history of southern California gold mining. The interpretive center at Paso Picaho features exhibits on the plants and animals of the region. And a museum at park headquarters tells the story of indigenous cultures.

Anza-Borrego State Park

At 600,000 acres, Anza-Borrego is California's largest state park. Anza refers to the Spanish explorer Juan Bautista de Anza. *Borrego,* Spanish for *sheep,* refers to the bighorn sheep that are native to the area. The unusual pairing comes from combining two smaller parks of those names.

No qualifiers are needed here: This isn't dryland hiking or a semiarid climate. This is desert, pure and simple, guarded by the sabers and bayonets of cactus and yucca and agave, home to rattlesnakes and desert toads, a dusty dry place where even the wind blows hot like a blast from an oven and every breath you take warms you from the inside. The PCT, you will be relieved to learn, does not go through the middle of the Anza-Borrego Desert—but it comes close enough, following along its edge for some 90 miles, sometimes in true desert, but more frequently in chaparral and even—at the higher elevations—forest.

As you're walking along the desert's edge, consider that only 10,000 years ago this parched and barren tangle of precipitous cliffs and steep defiles was a lush valley where Native Americans are thought to have hunted mammoths and camels. Instead of prickly pear, mesquite, ocotillo, and brittlebush, there were grasses and trees. Climate change after the Ice Age turned the area into a desert; the mammoths and camels became extinct; the residents, for the most part, moved on. But the desert preserved a wealth of information about the region's prehistory, including fossils ranging from shells to mammoth skeletons, sites of early human habitation, and petroglyphs.

More recent attempts at settling the Anza-Borrego Desert have been less successful. This is a land that has never been completely tamed. The trail passes above Chariot Canyon, an old mining area, where a few decrepit-looking contraptions still ply the earth for gold. More important for hikers: A detour to Chariot Canyon will usually yield something more valuable than gold—water.

The Anza-Borrego Desert was the last obstacle for those 19th-century settlers making the arduous 2,800-mile overland crossing from St. Louis to southern California. The settlers followed routes scouted and blazed by the Spanish, who in their time had relied on Native Americans to show them the water and the pasturage. In 1856 the short-lived Jackass Mail System charged $4 to deliver a letter from St. Louis to Los Angeles. In 1857 John Butterfield opened his Butterfield Stage, which took a southern route across the Continental Divide in New Mexico and connected St. Louis with Los Angeles. The fare was $200.

When gold was discovered nearby in the 1860s, thousand of dreamers jumped off the stage route here in the middle of dusty nowhere to search for their fortunes in the severe, unforgiving canyons. Prospectors staked claims, but the land was stingy, and after the gold rush peaked in the 1880s, the mines went dry and the miners moved elsewhere. Cattlemen built ranches, but the shortage of forage and water proved too daunting, even for hardy range cattle bred for harsh conditions. In 1933 the land was set aside as a park.

A unique visitors center is ingeniously located underground, its dirt roof covered with plants. Exhibits include descriptions of desert plants and their adaptations, as well as fossils of mammoths, giant sloths, camels, mastodons, and saber-toothed cats. There is also an artificial habitat for the rare and endangered desert pupfish, which can survive 100-degree temperatures and live in water four times more salty than the ocean.

The de Anza Expedition

Juan Bautista de Anza explored his eponymous desert in 1774, mapping water sources and pasturage and making contact with local tribes. (However, credit for the first European trip to the desert belongs to Pedro Fages, a Spanish officer, who had come this way two years earlier, looking for deserters.) In 1775 and 1776, Bautista led what was at the time the largest overland expedition ever amassed in the New World, a party of close to 300 people, more than half of whom were women and children, many under the age of 12.

The objective of the expedition was to settle and colonize the San Francisco Bay area. Alta California, as it was then called, was little more than a remote, unexplored outpost. Spain had established a series of missions along the California coast, but only about 70 Spaniards had managed to settle the area. Rough seas, strong winds, and a paucity of sheltered ports made it impractical to resupply the missions by sea, and the small size of the ships in use made it all but impossible to transport the large numbers of livestock required by prospective settlers. In 1769 the Spanish learned of a safe harbor in what is today San Francisco Bay. Settling the bay area would serve two purposes: first, to resupply, populate, link, and defend their already established missions along the coast; second, to exploit the harbor as a safe haven for treasure ships sailing from the Philippines to Spain.

Ocotillo in bloom

A land route was needed to link the missions, and settlers were needed to colonize the bay area. Landless Mexican peasants were promised acreage and supplies to lure them to join the expedition. De Anza began assembling volunteers in the Mexican city of Culiacan, enlisted more as he moved north to Horcasitas, then moved north again to his final staging area in Tubac, just south of Tucson, Arizona. Loaded down with tools, guns, clothing, and housewares, not to mention hundreds of cattle that would provide food for the journey and breeding stock for the future, the prospective settlers left Tubac on October 23, 1775. First they followed rivers—the Santa Cruz to the Gila, the Gila to the Colorado. From Yuma, there were no more rivers, and they were forced to strike out across a desert which, even today, shows up as a big blank expanse on a map. But despite the obstacles—which included an earthquake and snow—the party reached San Francisco Bay on March 28, 1776. Remarkably, only one settler died during the journey.

The de Anza Expedition is commemorated today by the Juan Bautista de Anza National Historic Trail, one of 11 national historic trails in the National Trails System. Like other national historic trails, the de Anza Trail is not, strictly speaking, a hiking path (although some stretches of the route are developed as hiking trails and can be hiked or ridden on). Instead it is a series of sites along de Anza's route that are marked to commemorate the expedition. The trail is supported by the Amigos de Anza organization, which works to preserve and enhance the trail's historical, educational, and recreational opportunities. For more information, contact

Amigos de Anza, c/o Heritage Trails Fund, 5301 Pine Hollow Road, Concord, CA 94521.

Desert Plants

Every hiker who travels this path must answer a fundamental question: What about water? If you look around, you'll see that every plant and animal that ekes out a living here has had to adapt to the problem of drought. There are infinite numbers of ingenious solutions. The creosote bush spreads a network of poisonous roots so it alone can catch any rainwater that falls within the vicinity. Some desert rodents extract and use water from plant foods so efficiently that they never actually drink. Most desert animals are nocturnal.

For sheer opportunism, you have to admire the ocotillo, a drought-deciduous plant (which sheds its leaves in times of drought) that grows in abundance on the eastern side of Grapevine Mountain in the San Felipe Hills. As you climb northward from San Felipe Creek, you'll find yourself walking through a forest of bare and dead-looking stalks that reach 10 or 15 feet into the air. But the stalks aren't dead at all, as you'll see if you happen to be hiking after the rare desert rain, when the ocotillo grows a new set of leaves that form a delicate layer along the stalk. The leaves grow quickly, taking only a few days to sprout, photosynthesize food, and die, leaving the stalk to lie dormant until the next rain. But even in the austere life of this efficient, inarguably ugly plant, there are moments of wild extravagance. In winter and spring, leaves are followed by flowers, pollinated by hummingbirds. Like a wallflower turned beauty queen, the ocotillo blooms in an extravagant display. Its flowers are the color of fire.

The cacti along the trail—commonly, you'll see beavertail, prickly pear, barrel cactus, and teddy-bear cholla—have developed different solutions to the problems of drought, heat, and nutrient-poor soil. Think about them as misers and hoarders, as penny-pinchers who operate on the assumption that what is abundant today will be scarce tomorrow. Their daily lives are consumed with two main tasks: storing water and minimizing water loss (two concerns, incidentally, that hikers also must consider).

Take the very shape of a cactus. Larger surface areas mean greater rates of transpiration (water loss), so cacti have, over eons, reduced their surface area and dispensed with leaves. Instead, a cactus is nothing more than a fleshy stem that has to transact all the routine business of being a plant: photosynthesis, reproduction, and—of course—storing water.

The leaves haven't entirely disappeared. What's left of them is the part of the plant that will put holes in your air mattress and prickles under your skin—spines. Instead of performing the normal job of a leaf, which is food production, spines have other functions. The first is defense: Spines keep animals from eating succulent tissues in search of water. The second is air-conditioning: Spines reflect the heat and decrease the internal tissue temperature of the plant. Stop and look on the next sunny day you encounter one of the densely spined teddy-bear cholla. You can see the spines shimmer in the sunlight, reflecting light and heat away from the plant. The ribs of the cactus also help with cooling by transferring heat from tissue to surrounding air. Seen prominently on silver cholla and cottontop, ribs dissipate heat on hot days and allow stems to expand when water is stored in them.

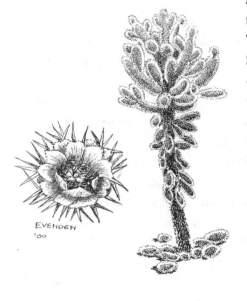

EVENDEN
'00

Teddy-bear cholla

To store water, cacti have succulent tissues that are protected by a thick stem covering, like a cuticle. This cuticle seals in water. Often, the waxy covering on the south-facing side of the plant will be noticeably thicker than the covering on the less sunny north-facing side. (Another cactus-based navigational tip: Barrel cacti usually grow tilting slightly toward the south). Another way cacti reduce exposure to the sun is to grow with leaves facing perpendicular to the sun rather than facing it. You can see this tendency in the prickly pear cactus.

Cacti have a different biological clock than other plants: You might call them night owls. Most plants transpire during the day through pores called stomates, which open to take in or to give off gases and water vapor. Cacti keep their stomates shut tight during the day and open them only at night, when temperatures are much cooler. This, however, has required an adaptation on the cellular level. Carbon dioxide and sunlight are both necessary for photosynthesis, and most plants take them both in at the same time. But cacti take in sunlight during the day, then take in carbon dioxide when their stomates are open at night. They have had to evolve a biochemistry that will let them handle this glitch in the food production assembly line by storing carbon taken in during the night as a weak acid until it can be used in photosynthesis during the day.

Barrel Cactus

Finally, most cacti have shallow but wide root systems that allows them to seize water—even a light sprinkling that quickly percolates through the sandy soil of a rain-shadowed hillside.

Wildflowers

With its relatively cool temperatures and profusions of colorful blooms, early spring is a wondrous time to be hiking the lower elevations of California's desert valleys. Wildly colored to attract pollinators such as the hummingbirds that frequently dive-bomb hikers along the trail, desert wildflowers run the colors of the rainbow, from delicate yellows to brilliant purples to flamelike oranges to timid blushing pinks. The desert wildflower bloom is one of nature's extravagances, but a rare and unpredictable one. Annual blooms depend on the amount of precipitation the previous fall. In the Anza-Borrego Desert, the bloom usually occurs sometime between late February and mid-April; later at the higher elevations. Early

Lifecycle of a desert wildflower

March is the best bet for those who need to plan in advance; even if you miss the peak bloom on the valley floor, you can always go a little higher up. Each year, naturalists go out into the field to predict the peak bloom. You can be notified approximately two weeks in advance if you send a request and include a stamped, self-addressed envelope to Wildflowers, Anza-Borrego State Park, Box 299, Borrego Springs, CA 92004.

Rattlesnakes

Several species of rattlesnakes inhabit the drylands of southern California, including the western diamondback, western rattlesnake, red diamond rattlesnake, sidewinder, speckled rattlesnake, and the much-feared Mojave green rattlesnake. In general, rattle-snakes are found up to the red fir belt, which is at about 9,000 feet in southern California, 8,000 feet in the Sierra, and progressively lower farther to the north. (But watch out for exceptions: On rare occasions, rattlesnakes have been seen as high as 11,000 feet.) Most commonly, however, PCT hikers see rattlesnakes at lower elevations, usually at or below the so-called transition zone, which is located in southern California between 5,000 and 7,000 feet. In southern California, rattlesnakes are most active in April, May, and June—precisely when thru-

hikers are traveling in prime rattlesnake country.

Rattlesnakes are commonly
referred to as cold-blooded, although
their blood can be anything but cold.
The technical term is *exothermic,*
which means that they cannot control
their body temperature. During the
day, a more accurate description
might be hot-blooded, because the

EVENPEN '00

Western diamondback

snake's body temperature rises with the temperature of its surroundings.
When ground temperatures and direct sunlight are too hot for snakes, they
hide in rock piles and sleep under the shade of thick chaparral shrubs. In
the cooler evenings, they are likely to be found basking on sun-warmed
open spaces—which includes the trail.

Rattlesnakes are pit vipers, identifiable by their wedge-shaped heads
and the pits under their eyes. (This information is of admittedly dubious
value: You don't want to get close enough to actually see the pits.) The pits
are heat-sensing organs that allow rattlers to sense temperature differences as subtle as 1 degree Fahrenheit. This, along with their ability to
feel the presence of prey through earth movement, makes them effective
nocturnal hunters—something to think about when considering a night
hike. Although some species, like the western diamondback, can be as
long as 7 feet and as thick as a large man's wrist (and can live as long as
26 years), you are unlikely to see them before they sense you because of
their excellent camouflage. Almost always you will be alerted to their presence when they break cover and rattle. Also keep an eye (or ear) out for
the foot-long juveniles.

Rattlesnakes eat rabbits, ground squirrels, voles, mice, California
quail, brown towhees, lizards, and smaller snakes. In turn they are hunted by kingsnakes, striped racers, and whipsnakes. They are not naturally
aggressive, but they can be stubborn, and in hot weather they prefer not to
move; they would rather intimidate you into walking around them.

While rattlesnakes are capable of delivering a fatal dose of venom, most
bites are not fatal. Nor does every rattlesnake bite actually deliver venom.
Bites are, however, extremely painful, and prevention is the order of the day.

Use your hiking stick as a snake detector, especially if you're stepping among rocks and boulders in snake country. When rock-scrambling, climb with your eyes: Don't put your hands where you can't see them. Step on obstacles, not over them. That way, you can check out what you're stepping into on the other side of the obstacle.

Know the snakes' habits. On a hot day, snakes will be hiding in the shade. On a cool day, they'll head for sunny rocks. If you hear a rattle, move away; then, from a safe distance, look for the snake so you can walk around it. At midday, torpid snakes may be disinclined to yield the right-of-way. If you're in thick chaparral where detours are impossible, a last resort is to fight for the right-of-way by throwing rocks from a safe distance. *Note:* A safe distance is as far away as you can get and still throw the rock—multiple lengths of the snake's body. Use small rocks, and aim to irritate, not to kill. The point is to get the snake to move. It may take a lot of rocks.

If you or someone in your party is bitten, treat for shock. Elevate the feet, keep the victim calm and comfortable. Try to provide shade; you can use a tarp or find a shade-giving tree. Do not use a snakebite kit: One expert on venomous snakes calls them "a license to kill." Apparently snakebite kits (like the old method of "cutting and sucking") actually spread the venom faster and can cause infection. The best thing to do is go for help—one reason that it's a good idea to have a map that shows alternate routes, side trails, and roads. If you are hiking alone or are more than 12 hours from help, you may have to walk out. Splint the injury without constricting it—and take your time.

Warner Springs

The hot springs in this quiet resort community have for centuries been a focal point of the area. Native Americans long used the springs as a traditional gathering place. In the 1820s, Spanish Franciscans began building a mission here, but it was abandoned. In 1844 Jonathan Warner was granted a deed, and the springs became a landmark to emigrants on the southern overland route—who probably looked as bedraggled, thirsty, and weather-beaten as the thru-hikers who straggle in today. The PCT passes the site of the old Warner's Hotel, an important relay point for Butterfield Stage, which ran through here from 1858 to 1861. Historical figures who passed this way include Kit Carson and the members of the Mormon Battalion.

Today the small community of Warner Springs consists of a golf course, a post office, and a restaurant—but alas, the hot springs are not open to the public.

Coulter Pines

North of Warner Springs, the trail climbs, and you'll soon encounter one other tree that deserves special mention in this section of the trail. You'll quickly recognize the Coulter pine, found in abundance when the trail reaches about 4,000 feet in elevation. Coulter pines grow throughout southern and central California, usually on dry, rocky ridges between 3,000 and 6,000 feet. These drought-tolerant pines are identifiable by their football-sized cones, which can weigh up to 5 pounds and are the heaviest of all the pines in the world. Indians once gathered and ate the large seeds; now, squirrels harvest the bounty. The cones are so striking that you might want to take one home as a souvenir. Unfortunately, in this dry country, if you're going to lug along another 4 or 5 pounds, it should be something useful, like water. The cones often litter the ground—which means that they frequently fall from above. So look up before you choose a campsite!

🚶 HIKING INFORMATION

Seasonal Information and Gear Tips

The best time to hike this section in its entirety is spring, usually in late April. Most of this section can also be hiked in winter, but the Lagunas often have significant accumulations of snow and require skills in winter travel and navigation. Fall temperatures are pleasant, but water sources will often be dry.

- Take plenty of sunscreen and a wide-brimmed hat.
- If you carry a tarp rather than a tent, you can make a sun shade during the day. Choose a dark-colored tarp; it blocks more light and casts deeper shade.
- You'll need enough sacks and bottles to carry water. National Park Service rangers recommend two gallons of water per day for hot-weather desert hiking.
- Be prepared for low nighttime temperatures at the higher

Lake Morena from Morena Butte

elevations. A 20-degree sleeping bag, or a 30-degree bag
with lots of extra clothes, is recommended in April and May.

Thru-hikers' Corner

- In most years, snow accumulation in the Lagunas makes it futile
  to try to start before mid-April. For current conditions, call the
  PCTA (1-888-PCTRAIL).

- If you're an experienced long-distance hiker, you may have
  developed the attitude that you'll start easy and break in on
  the trail. *Warning:* That's difficult to do in this section because
  of the distance between water sources.

- Your previous experience with water consumption may not be
  valid here. The high temperatures and extremely dry air may mean
  that you'll require more than twice as much water as you're used
  to drinking. Also, you need to acclimate to the heat; even if you're
  fit, the first few days can be uncomfortable. For these first days,
  take more water than you think you'll need, and pay attention to
  how much you use.

- Take frequent breaks to drink and to check your feet. The hot ground in this section can cause swelling, which can lead to blisters.

Best Short Hikes

- A day hike along the Desert View Trail (which is contiguous with the PCT along the crest of the Laguna Mountains) offers impressive views into the Anza-Borrego Desert. Start from the junction of the PCT with the Sunrise Highway (Highway 1). From Mount Laguna to the Pioneer Mail Trailhead Picnic Area (on the Sunrise Highway) is 10.1 miles.

- For a 26.9-mile backpacking sample of this section that takes you from open chaparral into cool Jeffrey pine forests with views of the Anza-Borrego Desert below, start at Boulder Oaks Campground and hike up into the Laguna Mountains, then continue on to the Pioneer Mail Picnic Area.

Resupplies and Trailheads

Campo, Mount Laguna, and Warner Springs are the most commonly used.

Campo (mile 1). The PCT's southern terminus is located about 1 mile south of the small border village of Campo, California. Campo is 50 miles east of San Diego. There is a small store, laundromat, and post office (92006). To find the trail terminus, turn south of Forrest Gate Road, make a quick turn left (east), away from Castle Rock Ranch, then turn south again and follow the dirt road to the border. Once you see the good border-patrol road, look around and you'll find the terminus monument. Campo is accessible by public transportation from San Diego, the nearest big city. Take County Bus 894 from El Cajon Transit Center in San Diego. The bus runs once a day. For more information and reservations (which are recommended; tell them you're traveling with a pack), call Southwest Rural County Transit System, 619-478-5874.

Lake Morena County Park (mile 20.2) has camping, showers, and a small store 0.3 miles from the trail.

Boulder Oaks Campground (mile 26.5) is a National Forest campground with a store nearby.

Mount Laguna (mile 42.9) has a store, motel, restaurant, and post office. Post office: General Delivery, Mount Laguna, CA 91948

Banner RV Park (mile 78.1) and store is 2 miles west of Scissors Crossing on Highway 78.

Warner Springs (mile 110.6) has a restaurant, a post office, and a small store. Post office: General Delivery, Warner Springs, CA 92086

Kamp Anza Kampground (mile 138.3) is 5.7 miles off-trail. Leave the PCT at Tule Canyon Road and go 2.5 miles west to Terwilliger Road. Kamp Anza is 3.2 miles north. To rejoin the trail without backtracking, continue on Terwilliger Road to Highway 371 to the PCT crossing on Highway 74 (Pines-to-Palms Highway). For info: Kamp Anza Kampground, 41560 Terwilliger Road, Space 19, Anza, CA 92539; 909-763-4819. (*Note:* You can also resupply in the nearby town of Anza; see page 63).

2

Pines-to-Palms Highway to Big Bear

122.6 miles

The Pacific Crest Trail is in one way misnamed: There is no identifiable Pacific Crest mountain range. True, central California has the unbroken line of the Sierra Nevada. And northern California, Oregon, and Washington have the continuous ridgelines from which erupt the volcanic giants of the Cascades. But the Cascades and the Sierra Nevada (as well as the Klamath Mountains of northern California, a subrange that the PCT also traverses) are distinctly different ranges, with different geologic histories.

To further confuse the picture, in southern California, there is no single crest for this crest trail to follow, no organized orderly progression along an identifiable ridgeline. The ranges run in different directions: either north-south (the San Jacinto and the Laguna Mountains are among the so-called peninsular ranges) or east-west (the San Bernardino and San Gabriel Mountains are among the so-called transverse ranges). It is a helter-skelter jumble of mountains, a tangle of ranges running this way and that, all thrown together and ripped apart by the heaving and buckling of the San Andreas Fault system.

In this section, the PCT offers a roller-coaster kind of hike. Think of the path of a basketball as it bounces from one end of a court to the other and you get a good idea of the trail's route: up to the mountains, down to a desert valley, back up to wind-sheared peaks, and—*slam dunk!*—down again into the broiling heat. In the San Jacinto Mountains alone, the variation in elevation is from 1,195 feet to 9,030 feet—and the 7,835-foot change in elevation between those points takes place within a mere 28 miles.

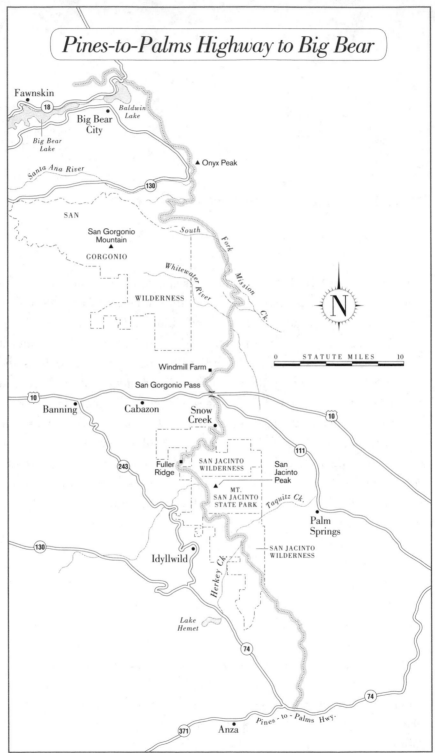

Pines-to-Palms Highway to Big Bear

Fawnskin

18

Big Bear
City

*Baldwin
Lake*

*Big Bear
Lake*

▲ Onyx Peak

Santa Ana River

130

SAN

San Gorgonio
Mountain ▲

South

GORGONIO

Fork

Whitewater River

Mission Ck.

WILDERNESS

N

0   STATUTE MILES   10

Windmill Farm ■

San Gorgonio Pass

10

Banning •

Cabazon •

Snow
Creek •

10

111

243

Fuller ■
Ridge

SAN JACINTO
WILDERNESS

San
Jacinto
Peak

▲
MT.
SAN JACINTO
STATE PARK

Taquitz Ck.

Palm
Springs •

130

Idyllwild •

Herkey Ck.

SAN JACINTO
WILDERNESS

*Lake
Hemet*

74

74

74

Pines - to - Palms Hwy.

371

Anza •

Paul Woodward, © 2000 The Countryman Press

To further complicate the situation, the mountains are surrounded by deserts. Some definitions: The Sonoran Desert—the driest and hottest—is the arid area east of the peninsular ranges, which include this section's San Jacinto Mountains. The Mojave—cooler, at least by the standards of southern California—is the arid area north of the transverse ranges, which include this section's San Bernardino Mountains. The Sonoran Desert is in turn divided into two distinct ecological zones: the upper Sonoran (higher and cooler) and the lower Sonoran (lower and hotter); the lower Sonoran is also known as the Colorado Desert. Finally—if you're not already confused enough—some ecologists consider the Mojave an ecotone, or edge, between the high, cold Great Basin Desert to the north and the lower Sonoran to the south.

"Our desert scenery is probably affected more by the presence of mountains than by any other geological feature," writes ecologist Michael Barbour, explaining the relationship between the high peaks and the deserts that separate them. "The monotony of the pale-faced basins is everywhere broken by the stern but colorful peaks and massive ridges which protrude islandlike from the vast sea of sand and gravel."

As for the trail, monotonous it isn't. Because of its variation in elevations, this section of the PCT goes through the lower Sonoran, upper Sonoran, transition, and Canadian ecological zones, sometimes within only a day or two of hiking. It contains more diversity than any other section in southern California.

THE ROUTE

The peak season for hiking this section in its entirety is spring, although the lower sections can be hiked in winter. In May and June, the old snow has only just melted, leaving springs full; the summer heat is not yet in full force. Fall temperatures are comfortable, but natural water sources are mostly dry.

Before leaving the Pines-to-Palms Highway (Highway 74) and heading into the San Jacinto Mountains in May and June, check with the Forest Service or the PCTA to see whether you'll need an ice ax up high. In the sparse transition-zone forest at the trailhead, snow may seem only a distant concern, but the mountains can be snow-clogged well into June.

Rising above 10,000 feet, the San Jacinto Mountains are the first major range the Pacific Crest Trail encounters. The footway is a little rougher than average, with slight ups and downs that seem just a bit mean-spirited, especially if you consider that your ultimate goal, the crest of the range, involves 4,000 feet of net elevation gain on exposed and sun-baked ridges—quite enough without adding in any extra nickel-and-dime ascents and descents. As you gain elevation, water sources become some-what more frequent, although you'll usually have to leave the footpath to get to them. Most are located on side trails, which means descending (sometimes half a mile or more) and losing elevation (sometimes several hundred feet). After you reach 8,000 feet or so, on-trail water is more common.

After about 7 miles, the trail crosses the watershed known as the Desert Divide. Western-side water ultimately drains into the Pacific Ocean; eastern-side water flows down to the Colorado Desert, where it drains into the sandy soil or evaporates—assuming, that is, that it even gets there. Climbing into the San Jacintos on a hot May afternoon, you may well con-sider the idea of a watershed more theoretical than real. Although the PCT crosses the Desert Divide at an elevation of nearly 6,000 feet, the desert below exerts a strong, hot influence here. Don't expect the cool Jeffrey pine forests of the Lagunas. Instead, the vegetation alternates between shadeless chaparral and skimpy forests of oak and pine. It takes another 1,000 feet of climbing before the trail reaches anything that could be reasonably expected to produce real shade: a forest comprising ponderosa pine along with incense cedar, black oak, white fir, and Jeffrey pine. Unfor-tunately, even then, shade continues to be elusive because the next sever-al miles of trail wear the scars of a 1980 wildfire. The trees are little more than charred skeletons.

But finally, about 20 miles north of the Pines-to-Palms Highway, the trail reaches a healthy high-country forest of spruce and fir. And here again, you might, depending on the season, encounter the conundrum of southern California's PCT: Within several hours of sweltering up sun-baked ridges, you could be bogged down in late-lingering snowpacks. It is possible for the trail here to be impassable even in May, and sometimes as late as mid-June. Several bail-out routes are available, depending on where you get into trouble. If you are traveling through this area in early

Seeking shade on a climb to the San Jacinto Mountains

season, it's a good idea to carry maps of the San Jacinto Wilderness and the San Bernardino National Forest.

If snow permits, side trips can be made to Tahquitz Peak's 8,846-foot summit (a 0.4-mile detour) and 10,804-foot San Jacinto Peak (2.3 miles and 2,000 feet of elevation gain). Another important side trail is the Devils Slide Trail, which you can take to resupply in Idyllwild—or to escape the snow. This resupply isn't exactly convenient—it requires a 4.5-mile (one way) detour and a 2,000-foot loss of elevation. The alternative is to finish crossing the San Jacintos and hitchhike along the Interstate 10 service road into Cabazon or along California Highway 111 to Palm Springs. *Be warned:* It can be a difficult hitch.

Once back on trail, you reach the high point in the San Jacintos about 28 miles from the Pines-to-Palms Highway at an elevation of 9,030 feet. From there the trail begins a largely waterless 28-mile descent to its 1,195-foot low point. (Southbounders: Reverse the numbers and plan carefully!) A potential trouble spot of this section is Fuller Ridge, which challenges the hiker with about 4 miles of scrappy, rocky, and at times just plain ornery trail. More problematic: The ridge is a snow catcher and a snow holder.

Even when the rest of the trail is dry, this north-facing ridge can hold snow until late in the season. If the trail has thus far been dry, any snow on Fuller Ridge will probably be only a minor annoyance. But if you've had to work hard to get here, you may a face a slick lingering snowpack and you may have no choice but to turn back and descend. You can back out by retracing your steps to the Marion Ridge Trail, then descending to Idyllwild, or you can use a network of trails and roads to circumvent the ridge entirely. If you resupply in Idyllwild, check in at the ranger station, which should have information about trail conditions on Fuller Ridge.

Continuing its descent, the PCT winds through forest until it reaches the chaparral zone on the north slope of the San Jacinto Mountains, a stark escarpment that was sculpted by the San Andreas Fault, then scoured and scarred by avalanches and wind erosion. From this vantage point, you can see all six of California's ecological zones, from the hot, dry bottom of San Gorgonio Pass to the arctic-alpine top of San Gorgonio Peak to the north, which at 11,499 feet is the highest point in southern California. John Muir, who knew something about such things (although he was admittedly inclined to hyperbole), called the view of the north face of the San Jacinto Mountains "the most sublime spectacle to be found anywhere on this earth."

On the descent the trail follows seemingly endless switchbacks, swinging from one side of the mountain to the other like some kind of cosmic pendulum. For almost the entire descent, you'll have a good view below of I-10, which never seems to get any closer. Some hikers, frustrated by the apparent lack of progress, abandon the trail in favor of a bushwhack straight down. This, they generally conclude, is a massive mistake. Because of the steepness of the terrain, the dense and thorny rattlesnake-inhabited chaparral, and the friable rocks underfoot, a straight-line cross-country route can take many hours longer than the meandering trail.

Once you finally reach the bottom, you'll find a water spigot attached to a pipeline that takes water from Snow Creek. The water not drunk by hikers will be used for swimming pools, golf courses, and cold drinks in Palm Springs, which is only a few miles away as the crow flies—but may as well be in another universe.

The PCT here leaves the National Forest and enters Bureau of Land Management terrain, where the trail makes an interesting change. This close

Chaparral succeeds itself after a wildfire.

to I-10 and well within the recreational orbit of Los Angeles County, BLM managers were concerned that a clear, constructed footway would attract off-road vehicle users, who are not allowed on the Pacific Crest Trail. Indiscriminate riding through vulnerable desert soils has an impact that lasts for many years. Elsewhere in California, for example, Patton's army tanks did training maneuvers and left tracks that still seem fresh more than 50 years after the fact. And 150-year-old ruts from settlers' wagon trains are clearly visible on some of the old emigrant routes. Construction corridors from the installation of pipelines and transmission lines have had a similar long-lasting impact. Desert plants grow slowly, and natural restoration of severely disturbed soils can be measured in centuries. The BLM elected to minimize the problem by not constructing a full-fledged trail. Instead, BLM staff and Sierra Club volunteers simply posted a route through the creosote bushes, leaving hikers to make their own path from one post to the next.

Once it reaches its low point (1,195 feet) just before San Gorgonio Pass, the trail starts back uphill to the ridge of the San Bernardino Mountains. Forty-two miles later, it reaches 8,750 feet. Although it's not one sustained uphill push—the trail meanders up and down before getting down to business and climbing for real—the 7,500-foot difference in elevation is the largest *northbound* climb on the entire PCT. (The largest *southbound* climb is the 7,800-foot ascent from San Gorgonio Pass to the San Jacinto

Switchbacked trail north of San Gorgonio Pass

Mountains just described in reverse.) You'll see a microcosm of southern California's ecosystems: the lower Sonoran desert, upper Sonoran chaparral, the transition zone, and finally the Canadian zone forests of pine and fir. The trail doesn't go through the Hudsonian and arctic-alpine zones— but you can see them where you look across to San Gorgonio Peak.

Water remains scarce. Except in a dry year, you will usually find water at the lower elevations in both Whitewater Canyon and Mission Creek well into June. As the trail gently gains elevation in the San Bernardinos, it becomes more shaded and cooler. In fact, it can be surprisingly cold. As in the San Jacintos, be sure to carry extra layers of clothing and some sort of shelter, especially if you're hiking in May, early June, and into the fall. Storms are not uncommon early in the hiking season. As the trail descends to the end of this section near Big Bear, it becomes much drier and hotter, reflecting its proximity to the rain-shadowed Mojave Desert to the north.

The section ends at Van Dusen Canyon Road (3NO9), a dirt route that leads 3 miles into Big Bear, (a resupply station for thru-hikers and a popular vacation destination for Los Angelenos).

WHAT YOU'LL SEE

Ecological Diversity

The 7,800 feet—almost a vertical mile and a half—difference between the high point and the low point in this section is the largest change of elevation on the entire Pacific Crest Trail. The extreme variation in elevation affects not only temperature, but also rainfall: At any given elevation, eastern slopes are much drier than their western counterparts. Thus one of this section's chief attractions is its wide variety of ecological communities.

Proximity to the wet oceanic air also contributes to the diversity. The presence of low passes through the mountains makes it possible for ocean-slope species to creep across to the eastern side of the mountains (a phenomenon that takes colorful form farther to the north, when the PCT passes fields of California poppies, long thought to be strictly western-slope plants, but flourishing in the eastern-slope of the Mojave Desert).

The San Bernardino National Forest contains a diverse array of plant and animal life, including 75 species of mammals, 55 of reptiles, 13 of amphibians, 297 of birds—and more than 2,000 species of plants, ranging from cedars, white firs, and Coulter, Jeffrey, ponderosa, sugar, lodgepole

Mount San Jacinto

EVENDEN '00

Black-tailed jackrabbit

and limber pines at the higher elevations, to chaparral on the hillsides, and creosote and cactus on the desert floor. High up the mountain slopes, animals include bighorn sheep, deer, mountain lions, raccoons, and skunks, while lower down are found coyotes, gray foxes, and black-tailed jackrabbits, along with an impressive collection of lizards and snakes.

San Jacinto Peak Aerial Tramway

The PCT does not go over the top of the range's highest peak, but 10,804-foot San Jacinto Peak is only a 2.3-mile detour from the trail. Day hikers have an interesting option: They can take the Palm Springs aerial tramway, which ascends nearly 6,000 vertical feet from the desert to the shoulder of San Jacinto Peak. The tramway affords an unparalleled view from blazing desert sands to brilliant snowcapped peaks. From the top of the tramway, it's a 5.8-mile hike to the summit. When you get done with your round trip, you can dine at the restaurant at the top of the tramway.

Tree Adaptations

Along the PCT in the San Jacinto Mountains, the trail climbs through a transition zone forest of Coulter and Jeffrey pines, then enters for the first time the Canadian zone—the lowest of the three so-called boreal, or northern, eco-zones. The Canadian zone is characterized by a conifer forest of red fir and lodgepole pine. While you might breathe a sigh of relief at entering the cooler, wetter, shaded highlands, the high ridges of the San Bernardino National Forest are, like many western mountain zones, actually a tough place for a plant to make a living, with extreme temperature variations, bitterly cold winters, a short growing season, and dry, moisture-stealing air. It's not only plants living in the deserts down below that must develop ways of coping with an inhospitable environment.

Conifers, however, are well-adapted to these conditions. The traditional

Christmas-tree shape actually has a function beyond providing a place for colored lights and seasonal baubles. The tapered top helps shed snow in winter, preventing branches from breaking under an insupportable weight. The limbs of conifers are flexible, which also helps the trees cope with heavy snow loads. Young conifers can survive even if they are bent flat to the ground by snow. This is most likely the explanation for weirdly shaped trees with trunks that run along the ground for a foot or two before curving upward.

The tapering shape also allows light to penetrate to the lower branches so that they can contribute to photosynthesis. But sometimes, in thick forest, very little light penetrates to the lower branches. When the lower branches use up more food and nutrients than they can produce through photosynthesis, mature conifers will sometimes simply shed them, giving literal meaning to the term *deadwood*. As a result, in some species of conifers, the lowest limbs may be 20 or 40 or 60 feet (or even more) off the ground. An extreme example: The lowest branch of the famous General Sherman tree in Sequoia National Park is 130 feet above the forest floor.

Conifer leaves, or needles, are also well adapted for the stresses they face: The tough waxy coating protects against cold and moisture loss. In summer, this coating keeps the internal temperature of the tissue low and acts as a barrier to evaporation; in winter, it provides insulation. The resin of conifers is also a sort of antifreeze—something to think about the next time you lean against a pine tree and get sap all over your back.

In the San Jacintos, the growing season is actually quite short, lasting only a few weeks in the spring when temperatures are neither too cold nor too hot and when moisture, largely from snowmelt, is abundant enough for plants to photosynthesize effectively. In such conditions, conifers have an advantage over deciduous trees: As soon as conditions are favorable, they can simply get to work producing food, rather than wasting time to grow a new set of leaves. Once conditions get too hot, conifers often go dormant, but because they keep their leaves all year long, some species can make up for lost food production by "waking up" during mild spells in winter and carrying on photosynthesis while the weather holds.

Conifers not only adapt to their environment, but they also affect it. Forests keep more moisture in the air by producing water vapor through

Snow plant

transpiration. Shade lowers the temperature, making life possible for understory plants. With more humidity in the air, the nights are warmer, reducing the chance of damage from frost. Moisture in the air turns to condensation, which is then available as a supplementary water source to other plants in the forest. Finally, the presence of forests deflects drying winds that would otherwise steal away the moisture.

Snow Plants

Not only trees, but smaller plants as well, have to adapt. During snowmelt, you will encounter another of the PCT's unusual-looking inhabitants, the so-called snow plant, a fleshy, bright red plant that grows in pools of snowmelt water. It looks like a combination of a succulent cactus, a fleshy-stalked mushroom, and a red azalea.

In fact it is almost the exact opposite of a cactus. Snow plants live in the deep shade of montane conifer forests, and their primary challenge is low light levels. Down in the drylands, cacti have developed adaptations that protect them from too much heat; here, the understory plants have developed adaptations to cope with a shortage of sunlight. The usual strategy is to overcompensate: Understory plants tend to have dark green leaves, jam-packed with chloroplasts (the cell structures that make chlorophyll, which is essential for photosynthesis). The leaves of typical shade-tolerant plants lack surface hairs, which could interfere with the absorption of light. They also tend to be big (because a leaf with bigger surface area can collect more sunlight) and thin (because a heavier leaf would droop and not collect as much sunlight.)

The snow plant, however, has taken a different course of evolution: It has simply given up photosynthesis altogether and moved one step up the food chain. Instead of making its own food, the snow plant draws nutrients from the forest humus. Since snow plants don't have to use their leaves to turn sunlight into food, the leaves are small and scalelike, and there isn't a speck of green anywhere on the plant. It is every bit as adapted to its cool, shady home as a cactus is to a sunny arroyo.

Colorado Desert

Not more than 25 miles from the cool shaded forests where the snow plants are likely to be soaking up the last of the season's snowfall, the PCT reaches its lowest point in all of California, at 1,195 feet. This is the realm of the Colorado Desert, which occupies much of southeastern California between the peninsular ranges and the Colorado River (it also includes the Anza-Borrego Desert to the south). It is California's hottest and driest desert, rain-shadowed by the peninsular mountains, receiving in some places as little as 2 inches of annual precipitation.

Here in San Gorgonio Pass—saddled between the San Jacinto and San Bernardino Mountains, which loom nearly 10,000 feet above—the PCT passes through the true desert of the lower Sonoran zone. Midday temperatures in May and June frequently creep above 100 degrees, and ground temperatures can be much hotter than that. Vegetation is dominated by cacti (jumping cholla, barrel, and pincushion are most common) and creosote. Colorado Desert trees are mostly deciduous, but in this case, deciduous has nothing to do with avoiding cold winters. Desert plants—examples include the palo verde, desert willow, jojoba, and ocotillo—shed their leaves not in autumn, but during heat and drought.

Three notable species you'll encounter on the walk across the pass are catclaw—(possibly the most vilified plant species in the American desert, although teddy-bear cholla and jumping cholla are close contenders), honey mesquite, and creosote.

Catclaw is also known as tear-blanket, devil's claw, and wait-a-minute. The origin of its many common names will become self-explanatory the first time you inadvertently brush up against one of these trees, which in the Colorado Desert may be no more than 15 inches tall. Size notwithstanding, the catclaw is indeed a tree—a

Catclaw

Colorado Desert

member of the genus *Acacia*. Alongside shaded and protected rock ledges, *Acacia greggii* can reach a respectable shrub size of 6 or 7 feet. In more moderate environments, it becomes an actual tree, about 15 feet tall.

The honey mesquite is a low-desert shrub that has found an interesting way to deal with water shortages. Just like a cattleman who drills a well to water his stock, the mesquite send its roots down to tap into subterranean water. The technical name for plant species that do this is *phreatophytes*. The presence of a healthy number of the honey mesquite is a fairly reliable way of identifying an underground water source, especially if the plants are thick and abundant. It's useful information if you happen to be drilling a well, but hikers, unfortunately, won't be able to put it to the test: The roots of a honey mesquite can be as long as 160 feet.

Arguably the most successful desert plant species in America is the creosote. In *Animal Dreams,* Barbara Kingsolver notes that "plants do everything animals do—give birth, grow, travel around . . . have sex. They just do it a lot slower." They also engage in war. There's even a word for it: *Alleopathy* is defined as chemical warfare between plant species. The creosote, ubiquitous in the low desert, is a perfect example of a warmongering plant.

Creosote poisons the competition. Unlike chaparral, which grows in impenetrable tangles and thickets, creosote grows in neat rows, almost as if it had been planted. It is easy to find a path between creosote bushes because they are spaced apart, surrounded by a circle of bare earth. The bare earth is courtesy of a toxin secreted by the plant, which rain washes to the ground. The toxin kills any surrounding plants so that the roots of the creosote have enough room to collect sufficient water from near the surface.

Creosote shrubs have other strategies for coping with unpredictable rain and periods of drought as long as 30 months. Touching creosote leaves reveals that they are covered with a thick, waxy substance that helps retain moisture so that water is conserved in internal tissues. The plant is also hardy. Although in a long drought it may look almost dead, creosote can seemingly pop back to life in response to the stingiest drizzle.

New creosote plants have the opportunity to become established only during periods of greater than normal rain, sometimes only once every few decades. So creosote plants also procreate by cloning. You'll be able to identify cloned communities of creosote plants: They grow in circular formations called fairy rings. These self-per-petuating communities expand

Creosote

over time. Scientists infer the age of the community from its size. Estimates differ, but the oldest known creosote communities are thought to be between 9,000 and 11,000 years old.

For plants (not unlike humans), success in warfare brings longevity and wide distribution. Creosote grows in southern California, southern Utah, Nevada, Arizona, New Mexico, Baja California, Texas, and central Mexico, existing throughout an area of some 275,000 square miles. In this section of the PCT, it dominates the Colorado Desert in the area of San Gorgonio Pass.

San Andreas Fault System

By far the most dramatic physical feature of this section is the San Andreas Fault system, the active agent in the sculpting of this region's landscape. The PCT crosses the fault near San Gorgonio Pass. The north face of the San Jacinto Mountains owes its starkness to fault activity.

Farther north, in the environs of Whitewater Canyon and the West Fork of Mission Creek, you'll see a jumble of topography in hills and gullies that are also products of earth movement.

Geologists argue about exact boundaries, but generally agree that the San Andreas Fault is somewhere between 800 and 1,000 miles long. The fault's northern end lies in Mendocino, north of San Francisco. About the southern end, there is more controversy. Depending on which geologist you talk to, the southern end extends at least as far south as the Salton Sea, and perhaps all the way into Mexico and the Gulf of California.

The fault is the product of tectonics, a word that derives from the Greek word for builder. Tectonics can be thought of as the process of building new shapes—mountains and ridges, and valleys, too. Tectonic plates are what we think of as the earth's crust, *terra firma*—which is not *firma* at all, but rather floats on a sea of semiliquid magma that lies between 3 and 35 miles beneath the surface. The Pacific plate is moving in a counterclockwise direction, while the North American plate is moving southward. The San Andreas Fault is the place where they meet.

It is handy to think of a fault as a single line: Step to one side, and you are on the Pacific plate; step to the other, and you are on the North American plate. The reality is not always so clear-cut. In many places the fault line is really a rift zone, which can be up to a mile wide. Additionally, the San Andreas fault is not just one single fault, but rather a system of 10 associated branches that have been created as tectonic plates periodically buckle and crash into each other. And there are hundreds of other, smaller faults as well in this system. In its entirety the system is responsible for much of the jagged topography of southern California's mountain ranges. It also produced three major passes, which can be thought of as interior gateways. Two of them—San Gorgonio Pass and Cajon Pass—are on the Pacific Crest Trail. These interior gateways have been important transportation arteries since the earliest days of European exploration and settlement in California.

The San Andreas Fault is a wrench fault, also called a strike-slip, lateral, or transcurrent fault. Translated into English, this means that when the two plates clash, the resulting movement—an earthquake—is horizontal. (Think of the *Titanic* grinding against the iceberg.) San Francisco and Los Angeles, being on different plates, are actually traveling toward

San Andreas Fault zone

each other. Usually this motion is slow, measured in inches per year. But
during an earthquake the movement can be much more dramatic. In the
San Francisco Earthquake of 1906, two centuries' worth of movement—
some 21 feet—took place in a matter of seconds. The cumulative dis-
placement of matter can, over time, add up to hundreds of miles.

Usually, however, tectonics is a slower process. Think of a rocket pre-
paring for liftoff. At first, very little seems to be happening, until a certain
amount of energy accumulates and must be released. What happens during
an earthquake is that energy, which has been accumulating as heat from
deep within the earth, is conducted to the surface where it is finally con-
verted to mechanical energy which can bend (fold) or fracture (fault) rock.

For all their power, fault lines are not always as easy to see as book dia-
grams make them out to be. Covered with vegetation and softened by erosion, they can blend into a landscape as cluttered and varied as that of
southern California. Indeed, sometimes it is easier to identify their presence by a small but prominent geological feature than by looking for a fault
line that marches through across the land as surely as a line on a map.
Near San Gorgonio Pass, the prominent feature is the San Jacinto escarpment. But the fault, too, is visible, especially in the hills near Whitewater
Canyon's Middle Fork and Mission Creek.

Windmill Farms

All passes are wind tunnels. But due to its location and geography, San Gorgonio Pass is an especially effective one. In *The California Deserts*, Edmund Jaeger quotes W. P. Blake's description of the winds through San Gorgonio Pass as a "constant, powerful current of air sweeping through the pass from the west. It pours from the Pacific in an apparently unbroken unvarying stream, passing over the surface with such violence that all the fine grains of sand are lifted from the dry channels of the stream and are driven along the descending slopes until they find a final resting-place to the leeward of the projecting spurs [of San Jacinto]."

The speed of these winds is caused by three factors: the cool coastal air, the hot interior desert, and the height of the mountains on either side of the pass. During April and May periods of coastal fog, winds from the coast are especially strong, and the pass is subject to violent sand and dust storms as air pours from the ocean to the interior. As cooler ocean air moves toward the hot interior, it heats and rises, and a vacuum is created that draws in more air from the coast. The flow of air increases as the air is compressed against the steep ridges. The result is a constant, powerful current of air that creates high-speed winds.

Just north of the pass, you will hear a low, almost unearthly sound. Those with a musical temperament might compare it to the drone of an organ. To others it might suggest a gathering of ghosts. Look up, and you'll see the

Windmill farms near San Gorgonio Pass

source of the sound. Just off the trail, hundreds of windmills perch on ridges, situated to catch the winds roaring through the pass. The wind farm is one of several such large-scale operations in southern California attempting to provide clean electrical energy.

Windmills are not without controversy. Sticking some 100 feet or more above the ridges in lines like an army of soldiers, they are ugly view-spoilers, as well as noisy. To build and maintain them requires the construction of roads, which contributes to erosion by disturbing the fragile desert soils. Older models can trap and decapitate birds. But windmills provide energy without pollutants. It is estimated that the energy produced by each windmill is equivalent to more than 1,000 barrels of oil per year.

San Bernardino Mountains

From an ecological standpoint, the climb from San Gorgonio Pass into the San Bernardino Mountains is the reverse of the descent down from the San Jacintos. Rising some 7,500 feet in 42 miles, the trail leaves the lower Sonoran Desert first for a high-desert ecosystem, where you'll see Joshua trees, a characteristic plant of the Mojave Desert to the north. Continuing up to the higher slopes of the mountains, you climb again through transition-zone forests and into the boreal zone of fir and lodgepole pine. The peaks often hold snow well into summer, and temperatures can be quite cool. But as you descend the 27 miles from the section's high point to its end at Van Dusen Canyon Road, drought-tolerant forests of pinyon and juniper show the influence of the Mojave Desert.

🚶🚶 HIKING INFORMATION

Seasonal Information and Gear Tips

This section is best hiked in its entirety in May and June—although in some years, the high country may not be passable until June. The lower elevations can be hiked in winter. In autumn, temperatures may be comfortable, but most springs and streams are dry.

- For the higher elevations in spring and fall, prepare for below-freezing temperatures at night with long johns (top-and-bottom polypropylene or the equivalent) and a light fleece jacket.

- A water- and wind-resistant jacket is good insurance against the surprise snowstorms that can occur well into spring.
- An ice ax is necessary in early spring and, depending on the snow year, may be required until late June. In an average year, you will probably not need an ice ax after mid-May. To decide whether to take an ice ax, check the latest information from the PCTA or the Forest Service.

Thru-hikers' Corner

Spring in the San Jacinto and San Bernardino Mountains can be stormy, cold, and snow-clogged. Or it can be sunny, warm, and all but snow-free. It is almost impossible to predict conditions more than a few weeks ahead. In 1997, for example, available information (aided by the irrepressible—not to mention often inaccurate—hiker grapevine) indicated a high snow year. But although snowfall was higher than average, spring was abnormally dry and warm, and the high ridges were snow-free by mid-May. But 1998 was an El Niño year, and thigh-deep snow persisted on Fuller Ridge until late June.

Because of the possibility of encountering impassable snow, hikers entering the San Jacinto Mountains before the snow has melted should carry maps that show not only the PCT, but also other routes and roads.

Best Short Hikes

- From the PCT's crossing of I-10 near San Gorgonio Pass, the trail heads north into the fascinating rift zone of the San Andreas Fault. Some of this area is accessible by road (especially if you happen to have a four-wheel-drive vehicle). If you're interested in exploring further on a day hike, get a map from the San Bernardino National Forest or the Bureau of Land Management. Because of the low elevations, this area makes for a good wintertime hike.
- A longer backpack that puts all the ecological and geologi-

cal diversity of this section on display starts at I-10 and
goes 64.3 miles to Van Dusen Canyon Road. This stretch
features excellent views of the fault zones, more water than
is usual in southern California, and ecology ranging from
low desert to cool Canadian-zone forest. The 6.8 miles
above Gold and Teutang Canyons are especially dramatic.

- The higher reaches of the PCT in the San Jacinto Mountains are accessible by side trails starting from either the
aerial tramway (see page 52) or the town of Idyllwild. There
are a number of trails and loops, all of which are shown on
the San Jacinto Wilderness map and the San Bernardino
National Forest map (see page 300 for contact information.)

Resupplies and Trailheads

Anza and Idyllwild are the most commonly used.

Anza (mile 0) is 6 miles from the trailhead on the Pines-to-Palms
Highway. It has restaurants, a store, and a post office, but no motels.
Post office: General Delivery, Anza, CA 92539

Idyllwild (mile 26.5). Resupplying in Idyllwild requires leaving the
PCT and descending 2,000 feet on a side trail. (And then, of course,
you have to regain those 2,000 feet when you want to get back to
the trail.) It's 2.5 miles down the trail, then another 2 miles on road.
Nonetheless this lovely mountain town is a popular resupply point for
long-distance hikers because it's located between the commonly
used resupplies at Warner Springs and Big Bear City. It's also a
good place to bail out and wait for the snow to melt if you arrive in
the San Jacintos too early in the season. Post office: General Delivery, Idyllwild, CA 92549

I-10 (mile 58.3). From where the PCT joins Tamarack Road near I-
10, you can hitch into Cabazon, Banning, or Palm Springs for resupply. The hitch can be difficult, since this is a major artery and every-
one is in a hurry. But it's your last chance to get supplies until Big
Bear City, about 64 trail miles away.

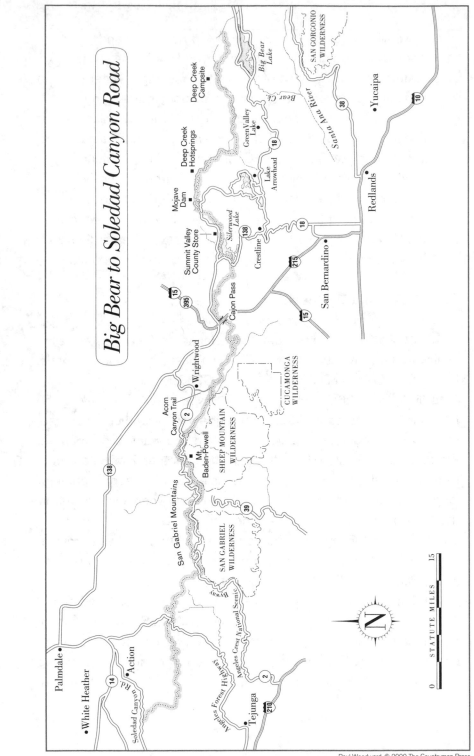

Big Bear to Soledad Canyon Road

San Gorgonio Wilderness

Big Bear Lake

Deep Creek Campsite

Yucaipa

10

Deep Creek Hotsprings

Green Valley Lake

18

Bear Ck.

Santa Ana River

38

Mojave Dam

Lake Arrowhead

Redlands

Silverwood Lake

138

Summit Valley County Store

Crestline

18

San Bernardino

215

15

395

15

Cajon Pass

CUCAMONGA WILDERNESS

Wrightwood

Acorn Canyon Trail

2

Mt. Baden-Powell

SHEEP MOUNTAIN WILDERNESS

138

San Gabriel Mountains

39

SAN GABRIEL WILDERNESS

Palmdale

Angeles Crest National Scenic Byway

White Heather

Action

14

Soledad Canyon Rd.

Angeles Forest Highway

Tejunga

2

210

N

0   STATUTE MILES   15

Paul Woodward, © 2000 The Countryman Press

3

Big Bear to Soledad Canyon Road

168.9 miles

This section consists of two distinct segments. The first segment (90 miles) starts in the transition-zone forest near Big Bear, but soon becomes largely a high-desert walk when it descends into the Mojave River drainage. It then crosses Cajon Pass and climbs the steep chaparral-covered south face of the San Gabriel Mountains. The second segment (80 miles) begins on the ridge of the San Gabriels, where it stays mostly high in transition-zone and Canadian-zone forests along the crest of the range. The PCT reaches its highest elevation in southern California (9,245 feet) at the junction with the side trail that leads to the summit of 9,399-foot Mount Baden-Powell. In the San Gabriel Mountains, plenty of trailhead parking areas enable you to fashion a hike of almost any length. The section ends with a 10-mile descent into Soledad Canyon.

THE ROUTE

Leaving the Big Bear area from Van Dusen Canyon Road, the trail is forested and shady—but not necessarily cool. Although the elevation starts out above 7,000 feet and stays above 6,000 feet for about 15 miles, the hot air of the Mojave Desert to the north seems to lie over the hillsides like a warming blanket. In these early miles, distances between water are reasonable (as always, within the context of southern California) and there is quite a bit of shade. But when the trail leaves the transition zone and its pine and oak forests, you can expect hot and dry hiking until you reach the

Big Bear Lake

crest of the San Gabriel Mountains, about 90 miles from the beginning of this section.

The first 35 miles of trail north of Big Bear boast two of the best places to camp along southern California's PCT. The first is 23.5 miles out, under a bridge that crosses Deep Creek. There's a small sandbar with ample room for a couple of tents. The pool of cold, clear water feels delicious, and if you happen to be carrying a fishing rod and a license, there's a good chance you'll be eating rainbow trout for dinner. The second site, 9 miles farther, is at the popular Deep Creek Hot Springs.

Because these sites are only 9 miles apart, most thru-hikers will be able to stay at only one of them. But short-distance hikers can plan to stay at both. *Warning:* After the hot springs, the trail parallels Deep Creek, but there are very few places where you can easily get from the trail to the water. Don't be fooled by how close together they look on maps! On leaving the hot springs, you're back in the sunshine and scrub, so drink up before you go, and carry a couple of quarts with you.

The trail gets even drier after it leaves the dam, 46 miles into this section. So if you are hiking on past the Mojave River Forks Reservoir, be sure to fill your water bottles. Despite the gargantuan size of the dam, the Mojave River itself isn't even enough of a river to reach the sea. For much

Deep Creek

of its course, the Mojave is what geologists refer to as an upside-down river, because its water sinks beneath the porous sandy soil of its riverbed and runs beneath the ground. And at some spots (different each year, due to varying levels of snowfall) it simply stops running altogether. Don't let the dam dupe you into thinking that there's actually a lot of water around.

After some more hot and dry meandering, the trail reaches Silverwood Lake State Park, which has water, bathrooms, and a small store, all of which offer a welcome respite. Leaving Silverwood Lake, the trail climbs gently, then descends to Cajon Pass following a route that is mostly dry and very hot, with only intermittent shade. At Cajon Pass, the PCT crosses Interstate 15, which makes for a convenient place to start or end a hike. There is a restaurant, a motel, a gas station, and a convenience store at the interchange.

From Cajon Pass, the PCT climbs very gently for about 5 miles before getting serious about the task ahead: an ascent of the southern face of the San Gabriel Mountains. Some hikers consider this climb the most arduous in southern California.

Warning: Do not leave Cajon Pass without enough water to climb 5,000 feet and walk 22 miles. There is a reliable stream that runs through Cajon Pass; you can also get water at the services at the interchange. Strong hikers who can do the 22 uphill miles in one day need an absolute minimum of a gallon of water—and will wish they had more. Hikers who plan to break up the climb by camping will need as much as two gallons. The route is steep, waterless, and almost entirely exposed to the sun. Be walking by first light.

Immediately after gaining the crest of the San Gabriel Mountains, most long-distance hikers temporarily leave the PCT via the Acorn Trail to descend into the small community of Wrightwood for resupply. When they rejoin the trail, they find that walking along the crest of the San Gabriel Mountains is both easier and cooler than the climb to reach the ridge.

After gaining the crest, the trail stays largely above 7,000 feet for 25 miles, then seesaws between 4,900 feet and 7,000 feet for another 45 miles. Occasionally crossing and often paralleling the Angeles Crest Highway, the trail in the San Gabriel Mountains is easily accessible for day hikers and weekenders. It also boasts a series of primitive campgrounds, most of which are equipped with latrines, picnic tables, shade, and a fairly reliable water source (although springs start to dry up in late spring or early summer). Throughout the entire section, the footway is excellent, although trail signage near and around road crossings can occasionally be confusing.

The trail concludes this section by leaving the San Gabriel Mountains and descending into Soledad Canyon.

San Gabriel Mountains

WHAT YOU'LL SEE

Deep Creek Hot Springs

The Deep Creek Hot Springs sit on a fault, and their steaming waters give evidence of the continuing geological upheaval and broiling energy beneath the surface. (Consider, too, that the nearby dam of the Mojave River sits on the same fault!) Although the hot springs are only a couple of hundred yards off the trail, it's not immediately obvious where they are. Some hikers have actually walked past them, so pay attention to your maps and your mileage. When you see an area that looks a bit greener than usual, you're probably there, especially if there are people about. Don't expect solitude—the springs are no secret. But there's lots of room. Hot water seeps out of the hillside in several places, and using rocks, local hot-tubbers have dammed these trickles into a series of private pools, each big enough for several people. Some of these backcountry bathtubs are immediately adjacent to the cold waters of Deep Creek, so you can alternate between hot and cold bathing.

The guidebook warns about a rare hot-spring-inhabiting amoeba that can invade the human body through the nose, causing a potentially fatal disease called meningoencephalitis. Reportedly one hiker died in the 1970s and another became seriously ill. However, thousands of people visit the hot springs each year, so the risk, if any, is slight. You can minimize it by keeping the water out of your eyes, ears, and nose and taking your drinking water from upstream of the hot springs. For immersion bathing, you can always take a cold-water swim in the creek itself.

Cajon Pass

Like San Gorgonio Pass, Cajon Pass was one of the interior gateways that made east-west travel possible in southern California. The first documented crossing of the pass by Europeans was the de Anza expedition of 1775–76. Other notable pioneers included Mormon settlers, who were coming to make a home in the San Bernardino Valley, mine for gold, or volunteer as part of the Mormon Battalion for service in the Mexican War. Today the pass is crossed by I-15, a railroad, and the PCT.

A natural gateway, Cajon Pass provides an easy and logical passage between the mountains. But to climb into the mountains is another story.

The south-facing slope of the San Gabriel Mountains resembles the north-facing slope of the San Jacintos: stark, steep, and altogether uninviting—and indeed, for a similar reason: Both escarpments are the result of fault activity. Even John Muir was taken aback. "The whole range, seen from the plain, with the hot sun beating upon its southern slopes, wears a terribly forbidding aspect," he wrote. "In the mountains of San Gabriel . . . Mother Nature is most ruggedly, thornily savage. Not even in the Sierra have I ever made the acquaintance of mountains more rigidly inaccessible. The slopes are exceptionally steep and insecure to the foot of the explorer, however great his strength or skill may be, but thorny chaparral constitutes their chief defense. With [little] exception, the entire surface is covered with it, from the highest peak to the plain . . . From base to summit all seems gray, barren, silent-dead, bleached bones of mountains, overgrown with scrubby bushes, like gray moss."

The view is much the same today.

Just north of Cajon Pass, a little interpretive nature trail identifies some of the rugged, ubiquitous plants that hikers have been seeing since their first steps from the Mexican border.

Chaparral

The word *chaparral* is derived from *chaparro,* a Spanish scrub oak. Chaparral is not a single plant, but rather a community of plants that grow well in dry, rocky, nutrient-poor soil. The name was first used by Spanish settlers, who saw the similarity between this plant community and that of their native Mediterranean climate. Chaparral includes such non-oaklike species as sagebrush and manzanita (of which there are 28 species; *manzanita* is Spanish for *little apple,* and in spring you'll see it blooming along the trail). Other common chaparral shrubs are chamise (also called greasewood because of its texture and flammability), mountain lilac, tobacco brush, ribbonwood, ceanothus, mountain mahogany, and poison oak. The shrubs often rise to the height of a hiker, blocking views. Sometimes the chaparral covering the hillsides can be as much as 15 feet tall.

True chaparral plants are well-adapted to heat and drought, with small, waxy leaves that reduce evapo-transpiration. Most varieties are evergreens. Like conifers, chaparral plants adapt to a short growing season by not having to waste time sprouting new sets of leaves. By midsummer they slip into near-dormancy to protect themselves from water loss. Other adaptations include extremely deep root systems and recessed stomates. (Burying the stomates deep in the plant tissue protects them from dry winds that could otherwise steal away water.) On some manzanitas, the leaves are an extremely light green, which better reflects the heat; other shrubs have shiny leaves to serve the same purpose.

Chaparral shrubs are also well-adapted to fire. Their seeds germinate after fire, and the shrubs can remain alive even when badly burnt, which gives them a competitive advantage over other species. Indeed, some species, like greasewood, actually encourage fire by being extremely flammable. Most unusual of all is chaparral's ability to succeed itself: It is both a colonizing community and a climax community. But this fire tolerance makes chaparral dangerously vulnerable to wildfires, which can blaze out of control and threaten local towns. Even a spark from a carelessly discarded cigarette can cause thousands of acres to turn into an inferno. Don't build fires when camping, and take special caution when using stoves, especially wood-burning stoves that require discarding ashes.

Chaparral plants are adapted for the dry life, but they know what to do with water. Given a moist year, these tough shrubs seize the moment and grow. In a matter of months, they can overrun a hiking trail with an obstacle course of spiky leaves, bloodthirsty thorns, and swordlike branches. Found on plains, mesas, and foothills, and common in southern California between 3,000 and 5,500 feet in elevation—especially on the desert side of mountains—chaparral is the most common plant community in California.

Poison Oak

Of all the plants that make up the ubiquitous chaparral community, one seems to dominate: poison oak. It's not your imagination. Some botanists think that it is the most common chaparral plant in southern California. The American Medical Association has reported that acute dermatitis (in other words, an allergic skin reaction) due to contact with poison oak was responsible for 50 percent of the cases of workers compensation cases in California. Nationwide, this pesky plant (and its close cousins, poison ivy and poison sumac) causes more skin rashes than all other plants, house-

EVENDEN
'00

Poison oak

hold chemicals, and industri-al chemicals combined.

Poison oak looks a little like poison ivy, with clusters of three unevenly lobed leaves. But poison oak can be hard to identify. It can grown as a shrub or a vine; some-times it even looks like a small tree. Where the trail is cut into steep slopes, look carefully, because poison oak sometimes clings to the side of the hill and hangs down from above, where it can brush against a face or an arm.

It's well worth your while to be able to identify the plant in all stages of its growth. If you're a native easterner, don't look for leaves that resemble those of the massive oak trees of an eastern hardwood forest. The shape of poison oak leaves can vary, but it tends to small, oval, and lobed, like the leaves of many western oaks. The oval-shaped leaves grow in triads and are usually thick and waxy-looking, especially in arid southern California, where their coating reduces transpiration and, therefore, heat loss. The size of the leaves can range widely. They tend to be smaller on hot exposed slopes, to reduce transpiration. In shady places, leaves are often quite a bit bigger. Leaves turn reddish in autumn, when the plant's small, white flowers yield small, white berries.

It's also important to be able to identify poison oak early in the season, before the leaves have sprouted. Poison oak branches (like poison ivy branches) are thin, flexible, and graceful looking. They often appear to be reaching out, then up, a little bit like the antlers of a deer. Sometimes the branches will hold leftover, shriveled white berries from the previous year.

All parts of the plant are poisonous. The irritant is a highly toxic sub-stance called urushiol, which is found in berries, flowers, leaves, stems, and roots. Most people—by some estimates, 70 to 85 percent of us—are allergic to urushiol; the allergy tends to develop with repeated exposure. Most people who think they're not allergic to poison oak will develop an allergy after enough exposure (the amount of exposure varying from person to person). So even if you think you aren't allergic, it makes sense to try to avoid contact as much as possible.

Wearing long pants and long-sleeved shirts affords protection, but beware: You can also contact poison oak from clothing that has urushiol on it. Washing clothes in water deactivates the urushiol, but in dry southern California, this isn't always an option for hikers. So even if you wear protective clothing, try to avoid plowing through a patch of poison oak.

There are some pre-exposure solutions, the idea being to put a chemical shield between your skin and the poison oak. But continually reapplying these solutions on a backpacking trip is impractical, especially if you can't wash between applications. A better choice is to carry a small amount of anti-oak lotion (available at your outfitter), which can also be applied if you know you've been exposed (or, less effectively, later when a rash develops). Otherwise, popular home remedies include washing with alcohol or yellow laundry soap. Use cold water, and avoid rubbing, which spreads the irritant. You'll know the poison oak rash when you get it: It itches like ten thousand mosquito bites, and in severe cases, it gets angry red with weepy blisters.

If you are very allergic, you might want to ask your doctor for a prescription of either a strong antihistamine (to stop the itching) or prednizone (which speeds healing of the rash).

Mormon Rocks

It's not just the chaparral that makes the southern slopes of the San Gabriels look so forbidding. Like the San Jacintos, the southern slopes of the San Gabriels owe their appearance to the action of the San Andreas Fault system, which cuts through Cajon Pass. Over time it has lifted the land on the north side of the fault to create the steep 7,000-foot escarpment that John Muir found so forbidding. A recent example of this uplifting occurred during the San Fernando Earthquake of 1971, which lifted the San Gabriel Mountains by an astonishing 6 feet.

Near Cajon Pass, there is also evidence of how the fault moves matter in an east-west direction. On the PCT, about a mile from Cajon Pass as you're hiking north, the trail passes a conspicuous formation known as Mormon Rocks. Although to human eyes these rocks look perfectly fixed in place, they are on the move, being carried northeast by the fault at a rate of some 2 inches a year. The Mormon Rocks have traveled a long way to get here: They originated about 25 miles away, and if you follow the fault in a southwesterly direction for 25 miles, you'll see the evidence. On the other side of the rift, there is a similar formation that geologists have determined was created at the same time and place as the rocks at Cajon Pass.

Since its formation some 30 million years ago, the San Andreas Fault system has continually rearranged the California landscape, in some cases moving matter as much as several hundred miles. In a sense, almost all of California seems to be on the move, headed for somewhere else. Geologists posit that if Los Angeles and San Francisco still exist a few million years from now, they'll be standing side by side.

San Gabriel Mountains

Aside from the hot and dry 20-mile climb to the crest, the San Gabriels are not nearly as thornily savage to today's hikers as they were to John Muir. Muir, remember, was wont to travel cross-country. In his day, maintained and graded recreational hiking trails did not tame steep slopes with gentle switchbacks and graded footways.

Back then the San Gabriels were prime habitat not for recreating humans, but for bears and bighorn sheep, which have now retreated into the most remote parts of the backcoutry, trying to escape the trails and roads that allow all manner of recreation use: not only hiking, but mountain biking, off-road driving, horseback riding, and skiing. (There are six ski areas in the Angeles National Forest; the thru-hiker resupply station of Wrightwood is a modest ski-resort town.) Paved roads bring the bulk of the visitors into these formerly impenetrable mountains. The Angeles Crest Scenic Byway runs between the towns of La Cañada and Wrightwood and is parallel tothe Pacific Crest Trail for some 35 miles. (*Note:* From some viewpoints along the highway, it is possible to see both the Pacific Ocean and the Mojave Desert.) Another paved road, the Angeles Forest Highway, intersects the PCT, linking the Angeles Crest Byway with Mojave Desert communities on the north side of the mountains, such as Palmdale and Lancaster. The frequent road crossings make it possible to plan short hikes of almost any duration.

These roads and trails have turned Muir's thornily savage and rigidly inaccessible mountains into one of the most accessible and popular recreation areas in southern California. The Forest Service call the Angeles National Forest Los Angeles's "backyard playground," and a "truly urban national forest," and claims that it attracts more than 32 million visitors each year. These distinctions are not likely to be attractive to backpackers and PCT thru-hikers, most of whom feel that if they wanted an urban playground, they could have stayed home. But not to worry: Despite the Forest Service's description, hikers are unlikely to find the PCT overly crowded, especially once you walk a few miles from the trailheads.

Limber pines atop Mount Baden-Powell

Mount Baden-Powell

The Angeles Crest boasts the highest point on southern California's PCT—9,245 feet, just below the summit of 9,399-foot Mount Baden-Powell. A side trail leads about a quarter-mile (and the remaining 154 feet up) to the actual summit. Named after Sir Robert Baden-Powell, the founder of the Boy Scouts, Mount Baden-Powell is something of a pilgrimage site for Scouts. It's also the terminus of the Scout-built Silver Moccasin Trail. Now designated as a national recreation trail, the Silver Moccasin Trail runs 53 miles through the San Gabriel Mountains and is a popular challenge for Scouts attempting to earn their hiking merit badge. For about 20 miles, it is contiguous with the Pacific Crest Trail. On the climb to Mount Baden-Powell (a well-trod trail, because the distance between parking lot and summit is only 4.2 miles), the Scouts have at random intervals built little markers showing distance and elevation. The distances are measured to the hundredth of a mile; elevations are given to the nearest foot. Doubtless such markers would become tedious over a long distance, but they last only a few miles. If you're interested, take the opportunity to field-test your internal pedometer and altimeter. Thru-hikers might find that after several hundred miles on the trail, they have become fairly accurate judges of distance and elevation.

The quarter-mile side trail to the summit of Baden-Powell is well worth the little additional effort to get there. If not blocked by smog, the view from the peak gives you a chance to see several hundred miles of your past and future route, laid out before and behind you. On a good day the views extend forward all the way to Mount Whitney in the High Sierra and backward to the San Jacintos.

Limber Pines

In southern California, an elevation of 9,000 feet means that you've climbed into the Hudsonian zone. At sea level, you'd have to walk to northern Canada to find similar conditions. On smog-free days, the view from the summit of Mount Baden-Powell can be dramatic, but even more arresting are the oddly shaped limber pines that hug the wind-sheared high country. Named for the flexibility of their tough rubbery twigs, which can sometimes be bent into a knot, the limber pines atop Baden-Powell are thought to be more than 2,000 years old. Their flexibility is an advantage on the storm-buffeted slopes of exposed ridges. Flexible trees are more able to bend with the wind; they are also better able to bend under large accumulations of snow.

Limber pine

Limber pines also grow at lower elevations—they are also found, for example, in Nebraska—and when their habitats are less exposed, they look a lot like ordinary pines, with symmetrical Christmas-tree shapes. But those that grow in the alpine zone allow themselves to be molded by the wind. The result is a tree with short, thick trunks and branches twisted into weird and fantastic shapes.

Soledad Canyon Road

In yet another of its precipitous changes of mood, the trail ends this section with a long descent into Soledad Canyon, where, at 2,200 feet, the terrain could not be more different from Baden-Powell's cold summit.

The descent into the canyon is the same kind of long and winding descent PCT hikers are well used to by now, becoming hotter and drier the lower you go. From the trail, you can see the bottom long before you get there. Most inviting of all is the prospect of water. The Santa Clara River runs through Soledad Canyon, clearly visible from the mountainsides. No need to worry about a water shortage here: In addition to the river, the canyon contains a series of RV and trailer-park campgrounds that welcome hikers. There are even a few swimming pools, their turquoise waters shimmering an invitation that is visible from high up on the trail. The downside is the noise. Whistle-blowing trains run through the canyon all night long, so if you plan to spend the night, bring earplugs.

🚶🚶 HIKING INFORMATION

Seasonal Information and Gear Tips

This section is similar in climate and challenges to the section covered in chapter 2. Most of the first 90 miles can be hiked in the winter, although you may have some snow around Big Bear. The San Gabriels have snow during the winter, but generally are clear by May or June. At the higher elevations, the hiking season extends into summer—although the springs and seasonal water sources may not be running.

- Three-season hiking gear, including a rain jacket and warm (20- or 30-degree) sleeping bag, is recommended during the spring. During the summer, a lighter bag and fewer layers will suffice.
- In late spring, gnats can be an irritation during the day in the San Gabriels. A head net is a big help.
- There are several very dry stretches in this section. Have enough water containers to carry 6 or 7 quarts (more if you

are overweight, out of shape, unacclimated to the temperatures, or plan to dry camp between water sources). Be sure to
pay attention to your water supply when you leave Mojave
Dam, Silverwood Lake, and, especially, Cajon Pass.

Thru-hikers' Corner

- Unless you are hiking in extreme early season or in an especially high snow year, you are likely to be slowed by snow
only on the slopes of Mount Baden-Powell.
- **Summit Valley Country Store,** on California Highway 173, is
0.3 miles off-trail just before the trail enters Silverwood
Lake State Recreation Area. It's a hiker-friendly resting
place where thru-hikers are invited to put their packs on a
scale and find out if what they've been telling folks about
pack weight is true. Your picture, plus the results of the
weighing, get put in the PCT album/register.

Best Short Hikes

- The first 46 miles (from Van Dusen Canyon Road to the Mojave
River Dam) of this stretch of trail offers perfectly spaced campsites with water for hikers looking for a four-day backpack.
Starting at Van Dusen Canyon Road, the mileages are 11 miles
(to Holcomb Creek), 12 miles (to a campsite under a bridge
spanning Deep Creek), 9 miles (to the Deep Creek Hot Springs),
and 14 miles (to the dam).
- Short-distance hikers will also find plenty of good options in
the San Gabriel Mountains. Frequent road crossings make it easier
to plan short hikes in the San Gabriels than in any other of southern
California's ranges. The Angeles National Forest is crisscrossed by the Angeles Forest Highway and the Angeles Crest
Scenic Byway. The PCT runs parallel to the Angeles Crest
Byway for 35 miles, and there are lots of trailheads, making it
possible to plan a hike of almost any length.
- The most popular day hike in this section of the PCT is the
4.2-mile climb from the trailhead on California Highway 2 to
the summit of Mount Baden-Powell in the San Gabriel
Mountains.

Resupplies and Trailheads

Big Bear City and Wrightwood are most commonly used.

Big Bear City (mile 0) is 3 miles off-trail via Van Dusen Canyon Road. It has restaurants, motels, laundry, a post office, and outfitters. The local fire department allows PCT hikers to camp in its yard. Post office: General Delivery, Big Bear City, CA 92314

Mojave River Dam (mile 46). There's nothing here in the way of supplies, but this is a good trailhead for the four-day hike mentioned above.

Silverwood Lake State Recreation Area (mile 54.8) has a campground, shower, and store.

Cajon Pass (mile 68.4). The PCT crosses I-15 at Cajon Pass. A half-mile off-trail is an interstate exchange with a motel, a convenience store, and (a few hundred yards closer to the trail) a hiker-friendly restaurant that maintains a trail register.

Wrightwood (mile 89.6) on California Highway 2. Resupplying in Wrightwood requires descending on the 2-mile Acorn Trail, then walking another 1.5 miles on roads. Nonetheless, most long-distance hikers stop here because it's the only convenient resupply point until Agua Dulce (chapter 4). Post office: General Delivery, Wrightwood, CA 92397

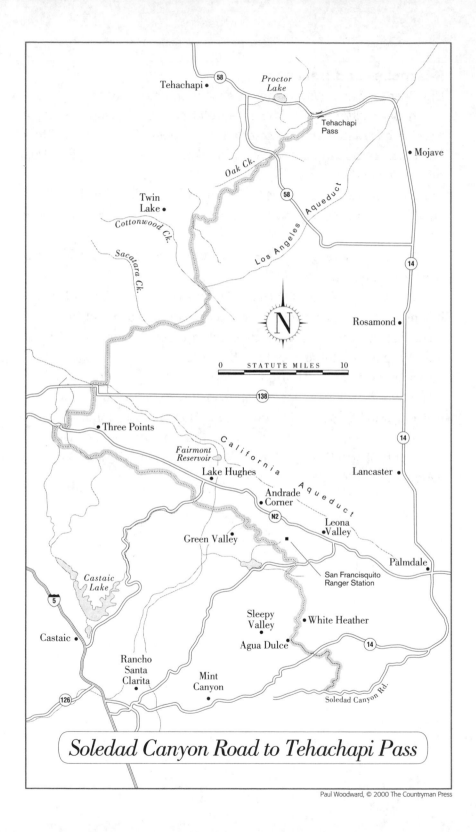

Soledad Canyon Road to Tehachapi Pass

4

Soledad Canyon Road to Tehachapi Pass

109.9 miles

This section of trail is one of the most feared in southern California.

The Mojave Desert.

Desert with a capital D, as in dry, dust-bedeviled, desiccated, deadly. Up till now, everything else has been just practice.

At least, so go the rumors. The reality is not nearly so bad. In fact, some hikers find this section a welcome change, if a challenge. In the right season, it can be one of the highlights of a PCT hike.

The focus of all the hullabaloo is the Antelope Valley, which is the western arm of the Mojave Desert. To correct one misconception right off the bat, the Mojave is not an especially hot desert. Ecologists put it in a sort of middling category, a transition area between the hot Colorado Desert to the south and the cooler Great Basin Desert to the north.

And, to correct another misconception, not all of this section of trail is in desert. True to form, the PCT heads for the hills whenever possible. It spends far more time on chaparral-covered hillsides than it does on the sandy desert floors.

All that said, the difficulties here can be more severe than usual. For thru-hikers, who usually arrive in late May or early June, the temperatures in this "cooler" desert can be more than 100 degrees—and, as usual, ground temperatures can be a sole-scorching 150 degrees or even more. (In summer, ground temperatures can rise to 190—which might make you wonder whether ecologists should be required to walk across a desert before they get to tell the rest of us whether it's hot or not.) The water situation is simply described: No natural water sources are reliable at any time of year. And if the trail often seems illogically routed and just plain ornery, that's because it is. The route is the gerrymandered result of political compromise between a well-funded corporate landowner, which did not want the trail on its property, and the U.S. Forest Service, which simply wanted to get the trail finished and done with. As a result, this section was the last on the entire PCT to be completed. Its route has been criticized by many in the trail community. Criticized or not, the trail's completion is marked by a monument in Soledad Canyon.

Ironically only a small percentage of the millions of people who annually hike on the PCT will ever see the monument. For the most part, this section is used by local outdoorspeople, long-distance hikers, or PCT section hikers. This section's difficulties, both reputed and real, make is less than attractive as a destination in and of itself. That is unfortunate, because the Mojave offers a spring wildflower bloom that is well worth traveling to see.

THE ROUTE

Starting at Soledad Canyon Road, on the northern side of the San Gabriel Mountains, the trail follows a meandering route past parcels of private property before arriving on the paved main street that runs through the small ranching town of Agua Dulce. Although Agua Dulce has limited services (no motels or campgrounds, and in some years the post office has been shut due to a lack of personnel to run it), the town's friendliness, hospitality, and involvement with the trail community, not to mention its well-stocked store, have earned it high marks as a thru-hiker trail town. It's also one of only four towns on the PCT that the trail actually passes through. (Two others are in California: Belden, a trailer park settlement so small that it barely merits being called a town, and Seiad Valley, which is only marginally bigger. Cascade Locks, on the Oregon–Washington border, is the fourth.)

From Agua Dulce, the trail roller-coasters through the dry San Pelona Mountains, then passes close to Lake Hughes, a recreation area 2.2 miles off-trail that is a good rest and resupply stop. North of Lake Hughes, on a ridge along Leibre Mountain, you can sometimes see the Pacific Ocean. But sometimes not: Smog limits the number of clear days.

Dropping into the Antelope Valley, the trail changes character, reflecting southern California's schizophrenic rural culture. Influenced by the proximity of the Los Angeles metropolitan area and the rapid growth of nearby towns like Palmdale and Lancaster, this part of the desert seems like a battleground between human civilization and the Mojave's refusal to be civilized. Following not only trails, but also dusty dirt roads and occasionally (where there is no clear footway) a series of posts, hikers pass the artificial rivers of the California and Los Angeles Aqueducts, furiously flowing to meet the endless needs of southern California.

From any height of land, you can look down onto grids of empty roads that—despite names like Avenue C or 270th Street West—seemingly go from nowhere to nowhere in ruler-straight lines that disappear into the haze of heat. Street signs are riddled with bullet holes, and on the ground are piles of shotgun shells. Occasionally there's a trailer dwelling surrounded with ATVs and cars that may or may not have been started in the last decade. Dirt-bike tracks are everywhere; occasionally you'll see someone riding about, as likely as not wearing camouflage gear.

But there is also space, and—on the rare windless day—that big desert silence is as vast and encompassing as the star-studded nighttime sky. There is a fabulous assortment of varied vegetation, like the ridiculous-looking Joshua trees and the brilliant California poppies. And there is the glorious spring wildflower bloom that splashes the sand and gravel with a carpet of color.

This section is subject to extreme conditions: high winds, hot spring and summer temperatures, and winter frost. Bring plenty of water, because none of the water sources are reliable. An important water source is Cottonwood Creek (87.3 miles into this section and smack in the middle of the desert valley). The next reliable water, in Oak Creek Canyon, is 22.7 hot, dry miles away. Check the PCT hot line (1-888-PCTRAIL) for the most recent info on Cottonwood Creek.

Once across the desert valley, the trail remembers its affinity for higher country and climbs up into the Tehachapi Mountains, which are considered by some geologists to be the southernmost spur of the Sierra Nevada Range. Elevations rise to above 6,000 feet, offering good views of the San Gorgonio and San Jacinto Mountains to the south. The path follows its compromise route along the boundaries of the Tejon Ranch, and because the trail's location was determined by politics and not the landscape, it often seems to defy the rules of commonsense trailbuilding. This section ends at Tehachapi Pass, the official beginning of the Sierra Nevada Mountains.

WHAT YOU'LL SEE

Trail History

Perhaps more than anywhere else on the PCT, this stretch of trail demonstrates some of the difficulties faced by trail mangers and public lands administrators in the construction of a long-distance footpath.

Most of the PCT boasts an extraordinarily scenic route. The trail has benefited from the fact that the major mountains ranges of California, Oregon, and Washington are part of our system of public lands. But there isn't an unbroken corridor of public land from Mexico to Canada: About 12 percent of the PCT crosses private land. Much of that land is owned by large corporations that are active in such traditional western land uses as timber cutting (especially in Washington) and grazing. That is the case here, where the Tejon Ranch sits atop the crest of the Tehachapi Mountains, exactly where trail planners envisioned that the PCT should go. The ranch's owners did not agree.

Like many rural landowners, the Tejon Ranch cited a litany of issues familiar to anyone who has worked to put a long-distance trail on the ground—whether it's in the Appalachians, or Montana, or New Mexico, or southern California. Landowners fear that hikers will leave gates open, scare the cattle, bother the dogs, leave litter, start fires, pollute the water, vandalize buildings, and pave the way for hunters to come. In many cases, the reluctance is fueled by anti-government sentiment or by fear that if a landowner gives an easement to a trail, the government could come back in future years and request—or demand—more land.

In any case, for years the corporate-owned Tejon Ranch sat smack in the middle of the trail's proposed route, and armed guards patrolled its perimeter, determined to keep trespassers out. Hikers, meanwhile, followed a temporary route through the middle of the Antelope Valley. This old route followed the Los Angeles Aqueduct straight across the desert toward the town of Mojave, then paralleled California Highway 58 up to Jawbone Canyon, where it turned west and climbed back into the mountains.

In 1988 most of the PCT was complete, and the 20th anniversary of the National Trail System Act brought the PCT publicity and increased public interest. Trail managers were determined to finish the trail and turned their attention to the pesky problem of the Tehachapis. Attempts to negotiate a right-of-way were rebuffed, and with no solution in sight, PCT managers did something they had never before done: In 1991 and 1992 they started condemnation proceedings to legally force the owners of the Tejon Ranch to allow the trail to pass through the property.

Condemnation is a powerful tool, but it has powerful, sometimes unwanted, repercussions. Forcing a landowner to sell property or an easement to the government often poisons relations between the trail and local communities for years. Realizing this, the PCT Advisory Council considered condemnation to be the tool of last resort. But with no compromise in sight, they felt they had no choice.

Facing with condemnation proceedings, the Tejon Ranch finally agreed to permit the PCT to pass through a small portion of its property. As a result, the PCT here follows some dirt roads, avoids ranch property whenever possible, and skirts along the fence line, following a bulldozed route that simply goes wherever the property line does—whether it makes trail sense or not. The guidebook calls the route a "hot, waterless, dangerous, ugly, and entirely un-Crestlike segment," which might be overstating the issue. As with the rest of the southern California's PCT, hiking through this largely waterless segment dictates careful planning and heavy water loads—but no more so than many other sections of trail to the south.

The route was clearly a compromise, but it was a route, and it was finished in time to celebrate the 25th anniversary of the National Trails System Act in 1993 by erecting a monument in Soledad Canyon. PCT managers and land administrators, as well as representatives from the Tejon Ranch, were on hand to celebrate the Golden Spike ceremony that marked completion of the PCT from Mexico to Canada.

Many hikers in the PCT community hope that in years ahead, a more pleasing route might still be established. In the meantime, hikers can help by being good guests. Follow posted regulations on ranch property, shut gates behind you, avoid making fires, follow minimum-impact guidelines, and pick up litter.

Los Angeles Aqueduct

In the Antelope Valley, hikers have the unusual experience of standing in the blazing sun, surrounded by cactus and Joshua trees, while hearing the roar of the artificial river of the Los Angeles Aqueduct running beneath their feet.

Spanish explorers first discovered the lazy, willow-choked Los Angeles River in 1769 and declared that the surrounding area had "all the requisites for a large settlement." All, that is, except for a truly adequate supply of water. In 1781, the city of Los Angeles was founded. Today it has a population of more than 3 million people, and Los Angeles County (through which the PCT passes) is home to more than 16 million. Without the imported aqueduct water, the Los Angeles River could, by itself, support perhaps a quarter-million residents.

Built in 1913, the Los Angeles Aqueduct was the brainchild of William Mulholland, water superintendent for Los Angeles County at the turn of the century. Mulholland realized that Los Angeles was fast outgrowing its water supply. In 1905, Los Angeles voters approved a bond issue authorizing the city to buy land and water rights in Owens Valley, where spring snowmelt falls in torrents from Sierran peaks.

More than 200 miles from Los Angeles, the Owens Valley was, prior to the aqueduct, a well-watered agricultural area. With a water table only a few feet below the surface, the valley was one of the few areas in California where Native Americans practiced agriculture. Nineteenth-century emigrants also settled here to raise crops. But when the aqueduct, called Mulholland's Ditch, opened in 1913, it took so much water that eventually even Owens Lake ran dry.

Seeing their farms become desiccated in this previously well-watered valley, Owens Valley farmers tried litigation, starting an era of water wars that combined the gunslinging drama of the Wild West with 20th-century big-city politics. Meanwhile, between 1913 and 1930, the population of Los Angeles grew from 200,000 people to 1,200,000, and the burgeoning city cast its eyes farther upstream, to the Mono Lake Basin, 105 miles north of Owens Lake. Taking too much water from the basin that fed the vulnerable habitat of Mono Lake almost destroyed this unique ecosystem, which is an important habitat for nesting birds and migratory waterfowl.

And still the city, and its thirst, kept growing. In 1970 the second Los Angeles Aqueduct was built. Today these two aqueducts bring in 430 million gallons a day and fuel 11 power plants. Los Angeles also gets water from northern California via the California Aqueduct (you'll cross its open culvert about 32 miles north of Lake Hughes). Yet another aqueduct runs underground at San Gorgonio Pass, this one carrying water from the Colorado River. So it's possible that some of the water you'll drink in a Los Angeles County restaurant started its life as a snowflake in Wyoming's Wind River Mountains or Colorado's Rocky Mountain National Park.

Walking along the L.A. Aqueduct, thirsty hikers might sentimentally remember the water fountain at Snow Creek, which tapped into the water supply for Palm Springs back at the northern base of the San Jacinto Mountains. The Los Angeles Aqueduct is not nearly so generous. While its location is perfectly obvious—a dirt service road traces the exact path of the underwater river, and every so often you'll see a capped siphon hole—the water is usually not accessible. In previous years, hikers were sometimes able to get water by removing the caps, but these days most of the caps are locked.

Mojave Desert

If you've been expecting a barren expanse of sand and cactus, you might be pleasantly surprised by the Mojave, especially if you happen to arrive during the peak of the spring wildflower bloom. Some biologists claim that the Mojave Desert is not an ecosystem unto itself, but is rather an ecotone, or edge, between the hotter Colorado Desert to the south and the colder Great Basin Desert to the North. Ecotones usually support large varieties of species—not only those endemic to each of the colliding ecosystems, but also those endemic to the unique environment that is formed where two different ecosystems meet. Adding to the biological diversity, the Mojave has great ranges in elevation (from below sea level to above 8,000 feet), and is proximate to other ecosystems, such as the southern Sierra, the Tehachapi Mountains, and the Coast Ranges. As a result, the Mojave boasts 250 species of annuals, 80 percent of which are endemics. In spring there can sometimes be as many as 70 plants per square yard; in wet years that number can exceed 400.

Thus valley oaks grow near Tehachapi Pass on the desert's edge, next to Joshua trees and cactus. Some plants grow here that were commonly thought exclusive to Pacific slopes. A bright example is the California poppy, which puts on a profuse display in the Antelope Valley, often near dense groves of Joshua trees. Plants growing here are a mixture of cold and hot desert species; often there will be an upper story of shrubs and a lower story of grasses and cacti.

Plants and animals here cope with the usual dryland challenges. Much of the Mojave Desert receives less than 5 inches of water a year, most of which falls in winter, sometimes as light snow. Despite the presence of the Mojave River, there is no outlet from the Mojave to the sea. The land is so dry that any water that falls is quickly absorbed by the porous soil. Compounding the problem are the Mojave's trademark high winds, which increase evaporation, stealing away much of the water that does manage to fall. Other factors that desert species must somehow adapt to include high salinity and alkalinity, scarce nutrients, frequent frost, and poor drainage.

Geologically as well as ecologically, the Mojave is one of America's most varied deserts, with rock forms and landscapes that show evidence of dramatic geological processes. Bounded by the Garlock and San Andreas Faults, this is an area of seismic activity. It is also highly mineralized. Over the last hundred years, miners have tunneled the earth in search of gold, silver, tungsten, iron, copper, lead, zinc, molybdenum, antimony, tin, uranium, and thorium. The Mojave is also one of the greatest borax-producing areas in the world

The PCT crosses the Mojave's western arm, the Antelope Valley. James Fremont came looking for a winter route across the Sierra with the 1844 U.S. topographical corps, and in 1845 some 250 Coast-bound settlers crossed here. In 1986 the Southern Pacific Railroad—with the help of the local Kawaiisu people, who lived in the nearby Tehachapis—put a railroad through.

Dust Devils

One of the most pervasive phenomena you'll encounter in the Mojave is the dust devil—also called a twister, and for good reason. A dust devil resembles nothing so much as a miniature tornado.

Dust devils usually occur around noon on a calm windless day, when

Antelope Valley

heated air rises swiftly and expands. Surface air moves into the vacuum to replace the rising air, and a whirl results, which gathers up sand, dust, and bits of vegetation and begins to move like a miniature tornado, made clearly visible by the debris it carries.

As the dust devil moves, it increases in height and velocity, sometimes impressively. Dust devils can (although they rarely do) reach heights of as much as a mile and can destroy parts of buildings. More commonly, and more modestly, dust devils are 10 to 50 feet tall—which is plenty big enough to wreak havoc with the tarp you've pitched to shelter yourself from the midday sun. On very windy days, it's good to have a bandanna on hand and wear it bandit-style as a dust mask.

Joshua Trees

Like the giant saguaros that announce that you are in Arizona's high Sonoran Desert, Joshua trees tells you that you are in California's Mojave. The plant is said to have been named by Mormon settlers who thought its raised branches looked like Joshua gesturing to the Israelites. It was also called—

Joshua tree

presumably by people of less religious sentiments—a cabbage tree.

In fact, the Joshua tree is neither a tree nor a cactus (and certainly not a cabbage), but rather a yucca—in fact, a relative of the lily. Joshua trees usually grow on alluvial slopes between 2,500 and 5,000 feet in elevation, hence they are more common in the higher elevations of the Mojave. Large colonies of Joshua trees often indicate that you are approaching the transition zone between the Mojave Desert and the higher mountain ecosystems that surround it.

Joshua trees can reach almost 30 feet in height and occasionally grow even higher. They are evergreen plants, able to withstand frost, drought, heat, and drying winds. The dagger-shaped dark green leaves are sharp, stiff, and leathery. In the spring growing season, a ring of new spikes encircles the tip of each live branch. Flowering varies from year to year.

Joshua trees play an important ecological role, supporting their own micro-ecosystem of plants and animals. One relationship is of particular interest, because the Joshua tree and a particular moth—the tegeticula—have a symbiotic relationship that is so codependent that without each other, neither species could survive. Like all lilies, yucca must be pollinated. Lily pollen is sticky—it is introduced by the surgical work of insects, not the random whimsy of winds. Surgical is not too strong a word. The moths are active at night and are attracted to white blossoms of the yucca. The female moth collects pollen, and when she has enough, she inserts a needlelike egg-laying organ into the "ovary" of the flower—the part of the flower that contains potential seeds. She lays her eggs and makes sure seeds will develop by depositing enough pollen. Later, her newly hatched offspring will feed on these seeds. But they will leave enough for a new generation of Joshua trees, which will in turn support many new generations of tegeticula moths.

Live Joshua trees are also home to insects; dead trees are home to termites and beetles, which process the dead wood and return nutrients to the soil. Branches provide shelter for woodpeckers, hawks, wrens, and the Scott oriole, which prefers to nest among the spikiest foliage. Other residents include yucca night lizards and wood rats. Intermittent visitors might include screech owls, red-tailed hawks, great horned owls, and rattlesnakes, all of whom regard the Joshua tree as a potential delicatessen and occasionally stop by in hope of a quick meal.

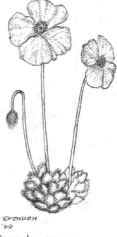

Great desert poppy

Mojave Desert Flowers

Plant life in the Mojave is very much affected by the amount and timing of the first rainfall of the growing season—not in the spring, but in autumn. Many of the annual plants germinate in late fall, when the area gets 1 or more inches of rain. Most of the annual rainfall in the Mojave comes in winter. The wildflower bloom is directly proportional to the rainfall. About once a decade, it is spectacular.

Because rain is erratic and scarce, flowering desert plants spend most of their life in a dormant state as seeds. The seeds have a hard waxy coating that protects the embryonic plant inside from drying out. A chemical in the seeds inhibits germination until enough rain leaches it away, allowing seeds to open only when there is an adequate amount of moisture. In December and January, these plants (called winter ephemerals) grow into small seedlings. Growth is slow, leaf by leaf. The young plants must endure cold nights and frost. Still, daytime temperatures are favorable—frequently between 50 and 80 degrees—and by late May, before the hot summer begins, the plants have managed to grow from seed to seed-bearer.

Desert candle

Scorpion

Types of flowers include brown-eyed primrose, Cholkley's lupine, thistle sage, California poppy (long believed endemic to eastern slopes, but able to migrate here through low passes), Mojave buckwheat, desert sunflower, red mariposa lily, the desert marigold, and a memorable oddity: the desert candle or squaw cabbage. Its yellow-green stems look like the plant has swallowed some billiard balls (think of a snake that has just swallowed an animal wider than it is). To top it all off, there's a bright tuft of purple flowers. If you add in the Joshua trees, you might well be excused for thinking of the Mojave as a place Dr. Seuss made up.

Wildlife

As Edward Abbey put it, virtually everything in the desert sticks, stabs, stinks, or stings. Certainly the plant kingdom lives up to this dubious reputation, and by this point in the PCT, most thru-hikers have had various prickly encounters with cactus, cholla, bayonet-sharp agave, and yucca.

But the animal kingdom, too, has its fair share of species with prickly attitudes. The Mojave is home to 10 or more species of scorpions, although you aren't likely to see them during the day, when they hide from the heat under clumps of debris or fallen Joshua trees. Scorpions are, however, active at night (one reason that some desert hikers prefer sleeping in tents).

Desert tortoise

Chuckwalla

If you camp out, check your boots in the morning, before inserting your feet!

The Mojave is also home to three species of rattlesnakes: sidewinders (so called because of their winding, writhing style of locomotion), speckled rattlesnakes, and Mojave green rattlesnakes. The last is a yellow-green version of the western diamondback, only more aggressive, with a more potent venom. (For more on rattlesnakes, see chapter 1.)

Other animals you might see include the desert tortoise, although you'll have to look closely: These big tortoises are becoming scarce, and during the day they hide in depressions under shrubs. But they are rambunctious in spring, and you may hear them snorting and banging their shells in a mating ritual.

Reptiles that inhabit the Mojave include iguanas, chuckwallas, zebra-tail lizards, desert-horned lizards, and collared lizards. You'll often see the latter stopping to do push-ups. It's not a mating ritual, as is often thought. Instead, the push-ups help the animal control its circulation and body temperature.

You're unlikely to see coyotes in the Mojave, but you're likely to hear them. Their canine chorus is a nightly serenade throughout the West. Nowhere is their howl more haunting than in the vast spaces of the open desert, where scarcity of game forces coyotes to cover vast distances to hunt, and therefore, to communicate with each other over long stretches of empty space. Coyotes are the best runners among the canids (a family than includes all dogs, from wolves to Chihuahuas), often cruising at 25 to 30 miles an hour, with sprints up to 40 miles an hour. In a normal night of hunting, a desert coyote pack might typically cover 15 linear miles, and sometimes much more. After dusk and before dawn, you'll hear them barking, yapping, and howling.

Desert coyote

Antelope Valley and the Los Angeles Aqueduct

Look for signs of coyotes on rocks in sparsely vegetated areas. If it looks like a good place for a hiker to have lunch—not too many plants to trip over, a comfortable rock, and a good view—it's a good coyote spot, too (although rather than appreciating the view, the coyotes are most likely looking for prey). Coyotes use scat and urine to mark their territories. They also dig holes—coyote wells—to get to water and then ambush prey that stop by for a drink.

Livestock Grazing

From desert tortoises, whose newly hatched young feed on foliage, to kangaroo rats that cache piles of seeds, desert animals are highly dependent on native annuals for food. Young desert tortoises, for example, depend on getting nutrition from spring wildflowers. Mice and rats depend on seeds. And carnivores depend on the success of these smaller creatures.

But the food sources—the plants and flowers—that support all this life are themselves under pressure from livestock grazing, which has had a significant impact on desert ecosystems. One flock of sheep munching its way through an area can reduce the biomass of annual plants by 60 percent. Livestock grazing also encourages the growth of nonnative species because they deposit seeds in their feces and because they do not eat many of these plants. The nonnative plants therefore have an advantage over the native plants and quickly take over. In the western Mojave, up to 70 percent of plants are now non-native species promoted by cattle and sheep. Grazers also eat shrubs, which provide shade for small animals. Fortunately new grazing restrictions were implemented by land managers in 1992 in an attempt to preserve desert tortoise habitat.

HIKING INFORMATION

Seasonal Information and Gear Tips
This is a good section to avoid in the summer. Even in spring, temperatures can rise above 100 degrees. In winter, the lower elevations make for fine hiking—but it may be surprisingly cold at night. The higher elevations in winter will have some snow.

- Bring sunscreen and a wide-brimmed hat for sun protection. Some hikers additionally protect themselves with lightweight, breathable long-sleeved shirts and long pants.
- You'll need extra water containers because the water sources are few and far between—and unreliable.

Thru-hikers' Corner
The tiny community of Agua Dulce has in recent years become renowned in hiker circles for its friendliness. In some years, either the church or local residents have allowed hikers to camp: Ask at the post office or the Century 21 Real Estate office.

In the Mojave Desert, local resident Jack Fair provides water for hikers at his home at the PCT crossing of California Highway 138. He also offers camping and a shuttle to a nearby convenience store for a small fee.

Alternate Route
Before the compromise route that was finally established in the Tehachapis, the PCT slashed straight across the desert following the

Los Angeles Aqueduct. This route was always intended to be temporary, but some hikers still take it. Two sources of information are Wilderness Press's old PCT California guidebook (now out of print, but available in some libraries). If you can't get your hands on the guidebook, be assured that you don't need specific step-by-step directions to navigate through this easy, open country, especially since all you'll be doing is following the aqueduct. A good source of information is the DeLorme *Atlas and Gazetteer* for California.

Here's the route: Leave the PCT at Elizabeth Lake Canyon Road, 40 miles into this chapter's section of trail. Descend on the road to Lake Hughes. Follow back roads past Fairmont Reservoir, then follow 170th Street west to the Los Angeles Aqueduct. Take the Los Angeles Aqueduct to near Mojave. After resupplying in Mojave, continue along the aqueduct to Jawbone Canyon. Go up into Jawbone Canyon, where the alternate route connects with the PCT 34.7 miles into the section covered in chapter 5.

The main argument in favor of the old route is that instead of a meandering, difficult up-and-down dry route through yet more chaparral, the old route introduces hikers to a completely new experience: a traverse of the Mojave Desert. Another advantage is that following the aqueduct is flat, straight, and fast. (It's also about 30 miles shorter than the new route.) While the official route crosses California Highway 58 at a point 9.2 miles from Tehachapi and 9 miles from Mojave—requiring a hitch in either direction if you want to resupply—the old route crosses California Highway 58 within 3 miles of Mojave. Resupplying doesn't require any hitchhiking. If you do use this route, remember to fill up with water at Cottonwood Creek because the aqueduct is sealed. There are, however, ranches and windmill farms where it may be possible to get some water.

Best Short Hikes

You won't see a lot of short-distance and day hikers on this section. But if you're interested in a sampling of this section's hiking, probably the most scenic stretch is the 22.7 miles from Agua Dulce to the San Francisquito Ranger Station. Expect lots of chaparral, a rolling-up-and-down hike, and some excellent views.

Resupplies and Trailheads

Agua Dulce is the most commonly used.

Soledad Canyon (mile 0) on Soledad Canyon Road boasts several campgrounds where hikers are welcome to stay. Some of them have amenities including vending machines, swimming pools, cafés, laundry facilities, and showers. Ask when you check in if pizza delivery is available!

Agua Dulce (mile 19.7). This is one of the few towns that the PCT actually passes through. The only disadvantage: There are no hotels or campgrounds. But there is a store, and in recent years, townspeople have sometimes generously offered PCT hikers a place to stay. Post office: General Delivery, Agua Dulce, CA 91350. (The post office is in Richard's Canyon Market.)

San Francisquito Ranger Station (mile 32.4) on San Francisquito Canyon Road. This trailhead has a reliable water supply. For resupply, you could detour 1.7 miles southwest to Green Valley.

Lake Hughes (mile 40.0) is 2.2 miles off-trail on Elizabeth Canyon Road. It has motels, showers, and limited groceries.

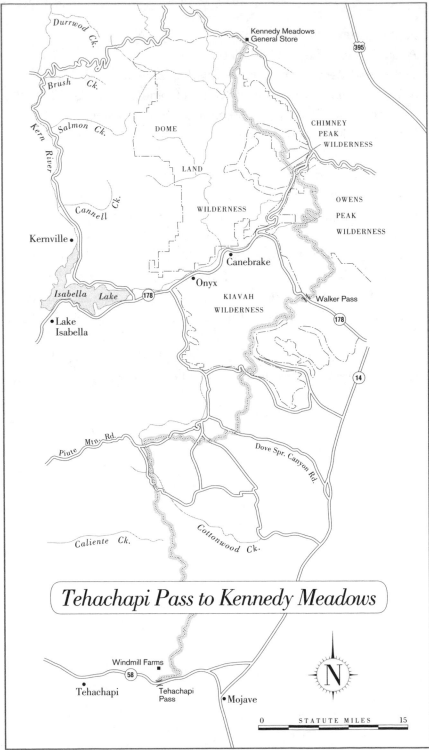

Durrwod Ck.

Kennedy Meadows
■ General Store

395

Brush Ck.

Kern River

Salmon Ck.

DOME

CHIMNEY
PEAK
WILDERNESS

LAND

Cannell Ck.

WILDERNESS

OWENS
PEAK
WILDERNESS

Kernville •

• Canebrake

Isabella Lake

• Onyx

178

KIAVAH
WILDERNESS

Walker Pass

178

• Lake
Isabella

14

Piute Mtn. Rd.

Dove Spr. Canyon Rd.

Caliente Ck.

Cottonwood Ck.

Tehachapi Pass to Kennedy Meadows

N

Windmill Farms
■

58

Tehachapi

Tehachapi
Pass

• Mojave

0   STATUTE MILES   15

Paul Woodward, © 2000 The Countryman Press

5

Tehachapi Pass to Kennedy Meadows

141.9 miles

Welcome to the Sierra Nevada!

The word *Sierra* refers to a range that is serrated, or saw-toothed. The word *Nevada* means *snowy*. In 1542 a Spanish ship captain was sailing along the California coast and recorded seeing *una gran sierra nevada* to the east of Monterey. The mountains we today call the Sierra Nevada aren't anywhere near Monterey—Captain Cabrillo was probably looking at the coastal range, although it is neither especially grand nor snowy—but for years the name was used on maps of California to indicate mountain

Climbing into the South Sierras

ranges. It wasn't until more than 200 years later, in 1772, that a Spanish expedition identified the mountains we today call the Sierra Nevada.

Running about 400 miles from Tehachapi Pass in the south to Mount Lassen in the north, the Sierra Nevada is the longest truly continuous mountain range in the 48 contiguous states. (The Appalachians and Rockies are subdivided into smaller ranges that have different geological histories.) But that 400 miles is crow-flying distance. If you happen to be measuring the distance on foot, switchbacking up and down countless mountains and meandering along the snakelike route of the PCT, you'll rack up close to 800 miles on your pedometer.

More facts: The Sierra runs through three national parks, nine national forests, and one national monument. It contains the longest wilderness, deepest canyon, and highest mountain in the contiguous states, as well as some of America's most spectacular scenery and most popular hiking trails.

The image of a trapdoor propped slightly open is often used to describe the shape of the range. The eastern side is short (as little as 6 miles from base to summit), steep, and dramatic; it forms one of the most striking escarpments in America. Mount Whitney, at 14,494 feet, looms two and a half vertical miles over the Owens Valley and is only 60 miles from Death Valley's Badwater Canyon, 280 feet below sea level. The western slope is much gentler, sometimes as much as 60 miles wide. There is also asymmetry on the north-south axis; elevations are higher in the south than in the north.

According to most geologists, the PCT enters the Sierra Nevada at Tehachapi Pass, where the Garlock and San Andreas Faults meet, forming a border between the Sierra Nevada and the Mojave Desert. Nonetheless, on arriving at Tehachapi Pass, you might feel hard-pressed to see much difference between the landscape ahead and that behind. Scruffy brown mountains are still covered in chaparral, and populations of lizards and rattlesnakes scuttle in the dry rustling underbrush. The occasional jackrabbit zigzags up the trail; coyotes sing at night. Joshua trees provide the only shade, and bayonet-sharp yucca spears nip at exposed skin. Water remains scarce. For the first 16 miles of this section, there isn't any at all. Geologists can say what they will; as a hiker, you may well feel that most of this section is far more like the familiar drylands to the south than like the dramatic pinnacles of the Sierra to the north.

THE ROUTE

Leaving Tehachapi Pass, the PCT crosses the Garlock Fault, California's second-longest. With two major faults and significant land movement, seismologists predict that this region is ripe for a major earthquake.

Shortly after Tehachapi Pass the trail passes above the Walong Loop, a rail route that is, because of its circular tunnel, one of the most photographed railroad sections in the world.

The trail climbs to the crest of the Sierra, leaving behind the Joshua trees and junipers and yuccas and rising to the cooler pinyon and oak woodlands. Once it reaches the crest, it pretty much stays there until Walker Pass, about 90 miles from Tehachapi Pass. Views alternate between mountain vistas and deep canyons, with the occasional panorama of the desert below, including Edwards Air Force Base, which has been used for landing space shuttles. Also along the route are windmill farms and the remains of old mines, testament to the mineral richness of the area.

The terrain through the section is transitional—no longer desert, not yet high mountains. It can be hot here during the hiking season (despite the word *Tehachapi,* which means *frozen* in a local Paiute dialect). But as you progress north, ever so subtly changes appear. The trees are taller and the

Transition zone in the South Sierras

shade is cooler. North-facing views open to higher mountains, some of them tipped in white. Springs become more reliable. A number of them have been boxed, piped, and otherwise protected from pollution by the BLM and Forest Service. The risk of forest fires is not as great, and even in the dry season, campfires are sometimes permitted. Although the trail has not quite broken away from the fetters of the drylands to the south, it is entering the orbit of the mountains to the north.

In this section, the PCT spends most of its time on public land and good cut trail. From Bird Spring Pass almost to Kennedy Meadows, the route is through a series of wilderness areas managed by either the BLM or the Forest Service. Nonetheless, like the previous section, this trail segment is primarily used by locals, by long-distance hikers, and by hikers trying to complete the PCT in sections. While it's perfectly pleasant, most back-packers using plane tickets and vacation time gravitate to the more spec-tacular country to the north.

You get your first distant views of the Sierra high country about 20 miles in. Between Golden Oaks Spring and Robin Bird Spring, the views open to the bigger mountains ahead: Olancha Peak (likely snow-covered during thru-hiking season) and Mount Whitney among them. If you're a thru-hiker, don't panic at the snow. True, the white-tipped panorama is likely to look a little intimidating—maybe a lot! But there are still 250 miles—at least two weeks of hiking—before you reach the real High Sierra at 12,000-foot Cottonwood Pass. A lot of snow can melt in that time.

The trail descends to Walker Pass, where there is a campground, made more lively in recent years by the visits of resident black bears. It's worth remembering that the Sierra Nevada is infamous for ursine campground robbers. If you haven't thus far been hanging your food at night, Walker Pass is a good place to start.

From Walker Pass, the trail is in a true transition zone, but almost with every mile, you can feel the high country coming closer. Finally, the trail reaches to the South Fork of the Kern River. The sun might still be still blazing and the footway dusty dry, but there is something new here: Water. Running fast and ice-cold, the South Fork of the Kern is fed from the melted snow of the high peaks—the first tactile, physical evidence that your long traverse through southern California's drylands is at last coming to an end.

This section ends at Kennedy Meadows, a Forest Service campground with a store that accepts food drops for long-distance hikers.

WHAT YOU'LL SEE

The Walong Loop

Eight miles west of Tehachapi, and visible from the trail, is the Walong Loop, an unusual circular stretch of railroad that dates from 1875 and 1876. The Southern Pacific Railroad had decided to connect central California (Bakersfield) and southern California (Los Angeles) with a route through Tehachapi Pass. Small problem: The Tehachapi Mountains stood directly in the way, and the grade was too steep for a railroad.

Like a modern-day trail builder, road engineers switchbacked through gullies and along slopes, inching ever higher—but they were still short 77 vertical feet.

The solution was to construct a tunnel that ran in a full circle, so that by the time the train had completed its loop, it had gained the necessary elevation. The resulting loop is 3,799 feet long. Today's freight trains can be more than a mile long, so frequently a locomotive going through the loop passes over (or under, depending upon direction) its own caboose.

The name *Walong* is of murky origin. It is thought to be the result of cultural and linguistic confusion between Americans and Cantonese railroad workers. There is no word *Walong* in Cantonese. One theory is that the name might be a combination of the Cantonese words for *Chinese people* and *road.* Another theory claims it means *coiled dragon.* Either seems appropriate.

Today the Walong Loop is operated by the Union Pacific and Santa Fe Railroads. It connects the San Joaquin Valley with Arizona and points east. As many as 40 freight trains a day execute the loop, carrying agricultural and petroleum products. It is the busiest single-track line in the United States.

Windmill Farms

Like San Gorgonio Pass, Tehachapi Pass is a natural wind tunnel that takes advantage of the fact that dry desert air rises and must be replaced by cooler air rushing in from eastward-blowing oceanic winds. Pressed against walls of ridges, air is compressed and wind speeds rise to more than 70 miles per hour. The region has been developed as one of the most extensive and productive wind energy systems in the world. More than 5,000 wind turbines are operated in the Tehachapi-Mojave Wind Resource Area and produce 1.3 terawatt-hours of electricity (or 1,300 million kilowatt hours)—enough for 500,000 residential users. Like the windmill farms in San Gorgonio Pass, the farms at Tehachapi Pass are considered by many to be an aesthetic nuisance.

A few miles north on the PCT, you'll see newer wind farms with more modern and efficient blades. The Sky River's 100-foot-high windmills occupy 5 miles of ridgelines and supply enough electricity for 300,000 people.

Pinyon Pines

Much of this area is dominated by pinyon pines, one of the more common trees in the transition zone. Pinyon nuts were an important Native American food. You'll see them if you're hiking in early autumn. Indians gathered the closed cones, heated them in a low oven, opened the cones, and then loosened and shelled the nuts. The protein-rich nuts can be eaten raw, or cooked. They can be used whole, but were more frequently ground into a flour.

Desert Protection

From Bird Spring Pass almost to Kennedy Meadows, the trail passes through the Kiavah, Dome Lands, Chimney Peaks, and Owens Peak Wildernesses. The California Desert Protection Act of 1994, which established new wilderness areas in semiarid environments, was designed to combat years of degradation due to mining, grazing, and more recently, off-road vehicles (you'll see tracks and roads especially in the Jawbone Canyon area). The Jawbone area, which you'll cross 35 miles past Tehachapi Pass, was of critical concern in the California Desert Plan because of its bird life. A total of 160 species of birds are protected there, including golden eagles.

Walker Pass

On the southern end of the Sierra, Walker Pass is the first reasonable opportunity to cross the mountains, and as such it was an ancient Native American route to the Kern River, which drains the Sierra. Natives fished along the Kern River in summer, then wintered along the coast. Later, in the 1860s, the pass was used by sheepherders driving herds of thousands of sheep into the high country for summer pasturage.

The pass was named by James Fremont in honor of Tennessean Joseph R. Walker, a guide with the 1843–46 Fremont Expedition. Earlier, in 1833, Walker had become the first European American to make an east-to-west crossing of the Sierra. (Jedediah Smith, who was the first European American to cross the Sierra, had gone the other way; see page 153.) Walker was leading an expedition of about 70 people in an exploration of areas west of Great Salt Lake. Traveling westbound, they first crossed the Sierra to the north, near Bridgeport. One member of the group, looking up at the eastern flank of the Sierra, is reported to have described it as a "dark and deathlike wall." When Walker returned, this time traveling eastbound, he crossed over the pass that now bears his name.

Walker's exploration credits include being the first white person to see Yosemite. His expedition returned with the report of big trees: "16 to 18 fathoms around the trunk at the height of a man's head from the ground." It was the first description of the giant sequoia.

South Fork Kern River

Perhaps the most compelling sign that you have finally and truly arrived in the Sierra is found near the end of this sec-   *South Fork Kern River* tion, when you first encounter the ice-cold evidence of the heights ahead. The snowmelt-fed South Fork of the Kern River drains much of the southeastern Sierra. Starting near Cottonwood Pass (hikers continuing north will get there in another 140 miles) the free-flowing South Fork descends through deep gorges, roars past large granite outcroppings and domes, and meanders through open meadows. It offers refreshing (if chilly) bathing and good fishing in summer months. (The river is habitat for the California state fish, the golden trout.) But it can be dangerous to cross during the snowmelt. The South Fork is part of the National Wild and Scenic Rivers System. In spring and summer, its lower stretches offer rafting; it's a popular whitewater destination. Outfitters can be found in Tehachapi.

🚶 HIKING INFORMATION

Seasonal Information and Gear Tips

This section is best hiked in the spring, when water is (relatively) plentiful and temperatures not too hot. In character, this section's terrain is much like the higher elevations of southern California. But there is more shade, less heat, more water—as you get ever closer to the higher mountains, the conditions become much less desertlike.

However, desert gear is still appropriate here: a sun-deflecting hat, clothes that protect you from the sun, and a tarp. In early spring and late fall, remember the origin of the word *Tehachapi* (frozen) and plan accordingly.

Thru-hikers' Corner

This section presents no unusual challenges for thru-hikers. However, despite the fact that this section is technically in the Sierra Nevada Mountains, don't expect to see the rocky pinnacles and snow-covered passes just yet. In many ways, hiking through this section is more like hiking in the San Jacinto and San Gabriel Mountains than it is like the heart of the High Sierra, just to the north.

Best Short Hikes
- Piute Mountain Road to Walker Pass on California Highway 178. This 40-mile stretch takes you through prime high-desert and transition-zone terrain.
- Walker Pass to Cranebrake Road. This 29-mile hike is mostly forested, with pleasant views and good camping. It ends 0.3 miles from the BLM-administered Chimney Creek Campground.

Resupplies and Trailheads
Highway 58 is the more commonly used.

Highway 58 (mile 0). From Highway 58, hitch to either Mojave or Tehachapi. Both have everything you'll need to clean up, rest, resupply, and get on your way. Post offices: General Delivery, Mojave, CA 93501; General Delivery, Tehachapi, CA 93561

Walker Pass (mile 83.5). To resupply in Onyx, go west 17.6 miles on Highway 178. Post office: General Delivery, Onyx, CA 93255

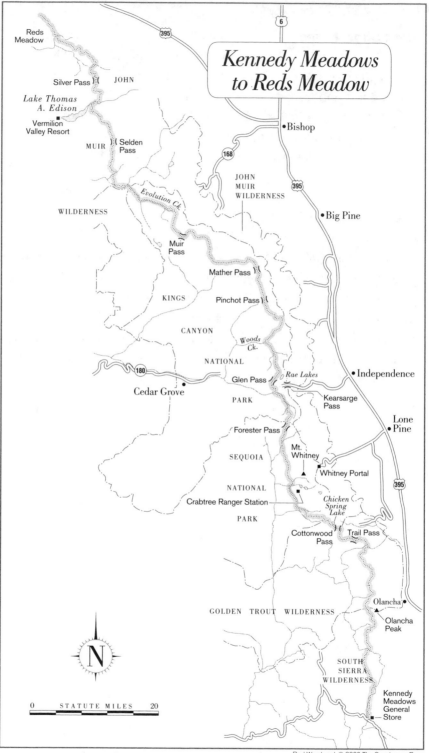

Kennedy Meadows
to Reds Meadow

Reds Meadow

Silver Pass

JOHN

Lake Thomas A. Edison

Vermilion Valley Resort

MUIR

Selden Pass

395

6

168

• Bishop

JOHN MUIR WILDERNESS

395

• Big Pine

WILDERNESS

Evolution Ck.

Muir Pass

Mather Pass

KINGS

Pinchot Pass

CANYON

Woods Ck.

NATIONAL

Rae Lakes

• Independence

180

Glen Pass

Cedar Grove

PARK

Kearsarge Pass

Lone Pine

Forester Pass

SEQUOIA

Mt. Whitney

Whitney Portal

395

NATIONAL

Crabtree Ranger Station

Chicken Spring Lake

PARK

Cottonwood Pass

Trail Pass

GOLDEN TROUT WILDERNESS

Olancha

Olancha Peak

SOUTH SIERRA WILDERNESS

Kennedy Meadows General Store

N

0   STATUTE MILES   20

Paul Woodward, © 2000 The Countryman Press

6

Kennedy Meadows to Reds Meadow

203.7 miles

It is 200 miles as the hiker walks from Kennedy Meadows (at the southern end of the High Sierra) to Reds Meadow (at Devils Postpile National Monument). In that 200 miles, you will not see a single road. You will not pass under an electric wire, nor cross a fence, nor see a telephone line, a store, or a vehicle. Not even your cell phone will work. This is Wilderness, pure and simple, capital-W Wilderness, the biggest in the 48 contiguous states, and the longest roadless section on any of the nation's long-distance hiking trails.

It is impossible to describe the High Sierra without resorting to superlatives. This is the Range of Light, sacred to John Muir and Ansel Adams.

"Surely the brightest and best of all the Lord has built," wrote Muir. "It has the brightest weather, brightest glacier-polished rocks, the greatest abundance of irised spray from its glorious waterfalls, the brightest forests of silver firs and silver pines, more starshine, moonshine, and perhaps more crystalshine that any other mountain chain, and its countless mirror lakes, having more light poured into them, glow and spangle most."

For many hikers, the High Sierra—the area covered by chapters 6 and 7—is one of the highlights of a PCT journey. Indeed, it may be one of the highlights of a backpacking career. Defined as the area above the main forests (about 8,000 feet) where peaks, lake basins, and other rock formations give conspicuous evidence of glaciation, the High Sierra extends from Cottonwood Pass (40 miles into this section) to the northern edge of Yosemite National Park (described in chapter 7). It is, quite simply, one of the grandest mountain spectacles to be found anywhere in the world.

It is also, for two reasons, one of the PCT's major challenges for long-distance and short-term hikers alike. First, the distances between convenient on-trail resupplies is long (see page 131), and leaving the trail to detour to a resupply station sometimes involves many miles of extra walking, not to mention thousands of feet of lost elevation (all of which must be regained). Second, there is a relatively short window of opportunity to hike the Sierra snow-free. Early-season hikers—and that invariably includes northbound thru-hikers—will find that the snowmelt creates obstacles both at high elevations, when hikers must cross the Sierra's high and still-frozen passes, and at low elevations, where the melted snow rages and roils in countless streams and rivers, confronting hikers with potentially dangerous fords. Late-season hikers—and that includes southbound thru-hikers—may well be caught in early winter storms in September or October.

If you're not a thru-hiker, it's not necessary to battle the Sierra's snow-pack. The PCT is a very different trail starting about mid-July. During the snow-free season, which typically extends from mid-July through September, the Sierra is characterized by *usually* gentle weather (although it can snow any day of the year). But while midsummer hikers have less to fear from snow and ice, the more crowded hiking season poses a challenge of its own: getting through the Sierra without losing your food to a hungry bear (see pages 120–122).

Despite its many challenges, this section of the PCT is for many hikers a favorite, a landscape to return to again and again.

THE ROUTE

For the first 40 miles, the trail out of Kennedy Meadows is still more transitional than alpine. Although there is often shade and sometimes running water, the trail has not yet fully broken away from the fetters of the desert. The path underfoot is still sandy, the all-too-familiar chaparral covers dry hillsides simmering in the sun, and rattlesnakes hide in shady crevices. The climbs can be dry and the distances between water sources are sometimes uncomfortably long—especially late in the summer, and especially if you've been lulled into complacency by the increasingly montane scenery.

Important note: In the 40 miles between Kennedy Meadows and

Cottonwood Pass, desert rules still apply. You don't need to carry excessive amounts of water, but you do need to consider your water supply when planning your climbs and your campsites. This is especially true in August when the ephemeral streams start to dry up.

For these first miles, the landscape alternates among familiar xeric hillsides, wide-open meadows, and cool upland forests, with tantalizing glimpses of sky-spearing pinnacles ahead. The trail is gently graded and rolling, but the overall direction is decidedly uphill. From Kennedy Meadows (elevation 6,150 feet), the trail gains more than 4,000 feet in the 40 miles it takes to reach Cottonwood Pass. Most hikers sooner or later notice that their breathing has become more labored; that it takes more effort to walk. This is a normal response to altitude, which affects hikers in different ways and at different elevations depending on a number of factors including age, fitness, acclimatization, and pace (slower is better).

Cottonwood Pass (elevation 11,160 feet) is the beginning of what's generally considered to be the High Sierra. It's also the first of the High Sierra's passes. If the snowpack is giving you trouble here, chances are you're in for a rough ride throughout the High Sierra. Because conditions vary from year to year and pass to pass, conditions at Cottonwood Pass are not entirely predictive of the trail ahead. But one thing is certain: If you are slogging in snow before and at Cottonwood Pass, you can expect snow ahead, especially at the higher elevations. Since the route requires climbing eight more high passes, the snow level is definitely something you'll want to consider before proceeding. If you decide to bail out, you can descend from Cottonwood Pass via the Trail Pass Trail and hitch to the town of Lone Pine.

Once past Cottonwood Pass, the trail reveals the glories of the High Sierra. Dramatic pinnacles, half-frozen tarns of aquamarine water, severe granitic rock, sculpted cirques, and cascading waterfalls all make this jaw-dropping, eye-popping country.

Twenty miles past Cottonwood Pass, the PCT reaches Crabtree Meadows, where a side trail veers east toward Mount Whitney. The PCT continues north. If you want to try climbing the highest peak in the 48 contiguous states follow the side trail 1.2 miles to Whitney Meadows and turn right (south) on the John Muir Trail. A climb of 8.6 miles and almost 4,000 feet will take you to the summit, which is also the southern terminus of the

212-mile long Muir Trail. North of Whitney Creek, the Muir Trail and the Pacific Crest Trail are largely contiguous until Yosemite National Park, where the Muir Trail turns off for Yosemite Valley while the PCT continues to Tuolumne Meadows. Most hikers planning to climb Mount Whitney camp at Whitney Creek, where there is also a food storage box and a ranger station. In thru-hiker season, the ranger is usually not yet on duty. Heading northbound again, the Muir Trail joins the PCT a mile north of Whitney Creek.

You'll have plenty of chances to practice your stream-crossing skills as you leave Whitney Creek and head toward Forester Pass, passing on your way the scenic Bighorn Plateau. Look from here to a granite wall about 9 miles to the north. That's where you're going—up and over.

Now, the route through the Sierra becomes a series of hurdles as you climb up to the base of each pass on gently inclining trail, switchback up and over the pass, and then descend back down into the following valley. At most of the high passes, the actual crossing of the pass—the hurdle—involves a short, steep climb of anywhere from 500 to 1,000 feet. During thru-hiker season, those hurdles are almost always snow-covered, even in a light snow year. During the snow-free midsummer months, you'll find the

Climbing to Forester Pass

climbs well-graded and mostly snow-free, although a few patches linger throughout the summer.

Forester Pass, at 13,180 feet, highest point on the entire PCT, was one of the last sections of the John Muir Trail to be completed. To cut a trail over this so-called pass—it's really more of a gap in the rock wall—required blasting into the wall, which is in some places so steep that it doesn't hold snow. But a late-lingering cornice on the south side poses a challenge in early season.

After Forester Pass, the route descends to Vidette Meadows, a popular campsite routinely visited by bears. It then climbs to Glen Pass, descends past spectacularly scenic Rae Lakes (another popular campsite), and descends to Woods Creek (crossed by a suspension bridge).

The up-down pattern continues with a climb to Pinchot Pass, followed by a descent past a series of pretty lakes and tarns to cross the sometimes raging South Fork of the Kings River. The next climb takes you up and over Mather Pass, from which you begin a descent down the long, steep, and tightly switchbacked Golden Staircase, the last section of the Muir Trail to finally be blasted and completed. At the bottom of this descent, you'll be at the Middle Fork of the Kings River. Then it's back up again. The next ascent, over Muir Pass, is gentle but extremely long, and

Muir Hut at Muir Pass

includes a glorious (in good weather) 10-mile stretch above tree line. In bad weather, this is an extremely exposed section of trail. There is a stone shelter at the summit of Muir Pass, but it gives new meaning to the word stone cold. The shelter is for emergency use only.

Once you've cleared Muir Pass, the hard work is behind you. The trail descends into Evolution Valley, then stays reasonably level (by High Sierra standards) for about 10 miles. It passes the turnoff for Muir Ranch (one of only two convenient near-trail resupplies on this whole 200-mile section). *Note:* Even if you're not going to Muir Ranch, the side trail is worth a short detour: There are natural hot springs on the other side of the South Fork of the San Joaquin River. Shortly after leaving the Muir Ranch area, the trail begins its easy climb to photogenic Selden Pass.

Leaving Selden Pass, the trail descends for 13 miles to the next turnoff for resupply, this time to popular Vermilion Valley Resort. It then climbs to Silver Pass—another easy ascent—from which it is 22 mostly downhill miles to the end of this section at Reds Meadow.

WHAT YOU'LL SEE

Glaciation

Early explorers and geologists used words like shock, trauma, and amputation to describe the High Sierra and the cataclysmic forces that they thought had created it. What else but a violent geological history could have made these sky-spearing pinnacles, these scoured cirques and mile-deep canyons, the cascading waterfalls and roaring rivers?

Snowflakes, said John Muir, a sheepherder, a walker, a writer, and an environmental activist, who in 1874 ascribed the fantastic forms of the region to the aeons-old movement of ancient glaciers.

"The Master Builder chose for a tool, not the earthquake nor lightning to rend asunder, not the stormy torrent nor eroding rain, but the tender snow-flowers, noiselessly falling through unnumbered seasons, the offspring of sun and sea."

Muir's theory was, to put it mildly, not well received. Josiah Dwight Whitney, head of the California State Geological Survey, characterized Muir as "a mere sheepherder, an ignoramus," and went on to say that "a

Descending from Muir Pass

more absurd theory was never advanced than that by which it was sought to ascribe to glaciers the sawing out of these vertical walls and the rounding of the domes. This theory, based on ignorance of the whole subject, may be dropped without wasting any more time upon it."

Clarence King, Whitney's colleague in the California State Geological Survey and author of the classic *Mountaineering in the Sierra Nevada,* concurred, adding, "It is to be hoped that the ambitious amateur may divert his evident enthusiastic love of nature into a channel, if there is one, in which his attainments would save him from hopeless floundering."

But Muir was right: The Sierra Nevada was shaped and sculpted by glaciation, and nowhere is this more evident than in this section's High Sierra. Evidence of glaciation is everywhere, in the scoured cirques, lateral and terminal moraines, hanging valleys, and countless lakes and tarns.

Some background: Geologists generally agree (although they argue about the details) that the Sierra Nevada began to rise from the bed of an ancestral sea some 60 million years ago, precipitated by the collision of the North American and Pacific Plates—the same agents whose ceaseless conflict sculpted so much of southern California's landscape. After a series of collisions that took place over a period of about 20 million years, the Sierra Nevada Range was established.

Then, about 2.5 million to 3 million years ago, came a frozen sheet of ice. At the height of North America's glaciation, 20,000 to 60,000 years ago, the sheet is thought to have been some 100 miles long, 60 miles wide—and in places as much as 4,000 feet deep.

Glaciers begin their life as snowfields, which are simply accumulations of snow that are so thick they don't have time to melt in the summer. If over a period of many years the rate of winter snowfall continues to exceed the rate of summer snowmelt, the snowfield eventually will start to change character. The snow crystals melt and refreeze many times, and as more snow falls and accumulates on top of old snow, the old snow is put under enormous pressure. Thus the process begins. Fluffy flakes become powdery snow. The crystals become denser, and air is squeezed out. The snow is subjected to pressure, melting, and refreezing, which turns the snow into the hard-pack. More pressure, more melting, and more refreezing compressed and packs the crystals together until they become ice (also called firn). Eventually, gravity takes over and the snowfield begins to slide downhill. It has become a glacier.

If you could take a time-lapse photograph over a period of centuries, you would see that the movement of a glacier resembles the movement of water. Like water, glaciers take the path of least resistance. Like water, they take the easiest path downhill. They cut through what can be cut, carve what can be carved, excavate and move whatever they loosen, and polish the rest.

Today, there are very few active glaciers in the High Sierra. The glaciers that do exist are small, and like most glaciers worldwide, they are receding. But hikers walk over plenty of evidence of the region's glaciation.

Among the most obvious are moraines, which are the ridges of rubble (sometimes covered with soil and trees) you'll often find yourself climbing over and around. When a glacier recedes or melts, it discards all the debris and rocks (also called till) that it has been carrying with it. The till left over at the front of the glacier's path is a terminal moraine; the till left on the sides is a lateral moraine. Moraines, which can be hundreds of feet high, are sometime found many miles from the peaks where the original glacier began.

U-shaped valleys are another indication of glacial action. The valleys that streams cut as they flow downhill are typically V-shaped. Glaciers, again following the path of least resistance, penetrate these valleys. The rubble they drag with them cuts into the valley walls and scours out wider, round-bottomed valleys.

Cirques are steep, bowl-shaped slopes, often encircling a tarn. These picturesque cliffs are formed by erosion, starting with large fields of durable ice that collect in a hollow. The ice deepens the hollow and cuts into the rock. Melting ice seeps into cracks, where it freezes and expands, breaking the rock into smaller chunks. Gravity administers the coup de grâce by carrying away loose debris, leaving behind steep scoured slopes. The cirque surrounding Chicken Spring Lake, just north of Cottonwood Pass, is a prime example of a glacial cirque.

Snowmelt on the trail near Glen Pass

Tarns are another beautiful remnant of glaciation. These high, jewel-colored lakes (there are some 1,500 named lakes and tarns in the Sierra Nevada) are, like Chicken Spring Lake, often surrounded by steep cirques, and provide some of the Sierra's loveliest and most photogenic high campsites—if you don't mind the cold air and the rocky ground. From the top of a pass, you can look down into the next valley, following with your eyes a chain of lakes, each on a lower shelf than the last, connected by threads of shimmering streams like pearls strung on a silver chain. One name for such strings of tarns is paternoster *(Our Father)* lakes, because they are said to resemble rosary beads.

High Sierra Ecology

Despite the accumulations of winter snow, the High Sierra is in many ways an alpine desert. Solar radiation is intense, winds are fierce, the rate of dehydration is high, there is little rain during the growing season, and the soil is thin or nonexistent, composed of disintegrated granite with little or no organic matter.

A good example is stunningly scenic Bighorn Plateau just south of Forester Pass. This wide plateau is surrounded by granite walls and pinnacles—the kind of place where if you dropped your camera, it would take a beautiful picture as the shutter clicked by accident. But the sparse and hardy vegetation tells the story; this is harsh and inhospitable terrain, subject to extreme environmental conditions, including avalanches, rockslides, freezing, and drought.

Go high enough in any mountain range and inevitably you will find harsh conditions. But several factors exacerbate these conditions in the Sierra.

As in all mountain ranges, the temperature decreases as the elevation increases (1 degree for each 300 feet in elevation). Similarly, as in all mountain ranges, the precipitation increases (here in the Sierra, at a rate of between 2 and 4 inches for each 300 feet). But the shape of the Sierra greatly affects the precipitation. The gently sloping western side is the wetter, ocean-facing side; the Sierran crest is some 60 to 90 miles from its western foot. By the time the rain-bearing clouds make it to 5,000 or 6,000 feet, most of the moisture has already been wrung out of them. Thus the long western slope creates a sort of rain shadow and even before the moisture-bearing clouds have managed to reach the top of the crest, there is little moisture left.

Two other weather facts are of interest to the PCT hiker who is monitoring Sierran conditions from home. In a typical year, one half of the Sierra's annual precipitation falls in January, February, and March, so it's futile to try to guess before April what the snowpack will be. And (good news for all hikers!) only 3 percent of the Sierra's precipitation falls between June 1 and the end of August. Although there can be severe storms in summer (which is why you will need adequate rain gear and an extra supply of warm clothes), the High Sierra in summer is the place where nature comes closest to offering a guarantee of good weather.

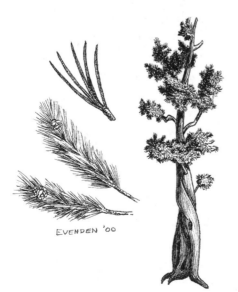

EVENDEN '00

Foxtail pine

High Sierra Forests

Only the hardiest trees can survive conditions in the High Sierra. The growing season is only two months long, and even summers are cold, with average daytime temperatures in the alpine zone rarely rising above 50 degrees. At night, temperatures frequently drop below freezing. In these conditions, trees cannot sustain buds, roots, or flowers.

EVENDEN '00

Mule deer

As is typical in western forests, conifers— better adapted for cold winters and short growing seasons—make up a larger percentage of Sierran forests than they do in more moderate environments. Twenty of the Sierra's 42 species of trees are evergreen conifers. In an eastern forest, by contrast, conifers may make up only about 10 percent of the total number of species. At the higher elevations, the trees are exclusively conifers: lodgepole pine, western white pine, mountain hemlock, whitebark pine, limber pine, western bristlecone pine, and foxtail pine.

Not surprisingly, given the meager resources, these trees grow at a slow rate. The trunk of a foxtail pine, for instance, grows only 4 inches per century and doesn't even start producing cones until the age of 50. You'll notice foxtail pines throughout the southern Sierra. They seem to grow in a corkscrew pattern, their red-brown trunks tapering to a white, bleached-looking top. The trees have asymmetrical foliage with branches that have dense clusters of needles at the end—hence the name foxtail. Foxtails thrive in rocky, inhospitable places just below the alpine zone. They grow neither in forests nor in groves, but instead alone, or perhaps in small clusters of a few hardy individuals independently staking their territory and sticking it out.

Surprisingly given the conditions, High Sierra trees are extremely long-lived. Some foxtails are thought to be as old as 3,300 years. But they are mere upstarts compared to the western bristlecone pines that live on Mount Whitney and elsewhere—and are estimated to be 5,000 years old.

Black Bears

It's sobering to consider that despite the fact that the High Sierra is the longest wilderness in the contiguous United States, many of its endemic animals are almost extinct—especially if they fall into categories hunted by humans: predators, fur-bearing animals, or game. Thus we find the grizzly, a predator, is extinct in California (despite being a state symbol). The population of two other predators, coyotes and wildcats, is also low. Mountain sheep, wolverines, fishers, and martens are extremely rare in the Sierra. Two of the animals that are doing just fine are the mule deer—because of a lack of predators—and the intelligent, adaptable black bear.

Ursus americanus, the American black bear, can be seen along most of the PCT. But it is in the High Sierra that bears are most commonly an issue for hikers. High Sierran bears seem to belong to their own special subspecies of park-spoiled bruins that are acclimated to humans and their food.

What's interesting about Sierran black bears is that they are completely out of their element. Black bears typically aren't found above the upper limits of the transition zone—here, about 7,000 feet in elevation. But in the High Sierra, they are commonly seen up to 10,000 feet, and sometimes higher. The explanation is simple. Bears have learned that backpackers carry food and they have become experts at stealing it. As a result, they frequently follow backpackers into areas where there is little natural food for them. Then the vicious cycle begins: Since there is little natural bear food, they have even more reason to seek out hikers' food.

It is unlikely that you will walk through the High Sierra without seeing a bear, especially in midsummer, unless you are traveling in an especially large group. You'll probably meet other hikers who have lost food to an ursine bandit—and you may lose some yourself.

The black bear (which can be any color from

Black bear

honey-tinted brown to russet to almost black) is extremely curious, extremely adaptable, extremely smart—and extremely hungry. Its natural diet consists of roots, berries, shoots, fish, grubs, worms, insects, small animals, and carrion. But its flexible palate also extends to oatmeal, freeze-dried shrimp Cantonese, vegetarian chili, Snickers bars, and granola. Toothpaste, on some occasions, apparently makes a delectable dessert. Or appetizer. Bears don't seem to care too much about what fits where on the menu.

For the hiker, having a bear steal food is always a nuisance, but in the High Sierra, it can be especially serious because the distance from the PCT to the nearest road can be a hungry hike of 20 or 30 miles—or more.

Bears that are unaccustomed to dealing with humans usually run (or at least lumber) away at the first sight of a person. But bears that have lost their fear of humans, or that are protecting cubs or defending a food source, can be cantankerous and even, occasionally, dangerous. By far the most common problems occur at night, when bears have several uninterrupted hours to figure out how to get your freeze-dried delicacies.

How, then, do you hike through the High Sierra without falling victim to a gang of ursine outlaws? In his *PCT Hiker's Handbook*, Ray Jardine recommends stealth camping, which he defines as avoiding popular tent sites near water, complete with fire rings and the tangled debris of failed bear bags. Instead, he suggests camping off-trail, away from water, in a place that is not an obvious tent site and has probably not been used before. He then recommends that hikers sleep with their food. This advice, however, is controversial (and roundly denounced by rangers). We ourselves have seen far too many bears to feel comfortable sleeping with our food in a tent in the High Sierra, and we do not recommend it. As a matter of fact, we know one hiker who, while so doing, woke up in the middle of the night to find a bear's mouth gently cradling his foot.

However, the advice about camping away from normal travel paths and campsites is sound. Of the more than 40 bears we've seen in the Sierra, most (but not all) were in or near popular tent sites. We've also woken up to the metal clank of bears checking out the food lockers, and we've seen them standing on their hind legs sniffing up at our regulation-hung bear bags. Our current strategy is to stay either at sites with food lockers or to sleep away from popular, frequently used sites, where we hang our food using the counterbalance method and surround the tree trunk with ice axes and ski poles. The idea is that if a bear tries to climb the tree, it will knock over the pile of tools, which will act as a burglar alarm. To hang food using the counterbalance method, you need to divide your food into two sacks. Throw your rope over a high tree branch and tie one sack to one end of the rope. Pull that sack up as high as you can, then tie the other sack to the other end of rope. Push the second sack as high as you can with a hiking stick.

Keep your eyes open for signs of bears—and camp elsewhere. In the High Sierra, you'll commonly see claw marks on trees, sometimes as high, or even higher, than a person can reach. Bears also use shaggy-barked trees as itching posts—you'll sometimes see clumps of hair clinging to the bark. On the ground, be alert for signs of digging (especially around logs and rocks) and carrion. Broken branches on fruit-bearing shrubs are also a sign of bears.

Official Bear Regulations

Strategies for bear-proofing a campsite have changed in recent years as the bears keep getting more and more savvy. Park Service regulations and recommendations keep changing too, so it's a good idea to check before your hike for the most current rules.

As of this writing, the Park Service policy in Kings Canyon, Sequoia, and Yosemite National Parks is to strongly discourage hikers from using the old bear-bag methods—even the counterbalance method described above. The High Sierra is one place where this practice is not foolproof. The Park Service has installed metal food lockers in many of the most popular campsites and strongly recommends—and in some parts of Kings Canyon and Sequoia National Parks requires—that hikers planning to camp where there are no bear boxes carry bear-proof food storage bags. (A bag that can carry five days of food, if you're not a big eater, weighs 3 pounds and costs $75. The bags can be rented in the national parks.)

Note: Northbound thru-hikers crossing the High Sierra early in the season are less likely to run into bears than are the hikers in July and August.

Marmots and Pikas

Two other animals you'll see throughout the High Sierra are marmots, which are the largest member of the squirrel family and the largest North American rodent, and pikas, which are members of the rabbit family.

Pikas

Marmots are closely related to woodchucks but are adapted to a different environment. While woodchucks live in lowlands, marmots inhabit the subalpine and alpine high country, from the lodgepole-fir belt to above tree line, at elevations between 6,200 and 12,000 feet. You won't mistake a marmot for any other animal: If you see something that looks like a woodchuck in the high country, between 18 and 27 inches long (including a furry 4-inch tail), it's a yellow-bellied marmot. If you disturb it, it will whistle and, if threatened, will plunge to safety in its burrow, which is usually found under large rocks or at the base of trees.

In the summer, marmots love to sun themselves, and you'll see them basking on warm rocks like sunbathers at the beach. They eat grasses, stems, and flowers (not to mention the occasional hiker meal). In the winter, marmots hibernate. Unlike bears, which merely sleep through the winter, marmots are true hibernators. They go into an almost comatose state in which their body temperature, heart rate, and respiration drop and they are so unresponsive that they can be dug up and handled without waking.

Pikas might look like rodents, but they are technically members of the rabbit family. Sometimes called rock rabbits, pikas look nothing like rabbits. They are rat-sized, with short round ears, no tail, and without the typical large hind legs of a rabbit. Like marmots, pikas find plenty to eat in the barren-looking high country: leaves, flowers, stems, nettles, and berries. They have the unusual habit of cutting and harvesting their food, then spreading it out to dry and carrying it into their burrows for storage. They even bring in food when it rains—and haul it back out to dry when the sun is out! Pikas don't hibernate, so this activity helps them store food for the winter. One industrious 5-ounce pika can store as much as 50 pounds of food for the winter. You'll hear pikas as you hike in the subalpine and alpine zones between 8,000 and 12,000 feet. Unlike marmots, which have a sharp, piercing whistle, pikas squeak.

Pikas and marmots are both known as glacial relicts, a group of animals (which also includes mountain goats and some birds, including the rosy finches you might see begging for food atop Mount Whitney) that were widely distributed during the Ice Age and now occur only in climates similar to the climate that prevailed during the Ice Age. It is thought that many of these species originated in Central Asia and came across the Bering Strait.

Pocket gopher

One other animal deserves mention, since you'll constantly see signs of it. This is the pocket gopher, another burrowing animal. In winter, pocket gophers lay out new tunnel systems between snow and ground—sometimes right above their old tunnels. They construct well-insulated nests of shredded grass under the snow, where they feed on grasses, sedges, leaves, and bark. When the snow starts to melt, they return to their underground burrows, which after the winter invariably need renovation. The gophers push the earth that has accumulated in their old burrows up, where it gets packed into the old snow tunnels. When the snow completely melts, it exposes the earth-packed network of tunnels, some of which are many feet long. They look like giant earthworms.

Mount Whitney

Question: Where can you see a building on the National Register of Historic places and a flying toilet at 14,494 feet?

Answer: Atop Mount Whitney, the highest summit in the contiguous states.

The building is the stone cabin built by the Smithsonian Institution as an observatory and now used as an emergency shelter. (*Warning:* The summit of Mount Whitney is not a good place to be in a lightning storm; the shelter is not a safe refuge, despite its lightning rods.)

As for the flying toilet: Dry, cold conditions on Mount Whitney prevent waste from decomposing, and the large number of visitors make waste management an expensive but necessary undertaking. Flying the toilet out

Smithsonian Hut on the summit of Mount Whitney

by helicopter is the unwieldy and expensive solution to maintaining America's highest latrine.

Whether you're hiking the whole PCT or a stretch of the Sierra, it's only natural to want to take a side trip to climb Mount Whitney. PCT hikers ascend Whitney from the western side, making a 17-mile round trip and gaining 4,000 feet of elevation. John Muir referred to the western slope as the "mule route," meaning it wasn't all that tough a climb. However, the eastern side is by far the most common approach, simply because it is easily accessible by road from Owens Valley and the town of Lone Pine. The western slope is accessible only to backpackers.

Nonetheless, the western side gets plenty of traffic, with Whitney Meadows a popular embarkation point for climbs of the mountain. From the meadows, you'll see lots of dramatic, sky-spearing peaks, but none of them are Mount Whitney, which is mostly hidden. From the western side, Whitney's summit looks like little more than a pile of rubble.

There's a long tradition here of summiting the wrong peak, starting with Clarence King, who in 1871 set out to be the first person to stand atop the highest mountain in the Sierra Nevada. On completing his climb, King declared himself successful, only to have his accomplishment debunked two years later by the California Academy of Sciences, which came to the conclusion that he had mistakenly climbed a lesser mountain. King hurried back to the Sierra, still hoping to make the first ascent. But when he

Climbing Mount Whitney

reached the true high point, he found a cairn and a note announcing the presence of two previous parties.

Credit for the first ascent belongs to three fishermen who earlier in the summer of 1873 decided to do a little peak bagging and escape the heat of Owens Valley. Although the mountain became locally known as Fishermen's Peak and the three were given credit for their accomplishment, the peak was ultimately named for Josiah Dwight Whitney, chief of the California State Geological Survey. Whitney's name had, in fact, been for some years attached to another peak, erroneously believed to be the highest point. When the true identity of the highest peak was finally established, the name and the mountain were reconciled.

Even John Muir was momentarily flummoxed by the hide-and-seek games of the highest peak. When he attempted to climb to the summit, he too found himself on the wrong mountain. Unlike King, however, he realized his error immediately, went back down, resupplied, turned around, and headed straight up again.

Nowadays the ascent to Whitney's summit is one of the most popular hikes in the Sierra. It requires a permit, which can be difficult to get, especially if you intend to climb from the more popular eastern side. To climb from the western side, you'll need to have a Whitney stamp affixed to your backpacking permit.

HIKING INFORMATION

Seasonal Information and Gear Tips

The snow-free season in the High Sierra is from early to mid-July through September. Nighttime temperatures in the high country can

dip into the 20s, even in midsummer, especially at the higher elevations. For summer hikers, alpine rules apply: Always be prepared for
unexpected weather, and take more gear than you think you need.

- It's most likely that the weather will be warm enough to travel
  in shorts and a T-shirt, but you need warm clothes for the
  nights and rain gear for emergencies. Sudden storms are
  always possible. A Gore-Tex jacket and nylon pants are
  adequate. Bring at least a layer of long underwear (top and
  bottom), a warm fleece jacket, and a hat.
- The trails over the passes are among the rockiest and boul-
  der-strewn on the trail, and the footway is more difficult
  than is typical of the PCT. So even sneaker-wearing, ultra-
  light thru-hikers will appreciate the added support and
  warmth of boots in the High Sierra, especially during snowmelt. Boots enable you to kick steps in the snow and ice
  slopes. Lightweight boots are fine. Gaiters help keep snow
  out.
- Tents offer warmth at higher elevations, where nighttime
  temperatures are frequently below freezing. They also offer
  mosquito protection during snowmelt.
- Speaking of skeeters, don't forget the DEET.
- For hikers in June (and, in heavy snow years, well into July),
  an ice ax is *absolutely essential.* Do not be fooled by tales
  from hikers who, after the fact, claim they hiked without an
  ice ax and had no problems on snowy passes: Time and
  hubris have dulled their memories. Had someone offered
  them an ice ax on a high pass, they would have taken it,
  with gratitude. After early July, ice axes *may* not be necessary, so early-summer hikers should check with the PCTA or
  Park Service to find out what the current snow levels are.
- Instep crampons are not strictly necessary, but they make
  the difference between nonchalantly walking across an ice
  slope or incessantly worrying that every step could turn into
  a misstep with dire consequences in a downhill direction.
  Instep crampons weigh only a few ounces and can give you

a little added traction, not to mention peace of mind. You do not have to take them off every time you hit rock or dirt. Simply put them on when the snow starts to make you feel insecure, and take them off when you're free of the snow. They can handle short stretches of rock and dirt between ice and snow. *Warning:* If you use instep crampons, be sure to take them off before glissading, because a point can catch in the snow, causing you to break an ankle or leg.

Fording Whitney Creek

Thru-hikers' Corner

Thru-hikers typically leave Kennedy Meadows sometime in the second week of June. Before then—unless it has been an extremely light snow year—the high passes are generally too snow-covered for hikers to make any progress, especially considering the heavy packs that result from having to carry enough food to get to the next resupply. If you arrive at Kennedy Meadows around the 15th of June, you're likely to find 60 or 70 (and sometimes more) other long-distance hikers getting ready for the challenge ahead. Solo-hiking the Sierra snowmelt is dangerous, so if you don't have a hiking partner, this is a good time to find one.

Southbounders will be racing winter here. Try to get through before the end of September. New snow is very different than old compacted snow: It's harder to walk through, and Sierra storms can pile it up deep.

Stream Crossings

Starting at Whitney Creek, early-season hikers encounter one of the High Sierra's major challenges: snowmelt-swollen streams to cross.

Four strategies will help you get across safely:

- Cross in the morning. During the night, the flow slows a little as low temperatures freeze the snowpack. Morning stream crossings will be literally ice-cold, but they may be less intimidating.
- If the crossing is especially rough, wear shoes or boots. This is a good argument for bringing an extra pair of footwear, perhaps amphibious sports sandals such as Tevas or booties made for scuba diving. In calm water, some hikers wear socks or go barefoot, but in churning rough water, sharp rocks can injure your feet or trap and twist your ankle.
- Don't assume that you should cross the river where the trail does.
- Trailwork is usually done in midsummer when the Sierra streams are friendly and meek.
- If you can stand the thought of packing both an ice ax and a pair of walking poles, you'll more easily be able to navigate both the snowpacked slopes and the snowmelt streams. Poles give you a third and fourth leg and make stream crossings incalculably easier and safer. (But the ice ax is the more important tool for the trip as a whole.)

Best Short Hikes

The real High Sierra begins at Cottonwood Pass. From the Horseshoe Meadow Road trailhead (23 miles from the town of Lone Pine), you can hike up the 2.1-mile Trail Pass Trail, which intersects the PCT 4.8 miles south of Cottonwood Pass. From this point north, the question is only how much food you can carry and how long you want to stay out. If you want to maximize your high-mountain time, Cottonwood Pass is the place to come in. However there is a big advantage to starting a hike at Kennedy Meadows: It gives you time to acclimate by slowly gaining elevation. You're less likely to come down with a case of altitude sickness.

Any of the trailheads listed at the end of this chapter can be used to access the PCT and create a hike of varying lengths. You can't go wrong: There is no mile on this segment that is anything but first-rate. But if you have to choose, the most stop-in-your-tracks-and-gape scenery is found between Cottonwood Pass and Evolution Valley, which is, not coincidentally, the section of trail that goes over the five highest passes. Coming in at Cottonwood Pass and leaving via the 18-mile-long Piute Pass Trail would give you a hike of 128 miles. If you want to add on the 16-mile side trip up and down Mount Whitney, plan for an extra day.

Short-Term Hiker Information

Long-distance hikers usually don't have too much trouble acclimatizing, because by the time they hit the Sierra, they've walked 700 miles, many of them above 8,000 feet. But short-term hikers just arriving in the mountains may feel woozy, headachy, nauseated, or cranky—all of which are symptoms of altitude sickness.

Altitude sickness is the body's reaction to the fact that as you gain elevation, the air pressure decreases. Therefore you take in less oxygen with each breath. How you react to altitude depends on a number of factors, including where you live (at sea level in New York? a mile high in Denver?), how fit you are, how much time you've taken to acclimatize, and your own individual body chemistry. People who live at sea level are especially susceptible: It's not at all unusual to be short of breath and fatigued at elevations as low as 6,000 or 7,000 feet. To prevent or lessen the symptoms of altitude sickness:

- Move uphill slowly. If you've just arrived from sea level, take a day or so to get acclimated to 5,000 or 6,000 feet, and then take a couple of easy days at the beginning of your hike. Don't push the mileage—and don't try to go too high too soon.
- Recognize the symptoms. A headache and nausea are classic symptoms of altitude sickness.
- Drink often, even if you aren't thirsty. Dehydration exacerbates the symptoms of altitude sickness. Compounding the problem is the fact that most people don't realize that they

are losing much more water than usual due to increased respiration and the dry mountain air.

- If you have symptoms of altitude sickness, avoid going higher until you've recovered. If you don't recover, go downhill to the last elevation at which you felt well.

Resupplies and Trailheads

Kennedy Meadows, Kearsarge, and Vermilion Valley Resort are the most commonly used.

Resupply in the Sierra is more complicated than anywhere else on the PCT. Of the resupply points on the 200 miles between Kennedy Meadows and Reds Meadow, Muir Ranch and Vermilion Valley are conveniently close to the PCT.

Kennedy Meadows (mile 0). Going north, your last vestige of civilization is the modestly stocked store at Kennedy Meadows Campground. The Forest Service campground lies at the dead end of a backwoods road, 24 miles from U.S. Highway 395, at which point it's another 25 miles to the sunbaked desert town of Ridgecrest.

Long-distance hikers need to resupply at Kennedy Meadows, because from there it's 200 miles to the next road crossing at Reds Meadow. Because of the distances involved in "going to town" from Kennedy Meadows, most thru-hikers send packages to the small general store. Coming from the south, you get to the store by going 0.7 miles southeast on paved road 22S05, which the PCT crosses 2.4 miles south of Kennedy Meadows campground. Contact: Kennedy Meadows General Store, P.O. Box 3A-5, Inyokern, CA 93527

The Kennedy Meadows trailhead is also a good entry point for hikers wanting to do a long hike in the High Sierra. Coming in this way gives you an opportunity to acclimate to the higher elevations of the Sierra. Hitching to the trailhead is problematic because there isn't much traffic on the dead-end road. A taxi from Inyokern (where there's a small airport) costs about $100.

Trail Pass Trail (mile 42). The PCT intersects the Trail Pass Trail, which leads 2.1 miles down to a trailhead at Horseshoe Meadow Road. From the trailhead, it's a 23-mile hitch to Lone Pine. For thru-hikers, the problem with this trailhead is that it's only a two-day walk from Kennedy Meadows. It's probably no more effort to carry an extra two days' worth of food than it is to hike an extra 4 miles, not to mention the time you lose in having to hitchhike and do chores in town. You be the judge. Post office: General Delivery, Lone Pine, CA 93545

Whitney Portal (mile 61.1). A side trail leaves the PCT at Crabtree Meadows and goes 1.2 miles to Whitney Creek. From there a 15.5-mile trail goes up the west side of Mount Whitney, crosses a high pass, and drops down the eastern side to Whitney Portal. This is the trail to take if you plan to climb Mount Whitney or if you plan to exit the High Sierra via Whitney Portal.

The Whitney Portal trailhead has some big problems for those hoping either to resupply or to start a hike there. If you intend to start a hike at Whitney Portal, you have to get a special permit. *Be warned:* Demand far exceeds supply. Nor is this a gentle introduction to the Sierra: You have to climb about 5,000 feet to get from one side of the mountain to the other (and another 1,000 if you want to actually go to the summit). Plan some really slow days to acclimate, because heading north on the John Muir Trail, you're going to be staying at consistently high elevations.

Thru-hikers: *Do not* resupply by the Whitney Portal Trail. Many thru-hikers climb Mount Whitney. Some of them reason that since they are already on top of the mountain, they might as well simply detour down the other side to resupply in Lone Pine. Big mistake. From the junction where you leave the Muir Trail to descend the east side of Mount Whitney, you have to walk 8.7 miles and lose 5,000 feet of elevation to get to the Whitney Portal trailhead—all before the snowpack is melted. From the trailhead, it is a 13-mile hitch into Lone Pine. And then you have to hitch back, regain that elevation (carrying a full pack), and repeat that mileage. Some thru-hikers who have attempted this resupply have actually hitchhiked back to the Cottonwood Pass trailhead, hiked up to Cottonwood Pass, then *re-hiked* the 16.7 miles back to Whitney Creek rather than attempt to go back over Whitney in snow with a full pack!

Kearsarge Pass (mile 87.4). This is probably the most sensible place for thru-hikers to resupply, unless they want to pack enough supplies to last all the way to Muir Ranch or Vermilion Valley. The

Kearsarge Pass Trail is also a good way for short-term hikers to get into the heart of the Sierra. But it does require adding on another high pass. From the PCT, it's a 9-mile walk to Onion Valley Road, from which it's a 15-mile hitch to the town of Independence. The side trail requires climbing over Kearsarge Pass, which is at about 11,600 feet. Post office: General Delivery, Independence, CA 93526

Muir Ranch (mile 153). Less than a mile off-trail, this is the closest resupply in the High Sierra. However, only people staying at the ranch can buy meals or supplies there. But the ranch will pack in and hold resupply boxes for hikers (for a fee). Contact the ranch regarding policies and fees: Muir Ranch, Box 176, Lakeshore, CA 93634.

Vermilion Valley Resort (mile 174.3). Almost all backpackers hiking the entire length of the Sierra stop at Vermilion Valley Resort, located six miles off-trail on the west end of Thomas A. Edison Lake. (A boat that runs several times a day cuts four miles off the trip.) The resort (more accurately, a backwoods fishing lodge) holds packages for hikers for a fee. It also serves meals and has a big tent for hikers to sleep in. There is a hot spring a few miles away (you'll need to bum a ride). The resort is accessible to vehicles from the western side of the Sierra via a poor-quality back road. Contact: Vermilion Valley Resort, c/o Rancheria Garage, Huntington Lake Road, Lakeshore, CA 93634

Other resupplies: The next on-trail resupply is at Reds Meadow, just over 200 miles from Kennedy Meadows (see chapter 7). Several other trails lead into the High Sierra, mostly from the eastern side. Most of them don't make sense for hikers needing to resupply, but they might be useful for hikers on shorter trips. Maps of the Sierra are available from the National Park Service and the Forest Service.

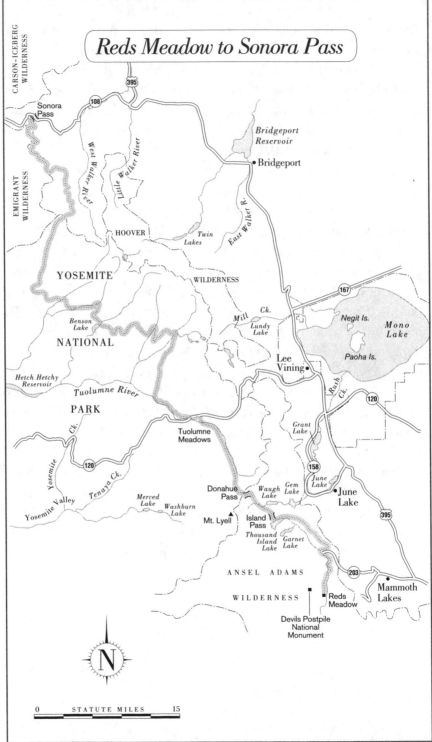

Reds Meadow to Sonora Pass

CARSON-ICEBERG WILDERNESS

Sonora Pass

EMIGRANT WILDERNESS

West Walker River

Little Walker River

395

108

Bridgeport Reservoir

• Bridgeport

East Walker R.

HOOVER

Twin Lakes

YOSEMITE

WILDERNESS

Mill Ck.

Lundy Lake

167

Negit Is.

Mono Lake

Benson Lake

NATIONAL

Paoha Is.

Lee Vining •

Hetch Hetchy Reservoir

Tuolumne River

Rush Ck.

PARK

Yosemite Ck.

Tuolumne Meadows

Grant Lake

120

120

158

June Lake

Tenaya Ck.

Donahue Pass

Waugh Lake

Gem Lake

June Lake

• June Lake

Yosemite Valley

Merced Lake

Washburn Lake

Mt. Lyell

Island Pass

Thousand Island Lake

Garnet Lake

395

ANSEL ADAMS

203

WILDERNESS

Reds Meadow

Mammoth Lakes

Devils Postpile National Monument

N

0   STATUTE MILES   15

Paul Woodward, © 2000 The Countryman Press

7

Reds Meadow to Sonora Pass

112.5 miles

The crown jewel of this section is the 70-mile traverse of Yosemite
National Park, one of America's classic landscapes. The trail's crossing of
Yosemite is diverse: At Tuolumne Meadows, it passes some of the park's
famous glacier-carved domes. It then embarks on an up-down course
through canyons and over passes before finally reaching Yosemite's lake-
dotted northern border.

The glaciated grandeur of Yosemite is bookended on either side by the
evidence of volcanic forces: Devils Postpile on the south end and lava formations near Sonora Pass on the north end. For hikers who don't have the
time or inclination to hike the entire High Sierra, this section offers man-
ageable shorter hikes that give an excellent view of what all the fuss is
about.

THE ROUTE

Since they joined a few miles north of Mount Whitney, the John Muir Trail
and the Pacific Crest Trail have been contiguous, but from Reds Meadow
to Thousand Island Lake, the two trails separate for about 13 miles. The
PCT follows a straight traverse along the side of a ridge, while the Muir
Trail (the more popular option) meanders through lake-dotted alpine
basins. Yet a third trail follows the San Joaquin River through the valley
separating the routes of the two other trails. Note, however, that during
peak hiking season, you can expect rangers to be checking your permit. If

Trail north of Thousand Island Lake

you've got a PCT thru-hiker's permit, stay on the PCT (or at least make sure that's where you camp).

The San Joaquin River Trail rejoins the PCT just past Badger Lake (where there is good camping); the Muir Trail rejoins it a mile or so farther at Thousand Island Lake, noteworthy not only for its many islets, but also for the towering presence of photogenic Banner Peak. There's no camping at Thousand Island Lake within a quarter-mile of the trail junction, but if you go off-trail and down the shoreline a few hundred yards, camping is permitted.

After Thousand Island Lake, the trail climbs to Donohue Pass, the last of the Sierra's high passes. One surprise in store for you is that you first must cross little Island Pass (10,200 feet) before your final ascent to the "real pass," about 5 miles farther. Donohue Pass (11,056 feet) is not especially steep, but the approach leading up to it can hold quite a bit of snow well into July. In a high snow year, you might need to do some careful navigating.

At Donohue Pass, the PCT enters Yosemite National Park. As you descend north from the pass, you'll have a good view of Mount Lyell (at 13,114 feet, Yosemite's highest peak) before entering Lyell Canyon, which leads directly to Tuolumne Meadows. You'll soon sense that you are in the

Dorothy Lake in Yosemite National Park

orbit of a major national park. Donohue Pass is only 13 miles from the Tioga Pass Road (California Highway 120), which runs smack through the middle of Tuolumne Meadows and is the major gateway to Yosemite's high country. So you're likely to have lots of company, both on the trails and at the pass—not to mention at Tuolumne Meadows itself, described by John Muir (in his typically understated fashion) as "the widest, smoothest, most serenely spacious, and in every way the most delightful pleasure park in all the High Sierra." With a store, grill, and post office, it's also a good resupply stop.

For the next 60 miles, from Tuolumne Meadows to the West Fork of the West Walker River near Yosemite National Park's northern boundary, the route goes against the lay of the land, crossing a series of steep ridges, then plummeting into deep canyons. The footway is more difficult than on the average stretch of PCT because it is both steep and at times very eroded. It can also be quite unstable, especially during the snowmelt, when water loosens the rubble and every rock underfoot seems ready to plummet to the valleys below. Later in the summer, the trail is much drier and markedly easier. If you're hiking early in the season—before July 1 in an average snow year—you'll probably encounter some leftover snow, but the passes are all

Near Sonora Pass

below timberline, so they are much easier than the higher passes to the south. At lower elevations, stream crossings can be a challenge well into July.

The reward for all your work is a series of dramatically scoured canyons, quite unlike any other section of the PCT. Highlights along this section of trail include Benson Lake (30 miles from Tuolumne Meadows, and 0.4 miles off the PCT), where a sandy beach makes a pleasant rest stop. In early summer, beautiful snowmelt-fed alpine flowers color the hillsides at the higher elevations.

Leaving Yosemite National Park, the trail briefly enters the Emigrant Wilderness before descending into Sonora Pass. For several miles just south of Sonora Pass, the trail does a spectacular high-country traverse of steep, open, windswept ridges. (*Note:* Once you climb up to the ridge, water and campsites are few and far between, so plan accordingly.) Here you'll notice that the landscape is changing. The mountains are altogether different colors and different shapes; even sunlight seems to reflect differently on their flanks. This change is the result of a new geology. While the High Sierra to the south was characterized by granitic domes and pinnacles, the northern Sierra, which you are about to enter, is characterized by volcanism. In the miles ahead, the PCT will pass through terrain that has been inundated by thick floods of lava. You'll see especially dramatic lava formations in the area around Sonora Pass, where this section ends.

WHAT YOU'LL SEE

Devils Postpile National Monument

Although the High Sierra is generally thought of as a glaciated granite landscape, volcanism has also been at work here, as seen in Devils Postpile, a 60-foot-tall columnar jointed basalt lava flow.

Devils Postpile, so named by Theodore Solomons after a sheepherder told him that he "recognized the handiwork of his satanic majesty," was designated a national monument in 1911. It was formed about 100,000 years ago when an eruption of basalt lava flowed from a vent and filled the valley of the Middle Fork of the San Joaquin River to a depth of about 400 feet.

The lava cooled slowly and evenly, but cracks on the surface formed as the lava shrunk. The fine-grained rock split into rectangular patterns along vertical lines (or joints) and the cracks deepened into long postlike columns.

Then, about 10,000 years ago, a glacier flowed through the valley and over the mass of lava. As it did, it scoured and excavated the rock in its way, including one side of what would become the postpile. This exposed the wall of columns (and sent fragments of some of them to fall into a jumble that lies at the base of the formation.). If you climb to the top of the formation, you can look down on the columns, which from that vantage point resemble tiles. The striations are the result of glacial polishing.

Also at Devils Postpile National Monument—and only 1 mile south from the Reds Meadow Resort and store—is Rainbow Falls, where the San Joaquin River drops 101 feet over a cliff made of erosion-resistant volcanic lava. (And yes, a rainbow is usually visible there, especially in the afternoons.)

At Soda Springs, there is yet more evidence of volcanic activity. The Soda Springs lie on a San Joaquin River gravel bar just north of the postpile. Gases are driven upward from hot areas deep in the earth and combine with groundwater to produce highly carbonated and mineralized coldwater springs. Iron in the water oxidizes on exposure to air and stains the gravel a reddish brown.

Finally (and more usefully), there are the hot-springs showers at Reds Meadow Campground—where you can consider the region's geology while enjoying a much-needed hot shower, the first on the trail since Kennedy Meadows!

Yosemite National Park

On June 3, 1864, Congress gave what is now Yosemite National Park to the State of California, the premises to be "held for public use, resort, and recreation . . . inalienable for all time." As a public park, Yosemite thus preceded Yellowstone by eight years. Yellowstone, however, is usually accorded the title of America's first national park because it was always under federal, as opposed to state, control.

Frederick Law Olmsted—considered the founder of American landscape architecture and one of the designers of New York's Central Park—was among the activists who lobbied Congress to preserve Yosemite by creating a park. Living in an era when the dominant myth about wilderness was that it was endless, Olmsted seems to have been well ahead of his time. Appointed to Yosemite's first board of commissioners, he established the following management goal in 1865:

The first point to be kept in mind is the preservation and maintenance as exactly as possible of the natural scenery; the restriction . . . with the narrowest limits consistent with the necessary accommodation of visitors, of all artificial constructions markedly inharmonious with the scenery or which would unnecessarily obscure, distort, or distract from the divinity of the scenery.

Olmsted couldn't have predicted how many battles over use and abuse were to take place over the next century. Trouble started almost immediately, when two entrepreneurs claimed that the land grant to the state violated private property rights. Despite Olmsted's passionate argument for preservation, the state legislature sided with the private property owners. The argument went back to Congress and finally to the Supreme Court, which ruled in favor of the park.

Between 1860 and 1870, about 5,000 tourists found their way to Yosemite, enduring a rough and rugged journey that ended with a 40-mile horseback or mule ride. By 1875, traveling conditions had vastly improved. Three stage roads were in operation, hotels had been constructed, and the number of tourists increased fourfold from the previous decade.

In 1890, prompted in part by newspaper and magazine articles written by John Muir, Congress declared Yosemite a national park, and control passed back into federal hands.

The first Yosemite rangers were U.S. Army troops, sent into Yosemite in 1890 to deal with sheepherders, squatters, and poachers. PCT toponyms from this era commemorate some of these rangers (McClure Meadows, Benson Lake, Smedberg Lake, Miller Lake) and the occasional sheepherder, too (Kerrick Canyon). In the 1890s, park superintendents were army officers. In 1898, civilian forest rangers (later to be called park rangers) began to serve, and in 1914 park management became a civilian rather than military responsibility.

Throughout Yosemite's history, managers have had to balance all manner of proposals, ranging from a scheme to use hydroelectric energy from Yosemite's waterfalls to light the trails at night to a suggestion that Yosemite be turned into an amusement park.

And as early as 1896, they were casting a jaundiced eye on campers, the majority of whom, one superintendent wrote, "are careless and negligent about extinguishing their fires and policing their campgrounds when leaving. The spectacle of empty tins . . . is abominable."

Visitor management took a new turn in July of 1900 when the Holmes brothers of San Jose entered the park by automobile. From 1902 to 1913, cars were banned, but in 1913, automobiles were officially admitted to the park, for the then-astronomical fee of $5. Today, Yosemite has 196 miles of road and receives millions of visitors each year—most of whom arrive by automobile, many of whom sit in traffic jams, and few of whom ever venture far from their cars.

John Muir and Ansel Adams

Of all the people who have loved Yosemite and worked to protect its matchless landscape, two especially stand out: Ansel Adams and John Muir. Two wilderness areas in the High Sierra are named after them, and the PCT goes through both of them.

Born in Scotland, John Muir came to the United States at the age of 11 and later attended the University of Wisconsin. In 1868 he visited

Yosemite for the first time; in 1869 he got a job as a shepherd and spent his famous first summer in the Sierra. It was the first of many spent exploring Yosemite and the surrounding high country. In *Treasures of the Yosemite*, he wrote:

> *One shining morning at the head of the Pancheco Pass, a landscape was displayed that after all my wanderings still appears as the most divinely beautiful and sublime I have ever beheld. There at my feet lay the great central plain of California, level as a lake, thirty or forty miles wide, four hundred long . . . And along the eastern shore of this lake of gold rose the mighty Sierra, miles in height, in massive, tranquil grandeur, so gloriously colored and so radiant that it seemed not clothed with light, but wholly composed of it, like the wall of some celestial city. Along the top, and extending a good way down, was a rich pearl-gray belt of snow; then a belt of blue and dark purple, marking the extension of the forests; and stretching along the base of the range a broad belt of rose-purple . . . all the colors smoothly blending, making a wall of light clear as crystal and ineffably fine, yet firm and adamant. Then it seemed to me the Sierra should be called not the Nevada or Snowy Range, but the Range of Light. And after ten years in the midst of it, rejoicing and wondering, seeing the glorious floods of light that fill it—the sunbursts of morning among the mountain peaks, the broad noonday radiance on the crystal rocks, the flush of the alpenglow, and the thousand dashing waterfalls with their marvelous abundance of irised spray—it still seems to me a range of light.*

But Muir knew that his range was endangered: "The glory of wildness has already departed from the great central plain. Its bloom is shed, and so in part is the bloom of the mountains. In Yosemite, even under the protection of the Government, all that is perishable is vanishing space."

The writer and wilderness lover became an activist. Muir was president of the Sierra Club from its founding in 1892 until his death in 1914. His most bitter and protracted battle took place not far from the PCT, when he unsuccessfully attempted to stop the proposed damming of the Grand Canyon of the Tuolumne River and the flooding of Hetch Hetchy Valley. Soon after the valley was flooded, he died, some say of a broken heart.

Ansel Adams, an early member of the citizens advisory board for the PCT, did in photos what Muir did in words. He turned photography into a tool for environmental action. Adams believed that if people could only see the spectacular wonders of the wilderness, they would have no choice but to rally and vote to protect it. His 1938 book on the Sierra Nevada, published by the Sierra Club, played a major role in convincing the Roosevelt administration to support a new kind of national park—a road-less wilderness, with no hotels, restaurants, or gift shops. That park is Kings Canyon, just to the south. (Yosemite, by contrast, has all of the above—plus a jail.)

Yosemite Valley

Fifteen miles after crossing Donohue Pass, the John Muir Trail again splits from the PCT. This time, the two trails part ways for good. The PCT con-tinues north to the high country of Tuolumne Meadows; the Muir Trail veers west for its terminus at Yosemite Valley. During the summer hiking season, when the facilities at Tuolumne Meadows are open, a shuttle van makes regular runs between the valley and Tuolumne Meadows. If you've never seen the valley, it's well worth the side trip to see one of America's— indeed, the world's—most dramatic landscapes.

One can only guess what Olmsted would have to say about the present state of affairs in Yosemite Valley. On a sunny summer afternoon, the roads are jammed with cars making their slow loop around the natural wonders, including El Capitan, Half Dome, and Yosemite Falls. Yet despite the crowds, Yosemite Valley remains one of the mythic landscapes of the world, one of the glories of the American West. Even jaded thru-hikers (who by this time are rightfully beginning to think they've seen nature at its most beautiful) will be surprised. If you've never been there, make time to go.

Bears

All the precautions discussed in chapter 6 apply here, especially between Lyell Canyon and Virginia Canyon, on either side of Tuolumne Meadows. Yosemite's bears are park bears at their worst, well-adjusted to people and well aware that what you're carrying in your pack tastes a lot better than anything they can find in the woods. Because the bears have pretty much mastered the art of getting food bags out of trees, rangers strongly suggest using bear-proof storage lockers (where available) and bear-proof food storage bags (which you can rent in the park). Check before you go on current regulations regarding food storage.

🚶🚶 HIKING INFORMATION

Seasonal Information and Gear Tips
The snow-free hiking season in this section is mid-July through September.

- Basic gear is three-season alpine: Shorts and a T-shirt for day, a layer of long underwear for night, some kind of rain protection (nylon wind-resistant pants and a rain jacket are a good combination here), a tarp or a tent, and—as always in high mountains—an extra layer of warm clothes and a hat.
- Be prepared for mosquitoes, especially early in the season. Yosemite in early summer can have some of the worst mosquitoes on the entire PCT. Come prepared with lots of DEET and some kind of mosquito clothing: Loose-fitting long pants, a long-sleeved shirt, and a head net can be sanity-savers. A tent rather than a tarp is also a good idea in bug season. If you use a tarp, consider rigging up some mosquito netting.
- If your knees gripe about steep downhills, take walking sticks for the hike between Tuolumne Meadows and Sonora Pass. The grades are steeper and the footway is rougher than is typical of the PCT.

Thru-hikers' Corner
In a typical snow year, thru-hikers will stop battling snow somewhere in this section. Donohue Pass, the last of the High Sierra's high passes, shouldn't cause any major problem for thru-hikers who have made their way across the more arduous passes to the south. The last big snow obstacle is on the south side of California Highway 108 at Sonora Pass. Sonora Pass doesn't present the problem; it is a low pass with a road running right through it. But the mountains

surrounding it present serious obstacles to early-season hikers. In most years, thru-hikers must have an ice ax to cross the exposed, steep, and dangerous slopes just south of Sonora Pass. (In an average year, the snow lasts into early July.) However, if you don't want to carry an ice ax past Tuolumne Meadows and don't care if you stay on the official trail, you can detour around the danger zone by descending 4.8 miles on a jeep road past Leavitt Lake to Highway 108, then walking 3.7 miles back up to Sonora Pass. North of Sonora Pass (and Highway 108), the trail is usually reasonably snow-free by mid-July. But in a high snow year, you may want to hang on to your ice ax for another week or so.

Note for mental health: Many thru-hikers celebrate the end of the "tough stuff" at Tuolumne Meadows. That may be premature—especially in a high snow year, when northern Yosemite's streams are swollen. The trail through Yosemite is a roller coaster that runs up over passes and down into canyons. Between frequent stream fords, steep climbs, and rubbly trail, it can be slow going. Give yourself a break and don't plan to speed up to major mileage until you reach Sonora Pass, when the footway gets much easier.

Caution: Thru-hikers should be aware that their thru-hiking permits entitle them to camp only on the PCT. Permit regulations are vigorously enforced in Yosemite, at times too vigorously. In three separate cases in recent years, rangers challenged the validity of a thru-hiker's permit, did not even know about such a permit, questioned whether a particular individual was in fact a thru-hiker, and (somewhat unbelievably) claimed that a hiker who was on the PCT was not on the PCT and threatened to have him arrested.

Given the freewheeling, laissez-faire attitude of the thru-hiking community and the law-enforcement training of the rangers, it's not surprising that conflicts occur. Please be aware that Yosemite National Park has in fact modified its rules to accommodate the needs of thru-hikers. Examples include accepting the thru-hiker permits and allowing thru-hikers to camp in the Tuolumne Meadows Campground even if they arrive there before the campground is open for the season. Rangers deal with theft, vandalism, ill-prepared hikers, bear problems (most caused by human carelessness or ignorance), preventable injuries, litter, and a host of other problems so severe that Yosemite Valley actually has a jail. So, overzealous rangers notwithstanding, give them a break by following the rules, practicing minimum impact, abiding by your permits, and saving the urge to party for someplace else.

Best Short Hikes

This section of the PCT can be conveniently divided into two shorter hikes, each of which starts and ends at a major trailhead. Both sections are superb.

- The first is from Reds Meadow to Tuolumne Meadows (35 miles).This section is not only shorter—it's easier, too, and it gives hikers who only have a couple of days a good taste of what lies south in the remote and inaccessible wildernesses described in chapter 6. You even get to go over one of the Sierra's classic high passes, Donahue Pass.
- The second is from Tuolumne Meadows to Sonora Pass (75 miles). This section is best hiked in August, after the snowmelt and the mosquitoes. Plan conservative mileage, because there are lots of ups and downs.

Resupplies and Trailheads

Reds Meadow (mile 0) offers a small store (which will hold your package for a fee), free hot showers at Reds Meadow Campground, and a shuttle to the Mammoth Lakes Ski Area (from which it is another 4 miles to the town of Mammoth Lakes).

Tuolumne Meadows (mile 35). This trailhead and resupply station in Yosemite National Park offers a campground, grill, lodge (reservations highly recommended), store, and post office. Stock up: The next convenient resupply is at Echo Lake, 160 miles away. *Warning:* In a heavy snow year, the road to Tuolumne Meadows (and its post office) and the road to Reds Meadow may not yet be open. If you are hiking in a heavy snow year, be sure to check with the PCTA for the most current information. Post office: General Delivery, Tuolumne Meadows, CA 95389

8

Sonora Pass to Donner Pass

139.9 miles

The character of the Sierra Nevada changes radically at Sonora Pass and the trail changes, too. The mountains are lower and the passes gentler. Joseph Hazard, one of the trail's early advocates, characterized the terrain as "a dependable granite land with rock lakes, flower meadows, primitive forest. Its very lack of extremes makes it ideal packhorse or backpacker country with convenient and sheltered campsites. Summer weather is cool, water pure and fairly plentiful, fishing most inviting. Passes are easy, streams fordable, gorges kindly."

This is ideal country for backpacking trips of less than a week. Lower passes, more trailheads, and frequent road crossings make it easier to plan a two- or three-day hike here than it is in the higher and more isolated mountains to the south. Day hikers, too, will find several parts of this section accessible because major roads cross the trail: California Highway 88 at Carson Pass, California Highway 4 at Ebbetts Pass, California Highway 108 at Sonora Pass, U.S. Highway 50 at Echo Summit, Old Highway 40 at Donner Summit, and Interstate 80 at Donner Pass. But accessibility comes at a price: There are several pockets of multiple use—especially grazing—in this section, and lots of dirt roads, which are ideal for vehicular recreation. Fortunately, much of the PCT itself is protected in four stunning wildernesses: the Carson-Iceberg, the Mokelumne, the Desolation, and the Granite Chief, making it possible for hikers on shorter trips to experience the PCT's high-mountain wilderness character. As a result, on a summer weekend, the trails can be quite crowded, especially within a mile or two of a trailhead.

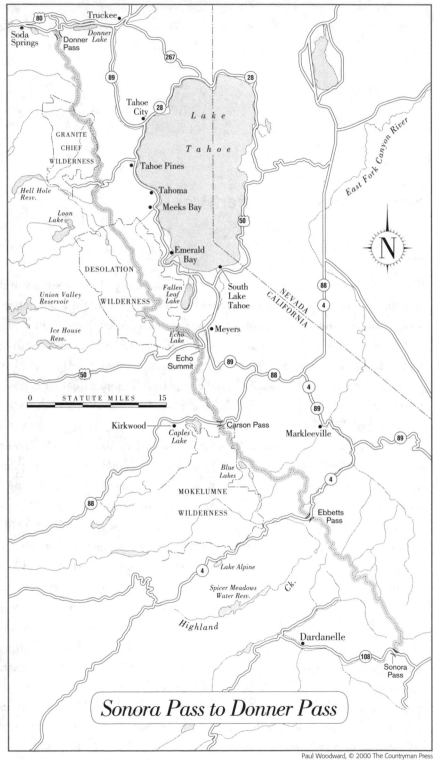

80 Truckee
Soda *Donner* Donner
Springs *Lake* Pass
89
267
28
Tahoe
City 28
L a k e
GRANITE
CHIEF
WILDERNESS *T a h o e*
Tahoe Pines
Hell Hole Tahoma
Resv.
Loon Meeks Bay
Lake
50
DESOLATION Emerald
Bay
Fallen South
Union Valley *Leaf* Lake
Reservoir WILDERNESS *Lake* Tahoe
NEVADA
CALIFORNIA
Ice House *Echo* Meyers
Resv. *Lake* 88
Echo 4
Summit 89
50 88
4
0 STATUTE MILES 15 89
Kirkwood Carson Pass
Caples Markleeville 89
Lake
Blue
Lakes 4
MOKELUMNE
WILDERNESS Ebbetts
88 Pass
4
Lake Alpine *Ck.*
4
Spicer Meadows
Water Resv.
Highland Dardanelle
108
Sonora
Pass

East Fork Canyon River

N

Sonora Pass to Donner Pass

THE ROUTE

This section starts with a spectacular climb out of Sonora Pass on open slopes dotted with lava formations that announce your arrival into the volcanic landscape of the northern Sierra. These are mountains that have been shaped not only by the slow, patient forces of glaciation, but also by the mercurial, violent forces of heat, pressure, and explosion. You'll see evidence in the many lava formations along the trail and in the rich volcanic soil, which nourishes brilliant fields of wildflowers in early summer.

After 3 miles, the ascent ends at a saddle at 10,500 feet. *Thru-hikers, take note:* This is the highest point on the PCT from here to Canada. Just over a mile later, the trail reaches another saddle at 10,250 feet. From there, it starts to descend and never again reaches a height of 10,000 feet. From here on, it's all downhill—or so you can tell yourself.

Entering the Carson-Iceberg Wilderness, the trail alternates between open high country, forest, and meadows, where in early summer a profusion of some 200 species of wildflowers carpet the mountains. Volcanic formations add startling shapes to the landscape, especially north of

Blue Lakes

Ascent north of Sonora Pass

Ebbetts Pass and near Raymonds Meadow, where there are prominent out-croppings and weirdly shaped features to capture your attention.

Now in the Mokelumne Wilderness, the trail remains generally gentle (although in the area near Blue Lakes it's not *quite* as gentle as the maps and guidebook make it appear; there are many more little ascents and descents than are indicated). After Blue Lakes, the trail skirts the edge of the Mokelumne Wilderness, so you'll see quite a few roads and the occasional car camper.

Seventy-six miles into this section, the trail passes Echo Summit, a convenient trailhead for short-term hikers and a resupply station (Echo Lake Resort) for long-distance folks. The PCT next enters the not very desolate Desolation Wilderness, which boasts the highest density of hikers per square mile of any of California's wilderness areas. No wonder, when it's a short drive from popular Lake Tahoe, which annually logs some 12 million visitor-days, about as many as Yosemite, Kings Canyon, and Sequoia National Parks put together. But it's not only accessibility that draws the crowds: This is one of California's most beautiful wildernesses.

The Desolation Wilderness is named not for its paucity of hikers, but for its paucity of trees. A layer of durable rock was dumped here by the glaciers; the resulting rocky soil has proved to be poor habitat for the trees that usually blanket the land at similar elevations. Consequently the wilderness has a little bit of the character of the High Sierra to the south, with granitic mountains and crystalline lakes and tarns. If you have a fishing rod and license, here's a good place to use them, although chances are you'll be sharing your lake with other anglers.

The trail hits another high point in the Desolation Wilderness: Dicks Pass, 9,380 feet, is the last time the PCT will rise above 9,000 feet.

Leaving the Desolation Wilderness, the trail wanders through about 10 miles of multiple-use Forest Service land before entering the Granite Chief Wilderness, where the highlight is a fine 4-mile ridgeline traverse along the wilderness's eastern border near the Alpine Meadows ski area. This section ends at Donner Summit on Old Highway 40. On a midsummer weekend, the trail near Donner Summit can be so crowded that you'll have to stand in line to cross the occasional lingering snowfield. And the parking area will be jampacked with cars. But easy interstate access and a convenient parking area (not to mention that you don't have to walk very

Volcanic ridge north of Raymonds Meadow

far to get a good view) make Donner Summit a good trailhead for short-distance hikers.

The trail then meanders for a few miles before passing under the interstate through a horse and hiker tunnel. There's a side trail to the interstate rest area, which has a large picnic area and rest rooms.

WHAT YOU'LL SEE

History of the Passes

Anyone who has hiked the PCT to the south knows the importance of a mountain pass in the 400-mile-long wall that is the Sierra Nevada. From the 1820s onward, much of the exploration in California was undertaken with the goal of finding viable routes from one side of the mountains to the other. The passes of the High Sierra were useless—impossibly rugged and snowbound for most of the year. South of the Sierra, the land was largely off-limits, first under Spanish control, then until 1848, under Mexican control. But north of Sonora Pass, the terrain was lower, wooded, and snow-free for longer periods of time. Here it was reasonable to look for an overland route to "Alta California."

Ebbetts Pass is named an after explorer and railroad man, Major John Ebbetts, who passed this way while leading an army expedition in search of a rail route to connect San Francisco and Las Vegas. But Ebbetts was not the first European American to cross the pass. That honor, if not the name, belongs to Jedediah Smith. When he crossed what is now Ebbetts Pass in May of 1827, he became the first European American known to have crossed the Sierra.

Smith's forays through the West—and his crossing of the Sierra Nevada—are the stuff of which pioneer legends are made. Born in western New York in 1799, Smith acquired an early case of wanderlust. At the age of 13, he took a job as clerk on a Great Lakes freighter; at 15 he joined the hordes of young men seeking fortune and adventure in the Pacific Northwest (the British having abandoned their claim to the region in the wake of their defeat in the War of 1812). In 1822 he was hired as a hunter and scout for the Rocky Mountain Fur Company; in 1824 he led the first party over South Pass in Wyoming, which was to become the crucial northern crossing of the Continental Divide for the emigrant trains of the Oregon Trail.

In 1826 Smith began the journey that would take him the length of the Sierra—although on a different route than that of the PCT hiker. He founded his own company and crossed from east to west over Tehachapi Pass, hoping to explore the country to the north for beaver. But once in San Diego, he ran into a problem: Mexican authorities refused to give him permission and ordered him to leave.

Smith and his party secretly headed north, still hoping to find good beaver country. They figured that at the end of their explorations, they would find a pass to take them over the mountains and back east. But it wasn't as easy as that, and by spring of 1827, they found themselves in the San Joaquin Valley looking up at what appeared to be an impenetrable wall. Each time they followed a river to its source, they failed to find a passage. The Kings and American Rivers both led to dead ends, deep snow, or both. Finally, in late May, they tried the Stanislaus River, following it to the crest where hard-packed snow and a break in the mountain wall finally permitted passage to the eastern side—over what became Ebbetts Pass.

Easy trail south of Carson Pass

Like Ebbetts Pass, Carson Pass—the next major pass on the PCT—is not named after the first European Americans to cross it (Mormons who were searching for a direct route between California and the Great Salt Lake). Instead, the pass commemorates Kit Carson—mountain man, scout, guide, soldier, and Indian agent—who left his tracks and name all over the West. Carson came through here as a scout for the second Fremont Expedition, which crossed the Sierra in the winter of 1844 on a trip that featured a series of explorations involving more than the usual number of mishaps and misadventures.

The expedition leader, John C. Fremont, was yet another of the West's legendary mountain men whose name can be found on topographic maps from Wyoming to California. Fremont was a second lieutenant with the U.S. topographical engineers. A skilled topographer, he made maps that were considered more accurate than those of his contemporaries, including Jedediah Smith and Joseph Walker. Between 1842 and 1854, he made five exploratory expeditions, looking for routes that could be used as major travel arteries through the mountains.

In the winter of 1844, due to a series of ill-fated decisions on route selection and timing, the Fremont Expedition found itself out of food on the eastern side of the Sierra—and desperately eager to find a way to the more temperate Sacramento Valley to the west. But nowhere in the Sierra Nevada was there anything remotely resembling a natural passage through the mountains that could be used in winter. With a combination of resourcefulness and resilience, the party pushed on. Confronted by deep snow, they made snowshoes. When they ran out of food, they ate what they could hunt, or concocted meals of pea soup, mule, and dog. ("It wouldn't have been so bad," wrote Charles Preuss, a German topographer, "if only they had a little salt.")

When they got lost, they climbed mountains to better see the land that surrounded them. Such was the case on February 14, 1844, when Fremont and Preuss climbed to the summit of what is now known as Red Lake Peak. This was a first ascent, and not only in the usual sense: It was the first recorded climb in the Sierra of an identifiable mountain. Another first: "a beautiful view of a mountain lake . . . so entirely surrounded by mountains that we could not discover an outlet." Fremont and Preuss thus became the first European Americans to see the clear waters of Lake

Tahoe. After the climb of Red Lake Peak, the party was finally able to find its way up and over the crest of the Sierra, and several days later reached sanctuary in the Sacramento Valley.

Of all the passes, Donner Pass is the name we know best. Donner Pass reminds hikers of just how powerful and unyielding these mountains can be. It whispers to thru-hikers to make haste in the heat of summer, lest they be trapped in the fierce and sometimes early winters of the Cascades, still far to the north.

The story is this: In 1846, the Donner brothers, both successful farmers in their 60s, left Illinois and headed west with their families to what they hoped would be greener pastures in California. Following the established emigrant route, they crossed the Continental Divide at South Pass in Wyoming. Somewhere along the way they learned of the so-called Hastings Cutoff, a shortcut that had been successfully used by previous parties. The brothers became the leaders of 91 people who broke off to take the cutoff, which would shorten their journey by more than 200 miles.

The cutoff was a disaster. The trail was barely traceable, and in some places disappeared entirely. In the Wasatch Mountains, the party had to hack out 36 miles of trail. The fierce heat and water shortages of the Great Salt Lake Desert decimated their livestock, which they relied on for food and wagon-pulling. The party was attacked by Paiutes and demoralized by internecine squabbling. And worst of all, the shortcut cost them three weeks' of time—and therefore, three weeks worth of food. They didn't have enough to complete the trip.

Volunteers went ahead, hoping to cross the mountains and bring back supplies. Meanwhile, the main party plodded on. In mid-October, one of the volunteers returned with seven mules loaded with meat and flour, and for a moment the future looked secure. But the group made one last and finally fatal mistake: They opted to rest rather than push forward over the Sierra. In late October, snow started to fall. The rest is grim history: Snow depths reached 22 feet, trapping the emigrants. Some despaired, some starved, some resorted to cannibalism. Of 91 people, 49 survived.

Ironically, Donner Pass, at an elevation of only 7,200 feet, is today the most accessible of all the passes of the Sierra. Its crest is broad and flat, and in the peak of summer, it is impossible to see how this gentle-looking saddle—crossed by a railroad and an interstate, not to mention the PCT—could have been the scene of such tragedy.

Donner Pass was in fact chosen for a major Pacific Railway crossing of the Sierra because of its gentle grade. But that didn't make building the railroad an easy proposition. Thousands of laborers, including Irish and Chinese workers,. were imported by the boatload and started laying tracks in 1866. But with 24 major storms, the winter of 1866-67 proved inclement even by Sierran standards. Crossing Donner Pass required constructing 15 tunnels, all cut through granite, the longest of which was 1,600 feet. The first train chugged over the pass in April 1868. The railroad still runs through the pass, along with I-80, the only four-lane crossing of the entire 400-mile-long mountain chain. In the winter, blizzards routinely close the pass.

Lake Tahoe

The lake that John C. Fremont saw from his perch atop Red Lake Peak—Lake Tahoe—is the largest of the 1,500 lakes in the Sierra Nevada: 195 square miles in size. At 6,247 feet in elevation, it's one of the largest high-altitude lakes anywhere in the world. And with a depth of 1,645 feet, it's the 10th deepest lake in the world.

Tahoe means *water* in the Washoe language, and for years Lake Tahoe was renowned for its clear water, where you could drop an object and watch it as it slowly sank far beneath the surface. Scuba divers consider visibility of 100 feet to be excellent. At Lake Tahoe, the visibility was sometimes twice that.

Then came development. Clinton Clarke was prescient in the 1930s when he wrote, "To keep this a wilderness and protect it from the ever constant encroachment of roads and recreational development will require active vigilance and determination. Conditions are critical and hard work only can preserve this matchless region."

Instead, strip malls, casinos, condominiums, and hotels were built, causing erosion. (Erosion at some construction sites can be as much as 12 times the rate of erosion at undeveloped sites.) Eroded soil carries algae. As a result, between 1969 and 1983, the amount of floating algae in the lake doubled and the clarity of the water decreased by 25 percent.

In response to these and other problems, in 1970 the Tahoe Regional

Planning Agency was created. Although critics question whether the agency is tough enough, it has managed to cut back on the rate of development and to confine development to the south shore of the lake. In addition, the National Forest Service, the state, and the county have all bought land to block development.

Air Pollution

The accessibility of this part of the Sierra to automobiles and the popularity of Lake Tahoe can be measured in another way: air pollution. Emissions from cars are causing a new and growing problem. Ozone is damaging conifers in much of this trail's section by interfering with cellular metabolism and structure, which causes needles to have shorter life spans. Needles, of course, perform photosynthesis, which is the way trees get food. So the affected trees—especially Jeffrey and ponderosa pines—suffer from a sort of arboreal malnutrition, with symptoms such as retarded trunk growth. White pines, sugar pines, and incense cedars are not as easily affected.

If the problem continues, ponderosas could cease to be the dominant species in the Stanislaus National Forest and the Lake Tahoe Basin. Instead there would be a mixed conifer forest of white fir, Douglas fir, incense cedar, live oak, and manzanita. Such a mixed forest is poor habitat for native wildlife—and it's also poor habitat for timber companies, in part because the mixed forest is susceptible to firestorms. So although timber companies and environmentalists usually glare at each other from opposite sides of the bargaining table, in this case they find themselves having to work together to support measures that will reduce air pollution in order to maintain the forests in their natural state.

Wildflowers

In early summer, this section of the PCT is one of the best places to see alpine and subalpine wildflowers. Prime flower viewing spots on the slopes on either side of the major passes are easily accessible to day hikers.

Desert and alpine areas look different on the surface, but from the point of view of a plant, they share some similarities. Both deserts and alpine areas are harsh environments. Anything that lives in either place has to develop adaptations to cope with extremes of heat or cold. So alpine flowers, like their desert cousins, have had to adapt in ways that bring to mind the plants of southern California.

Like the desert, the alpine environment is an open habitat. In summer that means lots of sunshine, along with desiccating winds. Soils are course and dry, favoring plants with large root systems. In addition, alpine flowers have developed small leaves in order to reduce transpiration.

Another factor is the mountain weather—unpredictable except in its harshness. Daily temperatures fluctuate wildly, and because the air is so dry, it doesn't hold much heat once the sun goes down. Nighttime temperatures are often below freezing. So alpine flowers live largely below the surface, with up to 80 percent of their biomass underground where it is not exposed to these conditions.

Because there is little precipitation in the Sierran summer, plants get most of their moisture from snowmelt, so you'll find sedges, rushes, grasses, and herbs in wet meadows near snowbanks. On less well-watered mountain slopes, you'll see plants like lupine, phlox, alpine everlasting, alpine daisy, and cinquefoil growing in scattered clumps, usually near or beneath late-lingering snowfields whose melt-off provides them with an ongoing water source.

Snowmelt flowers north of Dicks Pass

Lupine

In alpine areas the growing season is measured not in months, but in weeks. The timer starts ticking as soon as the snow melts. From then on, the flowers are in a race with the calendar. As a result, most alpine flowers are perennials: Annuals just don't have enough time to live an entire life cycle in the truncated growing season. Nor do the flowers bloom in stately procession, a few species at a time, as they do in the long drawn-out springs of more temperate areas such as the Appalachians. Here, some 200 species bloom all at once—usually between 10 and 20 days after the snowmelt—making the hillsides and meadows a riot of color.

Alpine flowers have something else in common with desert flowers: Most of them evolved without having to develop defenses against large herds of ungulates. So they have no defenses against cows and sheep, which apparently find a diet of mountain flowers delectable. Not only that, but under the hooves of large herds, the soil becomes compacted and susceptible to erosion. Although John Muir spent his first summer in the Sierra as a sheepherder, he quickly understood the damage caused by large herds and came to call sheep "hoofed locusts" because of their effect on the wildflowers. He wrote, "It is impossible to conceive of a devastation more universal than is produced among the plants of the Sierra by sheep . . . The grass is eaten and trodden until it resembles a corral."

Cinquefoil

You'll see herds of cattle in some of the multiple-use areas along the trail. It's not a coincidence that you'll see fewer wildflowers in those sections.

HIKING INFORMATION

Seasonal Information and Gear Tips

In the main hiking season—July through October—this is a temperate mountain climate with warm days, cool nights, and very little rain.

- As on any mountain hike, an extra layer of warm clothes and rain gear are recommended. After mosquito season (which ends in late July), a tarp is perfectly adequate.
- Bring a water filter. Some of the water sources are polluted by cattle.

Thru-hikers' Corner

- The region is usually mostly snow-free by early to mid-July, with only a few lingering snowfields to make things interesting. In a normal snow year, you won't need ice axes or instep crampons after the first week in July. However, if it's been a high snow year, you might encounter plenty of snow through much of July.
- In general, the trail is easy and relatively flat. If you're feeling good, it's time to up the mileage. Most thru-hikers comfortably do 20 to 25 miles a day here.
- Because this section is considerably lower than the mountains to the south, thru-hikers sometimes mistakenly think that if the High Sierra is still snowbound, they can skip ahead and start hiking here, then return later in the season to hike the High Sierra. In fact, these more northerly mountains get as much snow as the High Sierra, so skipping ahead rarely accomplishes anything. Just as in the High Sierra to the south, the snow-free hiking season is usually early July through October.

Best Short Hikes

All of the major road crossings in this section offer convenient trailheads and rewarding, varied walks for day hikers and backpackers alike. If you're starting at a pass, expect to climb at the beginning of the walk. And watch the altitude: Never in this section does the trail dip below 7,000 feet, and it spends most of its time between 8,000 feet and 9,000 feet.

- **Sonora Pass:** Going north from Sonora Pass takes you into wide-open high country dotted with misshapen volcanic outcroppings. The trail stays in the Carson-Iceberg Wilderness for most of the distance between Sonora Pass and Ebbetts Pass, about 30 miles away.
- **Ebbetts Pass:** This dramatic and scenic area offers good backpacking and day hiking in either direction. Heading north, you'll find excellent views and yet more dramatic volcanic formations, especially between Ebbetts Pass and Blue Lakes (about 20 miles). You run out of wilderness near Blue Lakes. After that, the trail winds past quite a few back roads until you get to Echo Summit.
- **Echo Lake Resort:** Going north from Echo Lake Resort takes you into the Desolation Wilderness, for true high-country granite and sparkling tarns. This is a day hiker's best chance to get a feel for the landscape of the High Sierra. But be prepared to see lots of other hikers doing just what you are doing. If you want a longer backpack, keep going and you'll end up in the Granite Chief Wilderness.
- **Donner Summit:** From Donner Summit, climb south for good open views. Choose a weekday for this popular day hike: On a sunny weekend, the trail is packed.

Resupplies and Trailheads

Echo Lake Resort is the most commonly used.

Sonora Pass (mile 0) at Highway 108. There are no towns, stores, phones, or other amenities at Sonora Pass, but there is a trailhead from which you may be able to wangle a ride down to Bridgeport (on the eastern side). Bridgeport, a big town with grocery stores, outfitters, motels, restaurants, post office, and self-service laundry, is 33 miles away (16 miles east on Highway 108 and 17 miles south on U.S. Highway 395). Post office: General Delivery, Bridgeport, CA 93517

Ebbetts Pass (mile 31.6) at Highway 4. Markleeville, with restaurants and a post office, is 18 miles northeast. Post office: General Delivery, Markleeville, CA 96120

Carson Pass (mile 60.4) at Highway 88. Caples Lake Resort, with limited supplies, is 4 miles west.

Echo Lake Resort (mile 76.2) has a small store with limited hiker supplies. It also has a small post office. If you need more supplies, you can hitch in to South Lake Tahoe. Post offices: General Delivery, Echo Lake, CA 95721; General Delivery, South Lake Tahoe, CA 96150

Donner Summit (mile 136.9) at Old Highway 40. Soda Springs, 3.2 miles west, has a post office, restaurant, and groceries. Post office: General Delivery, Soda Springs, CA 95728

9

Donner Pass to Belden

133.0 miles

This section ranges from the sheer-walled canyons of the Feather River to the impossibly teetering pinnacle of the Sierra Buttes fire tower, which looks for all the world like a fairy-tale mountain hideaway, perfectly situated for a wizard who spends his days mixing magic potions and his nights concocting mysterious spells.

The first 90 miles of this section vary in elevation from 4,500 to 8,300 feet, usually meandering between 6,000 and 7,000. In the remaining 43 miles, the trail twice drops precipitously, to cross the Middle and North Forks of the Feather River. The section ends at the North Fork of the Feather River at Belden, at an elevation of 2,300.

The 6,000 feet of elevation difference between the trail's high point near Donner Pass and its low point at Belden give this section more ecological diversity than the trail has encountered since southern California. In the high montane forests, red firs are adapted to terrain that may be snow-covered 200 days of the year, while down below, chaparral-covered hillsides in midsummer can remind hikers of the southern drylands, complete with water shortages and rattlesnakes. Also leaving their mark on this section and contributing to its variety are the forces of both volcanism and glaciation.

But while it's always interesting, the trail's character in these 133 miles is completely different than it has been in the mountains to the south. Most notably, there is only one small wilderness in this stretch. Much of the rest of the land shows evidence of multiple use: logging, grazing, and mining, as well as ORV use and recreational development. Frequently crossed by roads, the PCT is sometimes forced to detour around private property;

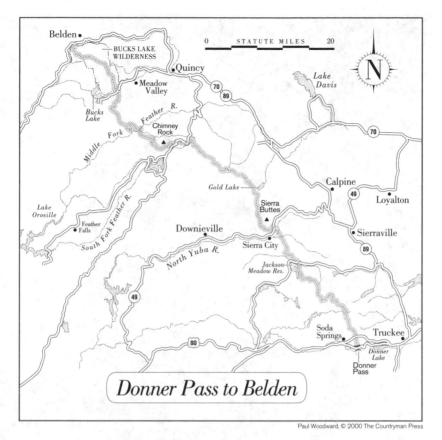

Donner Pass to Belden

Paul Woodward, © 2000 The Countryman Press

clearly, hiking is just one of many uses in this multiple-use region. Like the southern California sections described in chapters 4 and 5, this stretch of trail is most often used by people who live within reasonable driving distance, or hikers who are trying to complete the entire PCT (or, perhaps, all of California's PCT). Most of them find ample rewards here. But if you're only going to hike selected segments of the PCT—and especially if you need to take a plane trip and use vacation time to do it—this probably shouldn't be the first section you choose to do.

THE ROUTE

If you're being dropped off, you can access the PCT from the Interstate 80 rest stop at Donner Pass. If you need to park, there's a trailhead a quarter-mile south of the interstate.

Wolf lichen shows the snow level north of Donner Pass

From I-80, the trail climbs, soon passing the Sierra Club's Peter Grubb Hut, a shelter that is open to the public. One of the few huts or shelters on the entire PCT, this one makes a good case for eliminating them. Exceptionally run-down and poorly maintained, it's hardly a welcoming site—unless, perhaps, you arrive in a storm.

The route from here is easy, with good fast trail that meanders, climbing and descending gently, and frequently crossing logging and Forest Service roads. Just after snowmelt, the low-lying areas of this section can be infested with mosquitoes, especially near ponds and in meadows. Several stretches along open ridges offer escape from the bugs and good views of the largely volcanic landscape, which is punctuated with obvious lava formations and buttes.

About 27 miles from Donner Pass, the trail passes near Jackson Reservoir, an area popular with boaters. It's worth mentioning that there aren't many legal backcountry campsites here. You have the choice of camping in one of the official campgrounds (off-trail along the reservoir) or hiking on. Seven miles later, the trail reaches Milton Creek, along which there are many lovely creekside campsites.

Thirty-eight miles into this section, the trail crosses California Highway 49. Most hikers continuing on will detour 1.5 miles to resupply in Sierra City. Heading north from the highway, the trail gains nearly 3,000 feet as it switchbacks for 8 miles through shadeless chaparral. The climb is gentle and easy, if long, but on a hot summer day, watch your water, because the few water sources en route are not reliable. Once you've reached the ridge, a side trail leads to the Sierra Buttes fire tower, which is built into a steep rock pinnacle.

Continuing on, the PCT follows a route that carries you above and away from the Plumas National Forest's Lake Basin Area. This popular destination has suffered from overuse in the past, so the PCT was routed above it to minimize impact. Unfortunately, this makes for a rather dry stretch, so again, watch your water. Depending on the year, springs start to dry up in midsummer.

Around the headwaters of Nelson Creek, the trail's course is uncharacteristically meandering in order to avoid private land and mining and timber operations. The terrain here is difficult to categorize: Sometimes in forest, sometimes on open ridges, it crosses lots of logging and jeep roads and passes by the occasional logging operation. The trail undulates a bit before starting a descent to the Middle Fork of the Feather River. Here again, the springs tend to run dry in midsummer, so tank up. Relief is at hand when you reach the river, which has National Wild and Scenic River status, not to mention one of the best swimming holes on the PCT. This is a great place to schedule a long lunch or a midafternoon break. Campsites are good, too.

Take a good rest, because in the next 38 miles, the trail shoots straight back up again from 3,180 to 5,955 feet, drops 500 feet, climbs another 1,400—and then changes its mind and plummets 15 miles and 4,600 feet downhill to the North Fork of the Feather River, elevation 2,310. This section ends at Belden, a trailer park/campground where hikers can resupply.

WHAT YOU'LL SEE

Feather River

The Feather River carries twice as much water as any other river in the Sierra. The Middle Fork is its major tributary. The Middle Fork boasts one of the most spectacular and remote river canyons in America, along with (on its Fall River tributary) 640-foot-tall Feather Falls, the sixth-highest waterfall in the contiguous states. In 1968 the Middle Fork of the Feather River was named one of seven original federally designated wild and scenic rivers. This designation stopped the construction of dams that would have destroyed the river's wild character. Later, a stretch of the Feather River's North Fork was added to the system.

Downstream, after the North and Middle Forks converge, water is held in a reservoir behind Oroville Dam, which at 779 feet is the tallest dam in the United States. Thru-hikers might consider the long journey some of this water is about to make. About 2 million acre-feet of water a year are channeled into southern California. (One acre-foot equals 325,900 gallons; it's the amount of water that would cover 1 acre 1 foot deep.) Some of the Feather River water goes to Napa, Alameda, and Santa Clara Counties. Most of it travels via the California Aqueduct to the San Joaquin Valley and thence south to always thirsty Los Angeles.

PCT hikers cross the Middle Fork on a high bridge. From the trail, it's

The Middle Fork of the Feather River

an easy scramble down to the river, which is lined with granite rocks perfect for sunbathing and inviting pools that promise to rejuvenate even the most tired hiker. Afternoons are best for taking a dip, because by then, the water temperature has risen to a comfortable 70 degrees. In early season—or early in the morning—it can be quite a bit colder.

Gold Rush

Gold had been found in California as early as 1842, but it was the 1848 discovery of gold at John Sutter's mill on the South Fork of the American River near Sacramento that changed the history of the state.

Between 1848 and 1852, the population of California rose from less than 10,000 to more than 265,000. By 1861, immigration to the United States doubled. Miners arrived from nearby Oregon and the not-so-nearby East Coast, as well as from Mexico, Europe, Australia, Hawaii, Chile, and Peru. From the East Coast, it was an 18,000-mile journey by boat around Cape Horn—or an equally arduous overland trek. The trips were brutal: Between 1848 and 1850, some 90,000 people died in transit of diseases like yellow fever, malaria, and dysentery. But the miners kept coming. By 1850, legend has it that there were 600 abandoned boats sitting in San

Francisco's harbor, their crews having jumped ship to join the rush.

The 1848 gold rush made California the number one gold producer in the world, freeing the United States of its dependency on foreign supplies. It also transformed California from just another poor, rural, underdeveloped, underpopulated western state into a major political and economic player in the U.S. By 1865, an estimated $500 million in gold had been found—not much, perhaps, by the standards of today's Internet IPOs, but a fine sum 140 years ago.

The main gold belt extended from Mariposa to the North Fork of the Feather River. North of the Feather River, volcanic rock and lava beds made extraction unfeasible. However, a secondary vein ran northwest from the Feather River into Tehama, Shasta, and Trinity Counties and the Klamath Mountains—a path roughly parallel to the route of the PCT.

In this region, miners panned for gold in streams, looking for so-called "free gold" (as opposed to gold buried in the earth that has to be excavated). The finest grains of gold, called flour, are found farthest downstream from their origins, pulverized and eroded into fine particles. Upstream, bigger nuggets would be found, and maybe even chunks, fueling belief in the existence of a mother lode. In 1859 rumors of a solid gold lake brought some 2,000 treasure hunters into the Lakes Basin area of the Plumas National Forest—hence the name of Gold Lake, which is seen from the PCT a few miles north of Sierra Buttes.

Even today, mining companies cast covetous eyes at what might lie beneath the surface and miners and prospectors still stalk the elusive mother lode. You'll see handwritten signs announcing claims along creeks and rivers. And you may well wonder, as have so many before you: Is there still gold in them thar hills? Could I find it if I tried?

Sierra Buttes Fire Tower

Glaciation created the rugged pinnacles of the Sierra Buttes (as well as the Lakes Basin just ahead). From the PCT's junction with the Sierra Buttes jeep trail, it is a 1.5-mile walk (and 1,400-foot climb) to the Sierra Buttes fire tower, one of the most precarious-looking fire towers to be seen anywhere. Don't go if you're prone to acrophobia: The cabin leans out over hundreds of acres of mountains and below you is a nearly 600-foot vertical drop. But for those who can stomach the heights, the fire tower offers

The climb to the Sierra Buttes

an unparalleled view, clear back to the Desolation Wilderness and forward to Mount Lassen, still 150 trail miles away.

Trail Conflicts

If you find yourself occasionally thinking that the trail's route through some of this section doesn't make good foot-sense, you're right. It took until 1985 to establish the PCT's route through the Nelson Creek area (about 20 miles north of Sierra Buttes), making it the last section of trail to be completed in northern California. Land-use conflicts and difficulty obtaining easements delayed route selection and construction. Farther north, near Tom Creek Road, you'll see further evidence of multiple-use conflicts where the trail has been relocated onto an indirect route to avoid logging operations.

HIKING INFORMATION

Seasonal Information and Gear Tips

The trail in this section is generally snow-free from mid-June through mid-October, although at the lower elevations (especially in the southern half of this segment), the trail is sometimes snow-free until November. August and September are the best times to hike here; many hikers prefer September because the bugs and crowds are both gone and the temperatures are slightly cooler; however, some seasonal water sources will be dry.

Warm, dry summers allow you to carry lighter packs here than almost anywhere else on the PCT. It's a good place to experiment with ultralight hiking techniques, both because the terrain and environment are moderate and because a large network of Forest Service roads makes it possible to bail out.

Thru-hikers' Corner

If you're into lightweight fast-packing, this is the place to ditch your gear and fly. The footpath will be snow-free, and it's well-graded and easy enough to be hiked comfortably in sneakers. Warm, dry summers allow hikers to carry minimal clothing (although, as always in mountains, an extra warm layer and a rain jacket are recommended).

The only downside is bugs. Thru-hikers arrive here just after the snowmelt, and wet areas like meadows can be a-buzzin'. If you are hiking with a tarp, plan to camp on ridges, where the drier ground and higher winds help to alleviate the bug problem.

Best Short Hikes
- An accessible and dramatic day hike from Sierra City is the 16.8-mile round trip from Highway 49 to the Sierra Buttes fire tower (see page 170). The footway is easy, but the climb involves 3,980 feet total elevation gain, so it ranks as a difficult day hike. Bring lots of water and a camera.
- For a good day hike—or a leisurely overnight—start at Bucks Summit (mile 111.1), where you can park, and go 5.6 miles to a side trail that descends 0.7 miles east to isolated Gold Lake, with good camping.

Resupplies and Trailheads
Sierra City is the most commonly used.

Donner Pass (mile 0). There's only an interstate-highway rest area and picnic ground here, but it's a convenient place to get dropped off. A short side trail connects to the PCT.

Sierra City (mile 38.4) is 1.5 miles off the PCT on Highway 49. This town (population 250) has hotels, restaurants, a self-service laundry, a store, and a post office. *Northbounders:* Beyond Milton Creek, take a shortcut along an old road that leads 1 mile to Wild Plum Campground, from which it is 2.2 miles into town.

Bucks Lake Resort (Mile 106.2) is 3 miles off-trail. Take Big Creek Road 2.5 miles west, then take Bucks Lake Road half a mile to the resort, which has a store, restaurant, RV park, and cabins. If you continue on Bucks Lake Road for 3.8 miles, you'll reconnect with the PCT at Bucks Summit. This is a good alternate resupply if you think you'll be arriving in this area during biker week in Belden (see page 186).

10

Belden to Castella

216.6 miles

North of Belden, the Sierra Nevada gives way to a new mountain range—
the mighty Cascades—whose string of volcanoes will act as a beacon for
hikers for most of the miles between northern California and the Canadian
border.

The PCT through this section is hard to categorize. On the one hand, in
Lassen Volcanic National Park, the trail boasts features that can compete
with any of the PCT's scenic highlights. Some of Lassen Park's many thermal wonders are directly on the trail; others make for interesting side
trips. Attractions include fumaroles and geysers, Lassen Peak itself, and
a rare and perfect 600-foot-tall cinder cone, made of small loose cinders
piled around a volcanic vent. But also in this section is an infamous 30-
mile dry (although scenic) stretch through terrain that will make thru-hikers think they've taken a wrong turn and ended up back in southern
California's chaparral drylands. In the last 80 miles of this section,
between Burney Falls and Castella, the trail turns ornery as it wends its
way through a logged and roaded mess. Even Clinton Clarke, writing more
than half a century ago, felt this part of northern California was going to
offer less than a desirable trail experience. He characterized it as wan-
dering around logging trails and roads, partially lumbered forests, burned
clearings, sawmills, power and irrigation projects, swampy meadows, private lands, and commercialized areas. "Not much," he concluded, "can
be done."

Admittedly, today's route is better than all that would suggest. But for
the most part, this section is not up to par with the rest of the PCT.

Lassen Park, however, is well worth a visit, as are the Klamath
Mountains just to the north of this section (see chapter 11). If you have

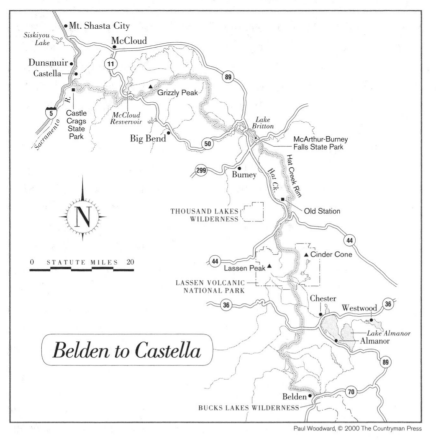

Paul Woodward, © 2000 The Countryman Press

limited time, make the best of it by hiking through Lassen Volcanic National Park, then skipping ahead to the Klamath Mountains.

THE ROUTE

The exact halfway point of the PCT changes from time to time because of trail relocations, but at the present writing, it is just south of the PCT's crossing of California Highway 36, precisely 46.2 miles north of Belden, where this section begins. If you're a thru-hiker, you'll probably spend the next few miles reflecting that for every mile you've walked in the last couple of months, you're going to walk one more in the months ahead!

The footway through this area is gentle and easy, even by PCT standards. Long-distance hikers and very fit section hikers often average daily mileage in the high 20s or low 30s.

For thru-hikers, Lassen Volcanic National Park marks another important milestone: Mount Lassen is the first in the string of volcanoes that stretches all the way into Canada. The trail's traverse of the park goes past some of the thermal basins, where the hissing and steaming and bubbling of countless vents, mud pots, fumaroles, and geysers demonstrate just how alive this volcanic area is.

North of Lassen, the trail's character abruptly changes as it enters hardcore timber country, where you'll walk not through forests but through monocultural timber farms, as businesslike and purposefully planted as any farmer's fields of corn. Interlaced with dirt and gravel roads, this area is easily accessible for vehicle-oriented recreation, and you'll see plenty of evidence of it in the scorched-earth campsites that line Hat Creek.

Next up is the Hat Creek Rim. Complete with rattlesnakes, chaparral, and a 30-mile stretch that is usually without water, the Hat Creek Rim is reminiscent of southern California's drylands, so be sure you have enough containers to carry several quarts of water. On this section, you'll get your first glimpse of Mount Shasta, the next major peak on your route. From this point on, Shasta will be intermittently visible all the way to the Oregon border, still some 300 miles away by trail.

Completing the Hat Creek Rim, the trail descends to cross California Highway 89 near Burney Falls, where hikers can take a side trip to see one of the state's most voluminous waterfalls.

North of Burney, trail quality is poor. The terrain itself is rolling mountains and thick forests, with occasional good views of Mount Shasta and Castle Crags (the 2.9-mile side trip to the summit of Grizzly Peak is especially recommended). But the area is also heavily logged,and the trail frequently crosses roads, many of which do not show up on Forest Service maps or in the guidebooks. The trail can be badly eroded and overgrown. A low population density and general lack of interest have created a shortage of volunteers, although recent thru-hikers, disgusted with the state of the trail, have traded their backpacks for axes and shovels and worked to improve conditions. Ironically, while this section of trail does not attract a crowd—it is hiked mainly by thru-hikers, section hikers, and hikers trying to complete all of California's PCT—this section of California does attract wealthy executives: Just a few miles to the south along the Pitt River, several major corporations maintain private fishing retreats.

This section ends at Castle Crags State Park, near Interstate 5 at Castella.

WHAT YOU'LL SEE

The End of the Sierra?

The northern end of the Sierra Nevada is no less difficult to pinpoint than the southern end. Somewhere in the general vicinity of Belden, the Sierra ends and the Cascades begin. If you want to identify the precise place where one mountain ranges ends and the other begins, you're going to run into controversy.

Guidebook author and geologist Jeffrey Schaffer sets the border just north of Belden, near Chips Creek, where, he says, the bedrock of granitic plutons that mark the Sierra give way to a continuous mantle of volcanic rock that is typical of the Cascades.

John Muir claimed that the Sierra extends north, past the volcanic cones of Mounts Lassen and Shasta. Geologist Mary Hill says that the Sierra Nevada ends south of Lassen. And writer and environmentalist Tim Palmer, who explored the Sierra Nevada for his book *The Sierra Nevada: A Mountain Journey*, puts the northern terminus underwater at Lake Almanor.

In any event, the tiny town of Belden is close to the changeover—and it's also within 50 miles of the trail's halfway point. So it's a good place for thru-hikers to celebrate two major accomplishments: completing half of the trail and hiking the entire length of Sierra Nevada.

Belden

Located at the confluence of the North Fork and East Branch of the Feather River (see chapter 9), Belden is named after a family that mined in the area. Between 1849 and 1852, more than 250,000 ounces of gold dust and nuggets were mined in a 4-mile stretch of river near Belden.

In 1903, the Western Pacific Railroad came through and Belden became a hub of activity. The railroad brought supplies in to the canyon, which were then transported to even more isolated local communities via the Belden-Longville Stage Coach Line. In 1935, the Feather River High-

Mudpots at Lassen Volcanic National Park

way (California Highway 70) was built, and ended the need for a stage line.

Today the small resort is mainly visited by recreationists and offers fishing, hiking, biking, rafting, and a host of other activities—including panning for gold.

Lassen Peak

This volcanic peak was known by local Natives as the Sweathouse of the Gods. Its English name comes from a Danish blacksmith who moved to California in 1840. In 1848 Peter Lassen led the first party of emigrants from Missouri along his newly opened Lassen Trail into northern California. But the route was difficult and was soon abandoned; Lassen himself turned to gold mining—unsuccessfully—and was finally murdered under mysterious circumstances.

Meanwhile, in 1851, another would-be entrepreneur, William H. Noble, built a wagon road, traces of which can still be seen and followed. (The PCT runs along it for a short stretch along the northern boundary of Lassen Park.) Thousands of emigrants and gold miners used this route, but because the Lassen area was some distance from the main gold fields, it was left relatively undeveloped. The region remains remote and relatively unpopulated even today.

Mount Lassen's last major eruption, beginning in May of 1915, is the

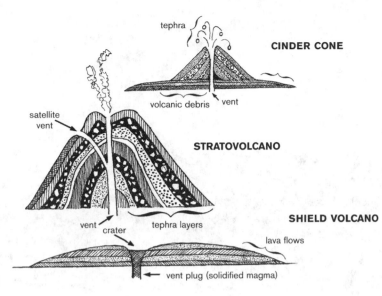

second-most recent volcanic eruption in the 48 coterminous states. (The 1980 eruption of Washington's Mount St. Helens, of course, is the most recent.) Clouds of dust reached into the stratosphere, and a train 100 miles away was stopped by ash piled high on its tracks. After the 1915 eruption, Lassen remained intermittently active until 1921. Since then, it has been relatively quiet, but there is plenty of evidence of continuing geological activity in the park, which, except for Yellowstone, boasts the largest number of active geothermal features in the United States.

Established in 1916, Lassen Volcanic National Park was one of the earliest national parks, as well as the only volcanic national park. (Mount St. Helens National Volcanic Monument, also administered by the National Park Service, was established after the mountain's 1980 eruption.) Lassen remains a major site for not only volcanology, but also for the study of landscape recovery after a volcanic eruption.

Lassen is also notable because, at 10,457 feet, it is the world's largest plug-dome volcano. All of the other major volcanoes in the Cascade range—Shasta, Hood, Adams, and Rainier—are stratovolcanoes.

Some definitions: A stratovolcano (also called a composite volcano) is a massive structure composed of multiple lava flows that have cooled and hardened on top of alternating layers of non-lava material. Lava is magma that arrives at the surface in liquid form. Pyroclastic (from the Greek for "broken by fire") material refers to volcanic matter that comes out in solid

Lava south of Humboldt Summit

chunks rather than as molten rock. In addition, composite volcanoes may have layers of volcanic ash and mud flows (called lahars). In a stratovolcano, each eruption places a new layer of lava or pyroclastic material atop previously existing layers. A cross-section would look like a layer cake, with distinct strata revealing the history of the mountain's eruptions. Most classic stratovolcanoes have steep upper flanks and moderate lower slopes; most of them have been reshaped by major eruptions, then eroded by glaciation, rain, and wind. The higher peaks all have glaciers on their upper slopes; most used to have glacier on their lower slopes as well.

By contrast, a plug dome volcano is composed entirely of lava. Plug dome volcanoes tend to be smaller and shorter-lived; commonly, they erupt only once. But Mount Lassen's Indian name—Sweathouse of the Gods—contradicts this. Indeed, the mountain has erupted several times in its history.

Other volcanoes in the Cascades include shield volcanoes (so named because have the shape of a warrior's shield). Shield volcanoes are formed when a volcano ejects thin lava which flows quickly for many miles before it solidifies. As a result, these mountains are usually less steep than other volcanoes.

Cinder cones are formed when lava ejected from the volcano "freezes" (or solidifies) while still in midair, and then piles up in a relatively cylindrical cone around the vent. They usually rise no more than 1,000 feet above the surrounding landscape. Large lava flows (such as those discussed in chapter 13) can often be traced to the base of a cinder cone.

Lassen is actually a second-generation plug dome volcano that sits on what used to be the edge of the crater of an ancient stratovolcano that geologists call Mount Tehama. About 600,000 years ago, initial eruptions built Tehama into an 11-mile wide, 11,500-foot stratovolcano. When, about 400,000 years ago, Tehama's volcanic activity declined, domes of lava started to erupt on its sides. What was to become Mount Lassen was the largest of these domes. As Lassen and other domes continued to grow and erupt, they weakened the original mountain, which began to deteriorate as hot steam and water from hydrothermic systems weakened its underlying structure. Wind, rain, and glaciers further eroded the original mountain, until all that is left are a few remnants of the original crater. Lassen, however, was covered by lava that solidified. Sitting atop a thermally active pressure cooker, it eventually became a volcano itself.

Hiking along the PCT, you'll pass plenty of evidence that the mountain is still alive. At aptly named Boiling Springs Lake, you'll see fumaroles (steam vents) and bubbling mud pots (caused by water from hot springs). Side trips to Bumpass Hell (just south of Lassen Peak itself; accessible by park road) and the 600-foot-tall Cinder Cone (an active volcano a few miles east of the PCT and accessible by a side trail) will round out the volcanic experience.

Hat Creek Rim

Just north of Lassen, the PCT was forced by land ownership patterns to take a dry detour along the Hat Creek Rim, a faulted escarpment that is in neither the Sierra nor the Cascades, but is atop a small part of central California's Modoc Plateau. Crisscrossed by fissures and tunnels, the plateau is dry because most of the water drains into a lost creek beneath the surface. For hikers, this means 30 potentially thirsty miles.

Three other potential annoyances here are rattlesnakes, ticks, and grass seeds that insist on crawling into your socks (gaiters help). If you get tired of all the fun and games, you can bail out by dropping down onto Highway 89, which offers (at the price of some traffic and the hard surface underfoot) cafés, plenty of water, and campgrounds.

Mount Shasta

"Lonely as God and white as a winter moon," wrote John Muir,

> *Mount Shasta rises in solitary grandeur from the edge of a compara-*
> *tively low and lightly sculptured lava plain near the northern extrem-*
> *ity of the Sierra, and maintains a far more impressive and command-*
> *ing individuality than any other mountain within the limits of*
> *California. Go where you may, within a radius of from 50 to 100 miles*
> *or more, there stands before you the colossal cone of Shasta clad in ice*
> *and snow, the one grand unmistakable landmark, the polestar of the*
> *landscape.*

Hikers in this section and the next will undoubtedly agree with Muir's sentiments. Beginning at Burney, the PCT makes a wide arc to the west, and as a result, you see Shasta from the south, the west, and the north. For more than 300 miles, no matter where you walk, or how far, you cannot leave the mountain behind you.

Unlike most of the other high peaks of the Cascades, which have been named for 19th-century Europeans or European Americans, Shasta takes its name from the Indians who inhabited the area in the 19th century. At 14,161 feet, Shasta is the second-highest mountain in the Cascades; only Washington's Mount Rainier is taller. Seventeen miles in diameter, and 80 to 84 cubic miles in volume, Shasta is really composed of four overlapping volcanoes, each of which was formed at a different time. The oldest of these is some 100,000 years old, but the summit cone and the prominent secondary peak (named Shastina) are much younger—only 10,000 to 12,000 years old. Shastina itself is 12,330 high—tall enough to make it the third-highest peak in the Cascades if you count it as a separate peak.

Shasta is less eroded than many of the other Cascade volcanoes because it lies at a more southerly latitude, so there has been less glaciation and erosion from snow and ice. Also, the large volume of lava that erupted from the mountain during its periods of activity has filled in the older gullies and cirques that were created by glaciation that occurred before the eruptions.

Unlike Lassen and Mount St. Helens, most of Shasta's volcanic activity took place before recorded history. But it has had six major eruptions in the last 2,000 years. In addition, Shasta may be the erupting volcano described by a Spanish explorer sailing along the California coast in 1786. A few small eruptions of steam and dust were reported in the 1850s, and in 1854, the first climbing party to reach the summit described "a cluster of boiling sulfur hot springs . . . located on the edge of a broad snowfield just below the summit pinnacle . . . and the rocks are hot enough to cook an egg in five minutes." Today there are only two hot springs near the summit, evidence that although the geothermal activity continues, it has somewhat subsided.

Muir's observation that Shasta is "a colossal cone rising in solitary grandeur [which] might well be regarded as an object of religious worship" has been shared by many others. One belief is that the mountain's interior is hollow and inhabited by Lemurians, highly civilized refugees and survivors of the ancient kingdom of Mu (said to be a sort of Atlantis of the Pacific). Lemurians are described as 7 feet tall, with a sense organ in the middle of their foreheads. The I AM foundation was founded in 1930 to spread this belief after one Guy W. Ballard reported meeting "a majestic figure, God-like in appearance, clad in jeweled robes, eyes sparkling with light and love."

Other groups also view the mountain as sacred, including Rosicrucians, the Knights of the White Rose, the Association Sananda and Sanat Kimara, the Radiant School of Seekers and Servers, and Understanding, Inc., as well as those who believe Shasta is a regularly scheduled stop for flying saucers traveling between planets. In the town of Shasta, you can find new-age bookstores selling materials that promote these (and other) belief systems. According to the Pacific Crest Trail Association, no PCT hiker has personally encountered a Lemurian.

Climbing Mount Shasta

The first ascent of Mount Shasta was in 1854, by a party led by a Captain E. D. Pierce. In 1870, Clarence King, the famed Sierran mountaineer and member of the California Geological Survey, climbed Shasta; in 1874, John Muir made an ascent. Backpackers who want to follow in their path can rent equipment in the town of Shasta (ice axes and crampons are required.) The round trip usually takes three days (two nights).

Burney Falls

Just off the trail, and well worth a visit, is 129-foot-high Burney Falls, among California's grandest. Called, perhaps over enthusiatically, by Theodore Roosevelt the "eighth wonder of the world," Burney Falls boasts a daily flow of 100 million gallons, more than any other waterfall in California—for eight months of the year. During late spring and summer, Yosemite Falls grabs the honor when its snowmelt-fed cascades swell into even bigger, albeit temporary, torrents.

The full name of the park—McArthur-Burney Falls Memorial State Park—commemorates Samuel Burney, one of the area's earliest settlers, and Frank McArthur, a wealthy cattle rancher who wanted to preserve the falls from hydroelectric development. In 1920, McArthur bought the 160 acres surrounding the falls and donated them to the state. In 1922, the park was established, making it one of the oldest state parks in California. In addition to being a popular tourist destination, it is a nesting site for bald eagles.

Logging

The upper montane forests of central and northern California are dominated by red fir. *Abies magnifica,* found almost exclusively in California, is one of the largest firs in the world.

Red fir

Trees that grow here must be able to tolerate having 8 to 13 feet of their trunks buried by snow for up to 200 days a year. You can see how deep the snow level is by looking up to where wolf lichen starts to grow on the trunks of the trees. Despite its appearance, wolf lichen is not parasitic; it is actually a photosynthetic plant.

Red firs are seldom found growing with deciduous trees, because deciduous trees cannot tolerate the long winters. Nor can shrubs, which would be buried for more than half the year. Red firs therefore grow alone, or sometimes with other firs, and the understory is clear. As a result, they are extremely attractive to loggers.

While walking through the roads and timber farms between Lassen National Park and Castella, you might consider the words of Supreme Court justice and environmentalist William O. Douglas, who wrote, "A road . . . would turn a place of beauty into a bald, devastated ugly place. The road—on whose construction the logger often makes a greater profit than he does on the timber he takes out—would be a road to nowhere, for with the forest, removed, the place becomes a ridge or basin of desolation. Even the game has gone; there is nothing to see."

HIKING INFORMATION

Seasonal Information and Gear Tips

The hiking season in this segment extends from mid-June through October. Summer temperatures can be in the 90s, especially at the lower elevations, and by early August, ephemeral springs and streams start to dry. Surface water is scarce between Lassen Park and Castella, especially in the Hat Creek Rim area.

- Extra containers for water will help get you through the dry stretches.
- In the Hat Creek Rim area, gaiters will help keep hitchhiking grass seeds out of your socks.

Thru-hikers' Corner

This is a stretch that can be dispiriting for thru-hikers. The difficulties are all psychological; there's nothing hard about the hiking. The realization that after months of walking, you have only just reached the halfway point can be shocking to even the happiest of hikers. So can the fact that not only have you not made it out of your first state, but the Oregon border is still more than 200 miles away! And then there is the uninspiring scenery of the heavily logged multiple-use lands. Cheer up! The lovely Klamath Mountains are just ahead, and well worth the detour.

Thru-hikers should be aware that Belden hosts an annual biker-bash. That's bikers, not hikers. Bikers as in Harley Davidsons, leather jackets, and tattoos. The hiking and biking communities get along (there seems to be a mutual appreciation for the nontraditional lifestyle), but the tiny town of Belden is busting at its seams during the weekend (usually in late July; for info, call 530-283-9662), and it just can't handle all the traffic. A long-standing tradition, the biker festival raises money for a local school. So it's a priority for the local folks. Campground space is therefore not available for hikers, and all the cabins are booked. The people at Belden feel that they can be a lot more hospitable if hikers try to time their arrival so that they don't show up in the middle of the festival.

Best Short Hikes

- An easy and interesting day hike in Lassen National Park starts at Drakesbad Road near Warner Springs Campground and goes 2.7 miles south on the PCT (also the Boiling Springs Lake Nature Trail) to Boiling Springs Lake.
- For an overnight hike that traverses most of the park, start at Drakesbad Road. (But first, if you have time, do the day hike south to Boiling Springs Lake.) Then head 20 miles north to Old Station, which is on Highway 89, just 0.3 miles from the PCT via any of several side roads.

Resupplies and Trailheads

Belden (mile 0) is just off Highway 70. This small town/campground has a store, a restaurant, cabins, campsites, showers, and laundry. It may accept UPS packages for hikers; call for info (530-283-9662). If you'll be arriving during the biker weekend (see above), it's best to resupply at Bucks Lake (see page 173). To use the post office in Belden, you'll have to go 1 mile west on Highway 70. Post office: General Delivery, Belden, CA 95915

Old Station (mile 88.5) is 0.3 miles off-trail on Highway 89. It has laundry, limited groceries, a restaurant, lodge, and post office. Post office: General Delivery, Old Station, CA 96013

Burney (mile 126.7) is 7 miles off-trail on Highway 299. It has motels, supermarkets and drugstores, restaurants, and a post office. Post office: General Delivery, Burney, CA 96013

11

Castella to Ashland

221.8 miles

From Interstate 5 at Castella, California, to Interstate 5 at Ashland, Oregon, the PCT swings in a wide westward arc, then changes its mind and swings back to the east. The driving distance is only about 60 miles. On trail, it's more than 200 miles!

Fortunately, it's well worth the detour: These 200-plus meandering miles include some of northern California's most scenic terrain. Thru-hikers who have been dispirited by the excessive logging of the previous section will appreciate the return to wilderness. (There's logging in this region, too, but

Castle Crags

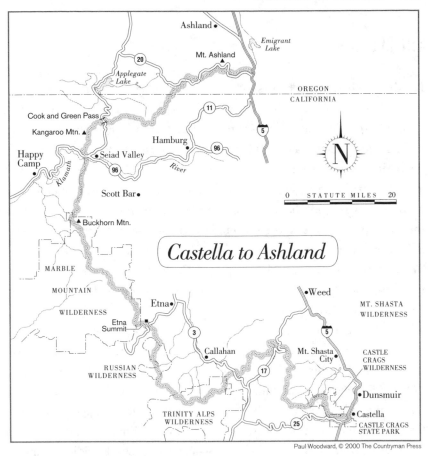

Castella to Ashland

Paul Woodward, © 2000 The Countryman Press

it's generally out of sight of the trail and prohibited entirely in the wildernesses.) This section is also appealing to short-term hikers: The mountains
are rugged and dramatic, and with a few well-placed roads, it's possible to
plan hikes of different lengths, depending on the time you have available
and the mileage you want to do.

Although most hikers loosely describe the PCT as following the Sierra
and then the Cascades, in this section, the trail in fact leaves the Cascades
for a foray into the Klamath Mountains. The reasons for this circuitous
routing include private property issues and water availability, both of
which are problems along the crest of northern California's Cascades. In
contrast, the Klamath Mountains offer adequate (if not abundant) water
and beautiful terrain, especially between Castle Crags and Seiad Valley,
where the trail goes through the Castle Crags, Trinity Alps, Russian, and
Marble Mountain Wildernesses.

THE ROUTE

Leave Castella early! The first 34 miles of this section is almost all uphill, gaining nearly 5,300 feet of elevation. You'll climb past the imposing Castle Crags and Castle Dome, granitic glaciated formations that are as jutting and dramatic as anything in the High Sierra. *Warning:* From the beginning of this section, it's 10 miles to the first decent campsite along the ridge of Kangaroo Mountain. Watch your water, because much of this climb is in exposed chaparral. Midsummer temperatures can climb well into the 90s, and late in the season, streams will start to dry up. Water is in especially short supply for the first 22 miles, until the Trinity Divide.

In addition to the excellent views of Castle Crags, there are frequent views back to Mount Shasta, which is visible through much of this section. And on a clear day, from just north of Scott Mountain, you can see south all the way back to Lassen and north into the Trinity Alps.

After Castle Crags, the trail passes in turn through the Trinity Alps, Russian, and Marble Mountain Wildernesses, which many hikers consider to have the most dramatic landscapes since the High Sierra. Keep an eye out for the side trail to Marble Mountain, which offers a spectacular view for those with a spare hour and the inclination to climb. Another highlight is Kings Castle, a dramatic peak that looms over pretty Paradise Lake.

The hiking is easy. *Note:* Although the region is dotted with lakes, the trail generally stays high, and only passes three of them. However, easy side trips of a mile or so will take backpacker (or fisherman) to many more.

In addition to the scenery and wilderness, thru-hikers have another reason to celebrate: From Buckhorn Mountain, about 131 miles into this section, you'll have your first unobstructed views into Oregon. You've still got 61 more miles to hike before you reach the border, but at long last, you have visual proof that your nearly 1,700-mile-long trek through the PCT's longest state is finally coming to an end.

One of the PCT's few road walks is a 6-mile stretch near Seiad Valley. The alternative—to build a bridge suitable for both foot and horse traffic over the Klamath River—was deemed too expensive. Therefore, the trail uses the highway bridge already in place. The land on either side of the river is

Mount Shasta

privately owned, so hikers walk on the road for 5 miles, cross on the bridge, and then turn around 180 degrees and walk 2 miles back to rejoin the trail.

Fording the river is a seductive shortcut, especially for hungry, hot hikers who have Seiad Valley's legendary pancake challenge on their minds (see page 198). The river is generally fordable in late summer, especially if the previous winter's snowfall has been moderate or light. If you choose to ford the river, you'll save between 2 and 3 miles, depending on exactly where you cross it. However, the shortcut isn't necessarily any quicker, since fording can be a slow process. Before tackling this crossing, you'll want to be sure you're a confident river wader, that the water level is low—and that your gear is packed to stay dry. If you stay on the official route and walk the extra miles, the reward in store is an arbor of blackberry bushes for snacking on. *Note:* The bushes are especially thick from Grider Creek Campground (where the road walk starts) to the river, so you're also likely to see bears, who take a proprietary interest in the juicy marble-sized berries.

North of Seiad Valley, the trail again climbs nearly 5,000 feet, so again, it's wise to start early. This can be another hot climb. When you reach Cook and Green Pass, 15 miles from Seiad Valley, you can actually walk a few yards off-trail and touch Oregon soil. But you can't say good-bye to California just yet: For the next 21 miles, the trail stays just on the California side of the border along an easy highline route with good views. You've left the wilderness behind. This is now multiple-use land, and multiple use means logging and cattle. You'll frequently cross logging roads, which detract from the wilderness experience (although they do offer early-season hikers alternate routes in years of high snow accumulations). You'll see some clear-cuts from the trail, but not many. Cattle are a more pressing nuisance. Be sure you've got a way to purify water, because the minimum-impact ethic of your bovine companions leaves a lot to be desired. You'll find that many of the springs are badly polluted.

Finally reaching the real California-Oregon border, you'll find a bullet-proof registration box where, if you're a thru-hiker, you can try to sum up what it feels like to finally complete 1,693.7 miles of California (if you're a northbounder) or 965 miles of Oregon and Washington (if you're headed south). Just before Ashland, you'll also get your last views of Mount Shasta, finally fading into the distance.

The 65 miles between Seiad Valley and I-5 near Ashland continue to be quite dry, although there are enough good springs if you pay attention to your water supply. There are also a couple of well-maintained and attractive shelters at Wangle and Grouse Gaps.

North of Jackson Gap, the PCT closely parallels Forest Road 20 as it makes its way toward Mount Ashland. If snow is giving you trouble, the road offers a convenient alternative.

WHAT YOU'LL SEE

Castle Crags

Naming geological features is always a bit of a hit-and-miss proposition. What looks like one person's Devil's Canyon may be another's Angel's Gulch. But it's hard to argue about Castle Crags, a crenellated series of ramparts and pinnacles that brings to mind a medieval fortress.

Castle Crags began life very much like the neighboring Cascades: They are the result of tectonic activity caused as the Pacific Plate pushed

Klamath Mountains

against the Continental Plate. But here, the process was different. When the Pacific Plate crashed into the Continental Plate, it was forced under the Continental Plate, into the hot mantle. This is called subduction, and in the Cascades, it resulted in magma being pressurized and shot out of the earth through volcanoes. But here, subduction heated a huge mass of granite far below the earth's surface. Because granite can retain heat for an unusually long time, the mass of rock slowly rose to the surface (like a hot-air balloon). Once on the surface, the granite was sculpted by wind, rain, and most of all, by ice. Glaciers removed all the softer rock, leaving only the hard granite, scoured and polished into dramatic crags and domes.

Klamath Mountains

The Klamath Mountains run through southwestern Oregon, south of the Coast Range and west of the Cascades, and extend into southern California. Their name is said to be derived from the Chinook word *tla-matl*, which was the name of a neighboring tribe.

Unlike their neighbors in the Cascades, the Klamath Mountains are not volcanic. At only 5,000 to 9,000 feet, the Klamath Mountains were less glaciated than were the High Sierra. Today, only a few tiny remnant glaciers exist on Thompson Peak.

Paradise Lake

The PCT's route passes through several subranges: the Trinity Alps; the Scott, Salmon, and Marble Mountains; and (on the other side of the Oregon border) the Siskiyou Mountains. Although *Siskiyou* is a Chinook word meaning *bobtailed horse*, the mountains were actually named by European Americans after a Hudson Bay Company official lost his favorite horse here.

The peaks in the Klamath range average about 5,000 feet. In Oregon, they rise to a high point of 7,530 feet atop Mount Ashland. In California, several peaks in the range top 9,000 feet.

The mountains here are geologically unique: They are the only range in North America made up largely of ultramafic rock. Ultramafic rock is both igneous and intrusive, meaning that it is molten matter that solidified while still in the earth's crust, then rose to the surface. Many of the rocks here were once beneath the ocean floor, but rose up when the plates collided. Much older than the Cascades, the Klamaths are the oldest range in western Oregon.

Despite their modest elevations, the terrain is both rugged and steep. Glaciation shaped the steep-walled valleys. High rainfall continues the work of erosion. (The average annual precipitation is 50 to 115 inches. Hikers will be delighted to learn that 90 percent of it falls between October and April.) Precipitation creates rapidly running rivers which have, over aeons, cut their way deeply into the mountains. One geologist claims that erosion in the Klamaths is occurring at a faster pace than at any other site in United States. The effects of erosion are easy to see. One example: the steep slopes on either side of the South Fork of the Scott River, where it's almost impossible to find a campsite because there's barely a square yard of level land.

Trinity Alps Wilderness

Containing 517,000 acres, the Trinity Alps Wilderness is California's second-largest wilderness. Although parts of this region had long been included in the Forest Service's primitive areas program, it was not designated as wilderness when the 1964 Wilderness Act went into effect, mostly because of the perceived value of its timberland. It was declared wilderness in 1984, with passage of the California Wilderness Act.

The other wildernesses are smaller, but added together, the Castle Crags, Russian, Marble Mountain, Siskiyou, and Trinity Alps Wildernesses comprise nearly 1 million acres of protected wild lands.

🚶 HIKING INFORMATION

Seasonal Information and Gear Tips

This section is generally snow-free from early July through October. Summers can be very hot, and in late summer some of the seasonal springs and streams start drying up. In addition, you'll find yourself sharing some water sources with cattle.

- Bring a water filter to help handle the polluted springs and streams.
- Because of its moderate to hot summer weather, this is a good section to experiment with lightweight gear.

Thru-hikers' Corner

This section is nothing but a delight for both northbound and southbound thru-hikers—who often cross paths here.

Castle Crags State Park has always treated PCT thru-hikers well.

Near Seven Lakes Basin

For many years, hikers were treated to the limitless hospitality of Milt Kinney, a local resident who died in 1995. A spur trail from the park back to the PCT bears his name. Campsite 25 in Castle Crags State Park is reserved for hikers arriving on foot. *Also note:* If you're traveling with a dog, you'll have to take the so-called Dog Trail back up to the PCT because dogs aren't allowed on other trails in the state park.

Best Short Hikes

This section's best hiking is in its wilderness areas, which are all found between Castle Crags State Park and Seiad Valley. That 156-mile stretch can be conveniently divided into two shorter sections by starting or ending a hike at the trailhead at Etna Summit (see below). Both hikes boast fabulous geological features, so length will probably be your deciding factor. From Castella to Etna Summit is 100 miles; from Etna Summit to Seiad Valley is 56 miles (50 miles, if you can arrange to start or end your hike at the trailhead at Grider Campground). In addition, several other forest service roads offer access and bail-out possibilities.

Castle Crags State Park offers good dayhiking. It's all uphill, so how far you get will depend on how high you can climb. But even if you go only a little way up, you're sure to enjoy the view of the crags and domes. For a good out-and-back overnight hike, go 10 miles up from Castella to the campsite on Kangaroo Mountain. The next day, you'll have time to look around a bit before retracing your steps back down.

Resupplies and Trailheads

Castella, Seiad Valley, and Ashland are the most commonly used.

Castella (mile 0) is 2 miles off-trail and has groceries, a restaurant, and camping in the state park. Dunsmuir, 6 miles north, offers hotels, restaurants, stores, laundry, and a post office. Post offices: General Delivery, Castella, CA 96017; General Delivery, Dunsmuir, CA 96025

Etna (mile 100.5) is 10.5 miles northeast of Etna Summit on the Somes Bar–Etna Road. It has a post office, B&B, motel, laundry, and restaurant. *Note:* It's 157.3 miles from Castella to Seiad Valley. Most thru-hikers don't resupply, and do this section in six to eight days. But most short-term hikers won't be doing 20–25 miles a day, and won't want to carry the ten or more days worth of food that a more leisurely pace would require. In this case, Etna is the most logical resupply, but if you have to hitch, be patient: there isn't much traffic on this road. Post office: General Delivery, Etna, CA 96027

Seiad Valley (mile 157.3) on California Highway 96 is a tiny community that has everything you're likely to need: campground, store, post office, cafe, and laundry. It's also got a legendary pancake challenge: eat the stack and it's free. Warning: we've seen 'em try, but we don't know of any hiker who has actually won the challenge! Post office: General Delivery, Seiad Valley, CA 96086

Ashland, Oregon (mile 208.0) is about 15 miles off-trail via Forest Roads 2080 and 200 via Bull Gap. This chapter describes the trail to I-5 (mile 214.9), from where you can hitch to Ashland. But if you take these forest service roads, you won't have to hitch. For more on Ashland, see the next chapter.

12

Ashland to Willamette Pass

187.2 miles

The PCT in Oregon is typically wooded, following long, broad ridges in coniferous forests dotted with lakes. Climbs are gentle, the footway well-graded. Strong long-distance hikers frequently cover up to 30 miles a day here—and sometimes more.

Oregon can lay claim to completing one of the earliest sections of the Pacific Crest Trail, although much of that original route is no longer in use. The mostly defunct Oregon Skyline Trail originally ran from Crater Lake in the south of the state to Mount Hood in the north. In 1937, when construction was completed on trails leading south from Crater Lake to the California border, and north from Mount Hood to the Washington border, Oregon became the first state to have a border-to-border trail.

Much of that old footway has been abandoned in favor of a higher route, chosen both because it offers a more truly crest-line path and because it avoids contributing to problems of overuse at popular lakeside campsites. But many segments of the old Oregon Skyline Trail still exist and are maintained as trails in national forests and wilderness areas. Some of these links are used by long-distance hikers as alternate routes because they pass close to backcountry lodges that will hold hiker boxes for resupply. They can also be used by weekend hikers to form loops.

Following Oregon's PCT is like following a row of beacons. The beacons, of course, are the volcanoes. The PCT circles around the shoulders of these giants, staying at relatively level elevations. Oregon's PCT ranges in elevation from nearly sea level at the Columbia River Gorge to more than 7,000 feet at Crater Lake. It spends the vast majority of its mileage

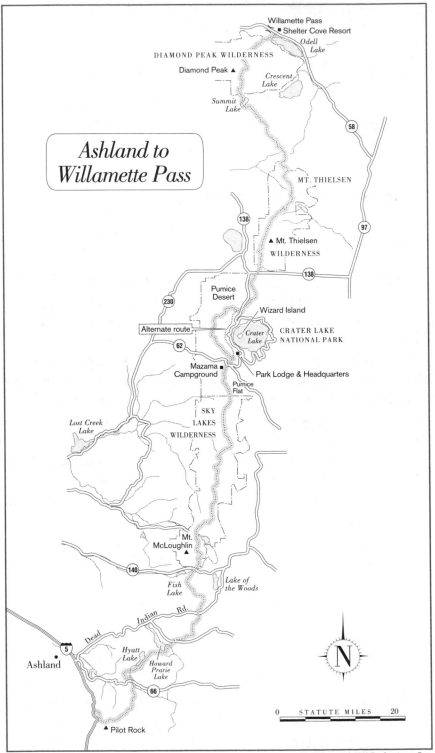

Ashland to
Willamette Pass

Willamette Pass
Shelter Cove Resort
Odell Lake
DIAMOND PEAK WILDERNESS
Diamond Peak ▲
Crescent Lake
Summit Lake
58

MT. THIELSEN
138
97
▲ Mt. Thielsen
WILDERNESS
138

Pumice Desert
230
Wizard Island
Alternate route
Crater Lake
CRATER LAKE NATIONAL PARK
62
Mazama Campground
Park Lodge & Headquarters
Pumice Flat

Lost Creek Lake
SKY LAKES WILDERNESS

Mt. McLoughlin ▲
140
Fish Lake
Lake of the Woods

Indian Rd.
Dead
5
Hyatt Lake
Howard Prarie Lake
Ashland
66

N

0 STATUTE MILES 20

▲ Pilot Rock

Paul Woodward, © 2000 The Countryman Press

gently undulating between 5,000 and 6,000 feet, and dips below 3,200 feet only on its final descent into the Columbia River Gorge.

By now, long-distance hikers are used to the dramatic differences in environment and ecology caused by the gain or loss of several thousand feet of elevation. The same changes, of course—from scrub to forest to alpine meadow to tundra—occur with changes in latitude. If you've previously hiked part or all of the trail in California, it's worth stopping for a moment here in Oregon to note how the change in latitude has affected what you'll see at different elevations. Most obvious is the much lower tree line. At 9,000 feet in the Cascades (assuming you were to climb that high), you would find the arctic rock and ice zone that you saw at 13,000 feet in the Sierra Nevada; in southern Oregon at elevations of 6,000 feet, you walk through forests of pine and fir, similar to those found above 9,000 feet in the San Gabriel Mountains.

One other difference: The character of the Oregon PCT is much more homogeneous than that of the California PCT. Particularly in the southern part of the state, the trail spends many miles in gentle forests, where dramatic views and changes of elevation are the exception rather than the rule. Still, this section spends much of its time in the Sky Lakes Wilderness and Crater Lake National Park—both well worth a visit, although preferably not in mosquito season.

THE ROUTE

From Interstate 5 at the beginning of this section, the trail heads east to rejoin the main ridge of the Cascades, which hikers will follow from here to the Canadian border, still almost 1,000 miles away. The first 54 miles north of I-5 are not the Oregon PCT's most scenic. Unfortunately, the BLM, which manages much of the land near Ashland through which the trail passes, has allowed old-growth forests to be lumbered. You'll see the evidence in checkerboard clear-cuts.

These first miles have always posed a challenge for trail builders. Oregon's original Skyline Trail stopped at Crater Lake, because trail builders didn't think the land between Crater Lake and the Oregon-California border was especially suited to a hiking trail. It was only when

Oregon at last! The author reaches the border on her thru-hike.

a Mexico-to-Canada route was proposed that Oregon's trail was extended. Even then, private property, water shortages, and incompatible land uses such as grazing and logging made trail building a challenge. In 1945, Clinton Clarke described southernmost Oregon as "a hotter and dryer climate, thinner forest and without special scenic value." In short, from I-5 to Fish Lake (about 54 miles) the main concern of the PCT is to get itself realigned with the crest of the Cascades, where it will stay all the way to Manning Park in Canada. While there is nothing especially difficult or unpleasant about these miles—assuming that hikers pay attention to their water supply—short-distance hikers might maximize the scenic value of their trip by starting at Oregon Highway 140 near Fish Lake rather than at I-5.

The trail rejoins the crest of the Cascades near Mount McLoughlin, then enters the Sky Lakes Wilderness, where the dry ridgeline trail manages to avoid every one of the wilderness's eponymous lakes (a distinct advantage in mosquito season). There is a large network of trails here, however, and lake-loving hikers will have no problem detouring to water.

Next up is the so-called Oregon Desert, which looks less like a desert than a patchy forest of scraggly lodgepole pines, any of which could have been used as a model for Charlie Brown's Christmas tree. Again, watch your water: From Jack Spring Spur Trail to Mazama Campground in Crater Lake National Park, there's a 15-mile dry stretch. That said, it's also worth pointing out that snow patches can linger here surprisingly late in July.

After Mazama Campground, the trail climbs to the rim of Crater Lake, where it looks down on America's deepest lake. For many years the PCT avoided walking along the scenic rim of Crater Lake because a trail here was not feasible for equestrians. Hikers wanting to see the lake (which included just about all hikers) left the trail and walked along the park road. Recently, however, the trail has been divided into hiker and equestrian routes. The equestrian route stays on the old path through the dry plateau; the new hiking trail takes a more scenic route along the rim, where it reaches 7,650 feet near the Watchman, a protruding andesite ridge produced when lava flowed out of a volcanic vent. This is the PCT's highest point in Oregon.

After Crater Lake, the trail passes near Diamond Lake Resort, a popular resupply stop with a post office, restaurant, store, and lodge. Next, the trail enters the Mount Thielsen Wilderness; then, at Emigrant Pass, the Diamond Peak Wilderness. This section ends at Willamette Pass (though a good argument could be made for the convenience of ending your hike at the small Shelter Cove resort, which is near the end of this section on Odell Lake).

WHAT YOU'LL SEE

Cascade Volcanoes

The Cascade Range, which you first encountered just north of Belden, in northern California, extends from approximately Mount Lassen to the Fraser River in Canada. Like the Sierra Nevada, the range changes in character as you move along it.

The southern Cascades are approximately 30 to 50 miles wide. On the western side of the range, elevations average around 5,000 feet. On that side, some of the volcanic flows are ancient—as much as 12 to 38 million years old. The eastern side, where the PCT spends much of its time, features the newer, higher peaks—including Jefferson and Hood and the Three Sisters (see chapters 13 and 14). Many of these major peaks tower a mile above the lower, more rounded mountains and ridges that surround them. However, you'll have to wait a while longer to see Oregon's most dramatic peaks. In this southernmost section of the state, the volcanoes are older and more eroded.

The volcanoes that hikers see in the Cascades are really part of a global structure, the Pacific Ring of volcanoes, which includes the Andes of South America, Alaska's Aleutians, Japan, and Indonesia. Volcanoes (like faults and earthquakes) are the product of plate tectonics. In this region, the Pacific Plate is expanding and colliding with the Continental Plate. As a result, the Pacific Plate has been subducted, or pushed down, beneath the Continental Plate. In the Klamath Mountains, this resulted in heated granite rising to the surface. In the Cascades, the heat of the earth melted rock miles beneath the surface into liquid magma, which is under enormous pressure. Once in a while, it shoots out of the earth. Hence the ring of fire-breathing mountains.

The Cascades are volcanically active today. At least seven Cascade volcanoes have been active in the last 150 years. Since the end of the Ice Age (about 10,000 years ago), the Cascades have produced, on the average, at least one major outburst per century. In the 20th century, we had two: Lassen, in California, and Mount St. Helens, in Washington. In addition, recent avalanches of rock and mud at Mounts Baker and Rainier (both in Washington) are thought to be the result of geothermal activity. Along Oregon and Washington's PCT, you'll walk past almost constant reminders of volcanic activity: huge lava flows, ash, pumice, obsidian, cinder cones, and the occasional (and welcome) hot spring. If you're the worrying kind, you can take comfort in statistics: Geologist Bates McKee says, "From an actuarial point of view, even active volcanoes are infinitely safer than are highways."

A volcanic eruption is a discharge on the surface of earth of magmatic material in solid, liquid, or gas form. The ejecta (whether solid, liquid, or gas) comes up from the heated depths of the earth via pipes or fissures. When an eruption takes place through a vertical chimney, the chimney is widened by the outward expansion and it slumps inward, producing a crater with flared sides. This is what produces the conical shape of the classic volcano. Lava may also erupt from satellite cones below the summit. A caldera is the gigantic depression within the walls of a summit, created at the volcano's main vent. A crater—typically much smaller than a caldera—occurs at satellite vents.

Mount McLoughlin

Long-distance hikers will appreciate the fact that Mount McLoughlin, elevation 9,493 feet, is named after a 19th-century trail angel. (They might not, however, appreciate the nugget of information that Mount McLoughlin is, as the crow flies, only 50 miles north of Mount Shasta. As the hiker walks it's—get ready for this—almost 300 miles!)

As an administrator for Hudson's Bay Company, Dr. John McLoughlin aided settlers arriving exhausted from the rigors of the Oregon Trail. At a time when both the United States and England claimed parts of the Oregon Territory—and almost came to blows over the location of the Canadian-American border—McLoughlin was famous for aiding all comers. The mountain, originally called Mount Pitt, was renamed in his honor.

Mount McLoughlin is the highest peak between Shasta and the Three Sisters. Like most of the major volcanoes in the Cascades, McLoughlin is a stratovolcano, made up of both lava, which is molten rock, and other matter that is pyroclastic in origin.

From a distance, the peak appears symmetrical, but views from the summit ridge reveal it as being severely eroded, with a large basin cut into its northeastern flank. Mount McLoughlin is older than many of the other major Cascade peaks—some estimates place its age at 100,000 years, and it probably reached maturity about 25,000 years ago, before the height of the most recent glaciation. So it has had plenty of time to become eroded and deeply scarred by glaciation. A small glacier survived on its summit until about 100 years ago.

The trail to the summit of Mount McLoughlin is 6 miles long. The best time of year to attempt the ascent is from late July through August.

To climb McLoughlin from the PCT, take Trail 3716. *Warning:* The last 1.5 miles is a trailless scramble. Be sure to keep an eye on the weather, because it's easy to get disoriented and lose the way back if the summit becomes fogged in. And take plenty of water. The reward: great views south to Mount Shasta and north to Mount Thielsen. On a good day, you can see the Three Sisters.

Crater Lake

Crater Lake—the deepest lake in the United States and the seventh-deepest in the world—is actually the remains of a volcano that blew itself up approximately 6,900 years ago. Geologists refer to the extinct mountain as Mazama (Spanish for *mountain goat*) and estimate that it might once have been as high as 12,000 feet—higher than Mount Hood, Oregon's current high point. All that is left today is a 20.25-square mile, 1,932-foot deep hole in the ground.

The power of Cascadian volcanoes can be appreciated by considering the extent of Mazama's eruption: It spewed 42 cubic miles of matter over some 350,000 square miles. Winds from the southwest carried its ashes over much of Oregon and Washington, as well as parts of Nevada, Idaho, Montana, Wyoming, Utah, British Columbia, Alberta, and even Saskatchewan. At the base of the mountain, ash accumulated in 20-foot deep piles; 70 miles away, a blanket of ash a foot deep covered the ground. One

Trail work is done with hand tools in wilderness areas.

writer postulates that the ash may have risen into the stratosphere, traveling (like the ash from Krakatoa) around the globe and creating colorful sunsets that might have astonished the ancestors of Druids and Gauls in England, half a world away!

Geologists estimate that the force of Mazama's explosion was equivalent to 40 times the force of Mount St. Helens' 1980 eruption. Consider: Although the eruption of Mount St. Helens was one of the biggest volcanic blasts in recorded history, it left most of the mountain standing. In contract, all that is left of Mazama is a huge hole that filled with snow and rain until it became a lake.

There is no outlet. The lake is encircled by the crater walls, which rise many hundreds of feet above the level of the water. Water can escape only through evaporation. In recent years, evaporation and precipitation have so exactly balanced each other that the water level of this nearly 2,000-foot-deep lake rarely fluctuates by more than an inch.

On the western side of the lake, below the Watchman, is Wizard Island, a small cinder cone that has erupted several times since Mazama collapsed. The island's high point is 763 feet above the lake's surface. You can get to the island by a boat operated by the Park Service. An easy climb takes you to the summit, from which you can peer into the 300-foot deep,

Oregon Desert

90-foot-wide crater, which is one of the best-preserved explosion craters in the Cascades.

Indians lived in the area at the time, and almost undoubtedly witnessed the eruption. Certainly the lake was a sacred place to the Native Americans who lived here when the first Europeans arrived. Shamans forbade their people to gaze at the lake. Perhaps that is why Natives did not tell Caucasians about it. The lake was only discovered by European Americans in 1853 when a group of explorers stumbled upon it while looking for the legendary Lost Cabin Mine.

Boat tours are available: a rare opportunity to see a mountain from the inside out.

Oregon Desert

Mazama's explosion is responsible for another phenomenon seen along the route. The so-called Oregon Desert is not technically a desert, but rather a dry stretch that was created when the volcano's explosion covered the surrounding area in ash and pumice. On the PCT, water is in short supply for almost 50 miles.

Look here for pumice, pieces of light-colored volcanic rock. Pumice is easy to identify because of its noticeably light weight. Pumice is ejected as liquid that "freezes" before it hits the ground. As it solidifies, air pockets are trapped inside. Put a piece in water: It's a rock that actually floats!

This pumice and the accompanying ash also covered the streams, which now largely run underground. Hence the long dry stretches of trail. The porous volcanic soil simply lets rainwater percolate through it, leaving little for thirsty hikers and trees. Trees that do grow here, like the scrawny lodgepole pines, are drought-tolerant and shriveled by the lack of water.

Mount Thielsen

Mount Thielsen, elevation 9,178 feet, is the next volcano on our route. It is completely different than its two predecessors, Mount McLoughlin and Crater Lake. A massive tower of eroded rock, Thielsen doesn't have the picture-postcard conical shape we think of when we picture a volcano. Instead, it looks like a skyscraper that's been hit by a wrecking ball. The dramatic souring is the result of the action of 100,000 years of glaciation and erosion on a landscape originally shaped by volcanic forces.

Mount Thielsen is one of Oregon's so-called Matterhorn peaks, named for their sky-piercing profiles. The Matterhorn peaks are easily identified by their gentle bases and very steep summits; all have lost all traces of their original summit craters. Far older than the more intact peaks like Hood and Rainier, the Matterhorn peaks also had the height of their volcanic activity far earlier, and all of them were extinct before the Ice Age ended. As a result, they've had a very long time to succumb to the eroding forces of glaciation, wind, and rain.

Despite their steep vertical profiles, the Matterhorn peaks are, interestingly enough, actually the remnants of shield volcanoes. As described in chapter 10, shield volcanoes (like the volcanoes of Hawaii) usually have a gentle, broad shape—like that of a shield placed on the ground—that is due to the ejection of thin lava that spreads over a wide area. The Matterhorn peaks began life as shield volcanoes. After a time, however, ejected material began to collect, building steep summit cones. The cones were "invaded" by plugs, which were pushed up by pressure within the earth. When these plugs were exposed by erosion, they became the pinnacles of the Matterhorn summits.

The PCT passes several other Matterhorn peaks in Oregon, including Mount Washington and Three Fingered Jack.

As might be expected, Thielsen's spire attracts both storms and climbers, who should take note of its nickname: Lightning Rod of the Cascades.

Evidence of lightning is found in the presence of a peculiar glassy substance called fulgurite, which is created when repeated electrical charges fuse certain kinds of rock crystals together. This glassy green-brown substance coats some of Thielsen's summit rocks like a layer of enamel. There's a safety lesson here: Outdoor experts suggest that if you're caught high on a ridge in a storm, you should lose elevation—even a few feet will help. Dropping down a couple of yards might seem a pathetic, even token, recourse when you're stuck up high, exposed to the fury of a full-fledged electrical storm. But consider this: The lightning-fused fulgurite atop Thielsen is found only on the top 5 or 6 feet of the summit area. Below that, you are (at least, statistically) safer.

HIKING INFORMATION

Seasonal Information and Gear Tips

August and September are the best months for hiking in Oregon. In July there may still be patchy snow, and there will almost definitely be mosquitoes, so bring a tent and plenty of DEET. In a high snow year, snow and mosquitoes can linger well into August. August is the driest month in the Pacific Northwest. September can also be dry and comfortable—but it's not unusual for early fall storms to roll in. For summer hiking, one warm layer plus rain gear should be adequate.

Thru-hikers' Corner

Oregon is a fast, easy hike for most thru-hikers, who usually arrive well after the snowmelt. The trail is well-graded, and big climbs are few and far between. In short, if you're interested in big mileage, this is a good place to do it.

The major challenge is resupplying. The PCT only goes near towns when it enters the state (near Ashland) and when it leaves it (at Cascade Locks). In between, going to town means long hitch-hikes, so most hikers resupply at the backcountry lodges which lie near the trail.

Even if you generally prefer to buy your food as you go, you might want to consider using mail drops for some of Oregon's resupplies, because the stores at the lodges vary from fully stocked to nearly bare. Most of these lodges do not receive rural mail delivery; they must pick up their mail at the nearest post office, which may be many miles away. So some of them require hikers to use UPS or another private delivery service that will actually deliver the package to their door. While the information at the end of this chapter under Resupplies and Trailheads is current as of this writing, please be aware that lodges change owners and policies. Write in advance to confirm that they will hold your package for you.

Best Short Hikes
- The highlight of this section is the 8.8-mile walk along the rim of Crater Lake starting from Crater Lake Lodge (mile 108.3) and ending at the junction with the PCT equestrian route (mile 117.1).
- An especially fine 30-mile, 2- to 3-day hike starts at the PCT's crossing of Oregon Highway 138 near the Cascade Crest (at mile 124.0). The Forest Service parking lot is 0.2 miles west. The trail climbs to the crest with fine views of Mount Thielsen, reaching a high point of 7,435 feet in 14.8 miles. There's an opportunity to scramble to the top of Mount Thielsen (see page 209), with views north to Mount Jefferson and south to Shasta. Figure a 2-hour round trip. Continuing on, the trail follows a high ridge past Tipsoo Peak (the summit of which is an easy 20-minute detour), then continues to Tolo Camp. This hike ends at Forest Road 60 in Windigo Pass.

Resupplies and Trailheads
Ashland (mile 0) is about 12.9 miles north of the trail, on I-5. With great food, microbrew bars, health-food stores, an outfitter, and the renowned Shakespeare Festival (if it's sold out, try to score tickets from people selling outside the theater the evening of the performance), it's got everything you need to rest, recuperate, and rev up

for the 1,000 miles ahead. From the intersection of the trail and I-5, hiker-friendly Callahans Restaurant is 0.9 miles north on Oregon Highway 99. Post office: General Delivery, Ashland, OR 97520

Fish Lake Resort (mile 54.3) is about 1.8 miles west of the PCT crossing of Highway 140. It has a café, limited supplies, cabins, and showers. It will hold packages if you send them UPS. Contact: Fish Lake Lodge, Highway 140 MM #30, Medford, OR 97501

Mazama Village and Campground (mile 103.8) is in Crater Lake National Park. It is 1.3 miles east of the trail on Highway 62 and has a motel, campground, showers, and groceries. However, it's best to send packages to Crater Lake Lodge, 4.5 miles north on the PCT. Contact: Crater Lake Lodge, 400 Rim Village Drive, Crater Lake, OR 97604

Diamond Lake Lodge (mile 132.1) is most directly accessed by the Mount Thielsen Trail #1456, which leads 4 miles down to the resort, where there are cabins, a store, a restaurant, and a post office.

13

Willamette Pass to Santiam Pass

92.9 miles

While much of the Pacific Crest Trail has been formed and shaped by the forces of volcanism and glaciation, nowhere is the work of fire and ice more evident than it is here, where shimmering glaciated summits tower over hundreds of lava-covered acres. This section includes two of Oregon's most memorable and unusual landscapes: the Three Sisters Wilderness and the Belknap and Yapoah lava beds on either side of McKenzie Pass.

The first 20 or so miles of this section are gently wooded, much like the trail to the south. Plenty of small lakes and a few larger ones make camping along this section of trail a pleasure (but in bug season, which follows the snowmelt, usually in mid to late July, bring a tent and plenty of DEET). Once you are north of the wilderness boundary near Irish Lake, the trail develops a more montane character with excellent views of all of the Three Sisters along with countless smaller peaks, cinder cones, and lava flows, which look as though the earth exploded only yesterday. If you're ambitious, you can even take a crack at South Sister, the tallest but easiest of the three peaks to climb.

All in all, this section stands out among the PCT's highlights, not just in Oregon, but along the entire three-state trail.

THE ROUTE

Leaving Willamette Pass on Oregon Highway 58, the trail climbs gently past cliff-framed Rosary Lakes, which offer excellent campsites. (There's

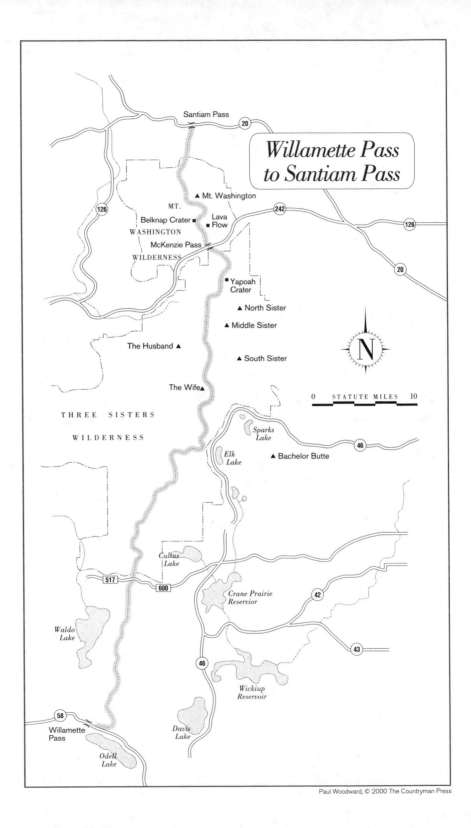

Willamette Pass
to Santiam Pass

Santiam Pass

▲ Mt. Washington

MT.
Belknap Crater ■ ■ Lava
                    Flow
WASHINGTON
McKenzie Pass
WILDERNESS

■ Yapoah
  Crater

▲ North Sister

▲ Middle Sister

The Husband ▲

▲ South Sister

The Wife▲

THREE SISTERS

WILDERNESS

Sparks
Lake

Elk
Lake

▲ Bachelor Butte

N

0   STATUTE MILES   10

Cultus
Lake

Crane Prairie
Reservior

Waldo
Lake

Wickiup
Reservoir

Willamette
Pass

Davis
Lake

Odell
Lake

an especially nice place to camp on the isthmus between Middle and North Rosemary Lakes.) For the next 20 or so miles, progress is uneventful—through forests, past lakes, with only gentle ups and downs. You might notice that some of the trail signs are placed 10 to 12 feet high on the trees: The trails here are popular with cross-country skiers. The sign placement tells you a little about snow depth in the wintertime. *Note:* It's worth watching your water and planning your campsites here; despite the number of lakes on the map, on-trail water can be hard to find until you reach the boundary of the Three Sisters Wilderness, just north of Forest Road 600 near Irish Lake. After that, for the next 30 miles, there are dozens of lakes. Note, however, that camping is prohibited at some of the more popular ones.

As you approach the Three Sisters, you'll have increasingly good views of the peaks ahead and the glaciers above. Underfoot, you'll see continuing evidence of the volcanism that formed this region. North of Sisters Mirror Lake, you'll pass the Wickiup Plain, a young lava flow near South Sister. Volcanic evidence is everywhere: The trail passes around the base of symmetrical Le Conte Crater, then descends onto the jumbled chaos of lava-covered Rock Mesa, winds past South and Middle Sisters, then crosses the Obsidian Trail, where hikers will indeed see shimmering black chunks of obsidian—"nature's glass"—strewn about, yet another clear indication of volcanic activity.

The trail then passes Obsidian Falls and climbs a bit to reach fine open views of North Sister. Continuing north, the trail makes its way through increasingly stark, severe lava flows. Eventually, you realize that you are surrounded by hundreds of acres of lava, only occasionally dotted with the odd, unfortunate, straggly, struggling tree that had the misguided idea that this would be a good place to call home. It is difficult to conceive of how a trail could ever have been built through this jumble of volcanic rock.

As you make your way north of North Sister, you'll be staying on the eastern edge of the lava fields, occasionally venturing into them. You'll contour around the Yapoah Crater, a modest-looking cinder cone that ejected much of the lava you are walking over. There are several springs and lakes between North Sister and McKenzie Pass (just ahead) and you should make sure you have enough water before proceeding. There is no water (and no shade) in the lava fields ahead, and on a hot day, the dark rock reflects a lot of heat.

Just north of the Three Sisters Wilderness boundary, the trail crosses Oregon Highway 242 at McKenzie Pass, where the Dee Wright Observatory offers an especially good vantage point just 0.2 miles west of the trail. You might not at first see the observatory. Built of lava itself, it is almost perfectly camouflaged in its rocky surroundings. The views here span virtually all of Oregon's major peaks. Ahead of you, lined up like sentries, are the Matterhorn peaks of Mount Washington and Three Fingered Jack (which you will walk past in the next few days), and Mounts Jefferson and Hood, still many miles away. Looking back, you can occasionally see as far south as Mounts Thielsen and McLoughlin. Just north of the pass, there's another worthwhile side trip: the short climb to the rim of Little Belknap Crater, another modest cinder cone that is responsible for some of the lava underfoot.

Continuing north, the trail then contours around the slopes of Mount Washington. *Note:* The minuscule Washington ponds are one of the few reliable (if not exactly clean) sources of water in this area, since Coldwater Spring, 2 miles farther, is sometimes dry. You'll have to keep a careful eye out for the turnoff for the ponds, which are out of sight from the trail. A brushy footpath leads the way.

Just north of Mount Washington, the trail crosses the Old Santiam Wagon Road, a route through Santiam Pass used by 19th-century settlers. Today, you'll encounter numerous mountain bikers and dirt bikers, even though *all* of the PCT is off-limits to any kind of wheeled vehicles, motorized or not. The next 3 miles are fast, flat, and relatively uninteresting. The section ends at Santiam Highway (Oregon Highway 20).

WHAT YOU'LL SEE

Three Sisters

This is a landscape of extremes, with scenery that is almost overwhelming. Underfoot, there is evidence of volcanic forces—easily seen in the extensive lava fields, lava ridges, cinder cones, pumice, and obsidian fields, all signs of a geologically young and active region. Looking up to the Sisters' 12 glaciers, you see the slower but no less dramatic results of the sculpting hand of ice.

This cluster of three major peaks (and several secondary ones) is unique in two ways. First, the Three Sisters are the most protected of all of Oregon's volcanoes. The other major volcanic peaks in the state are at least partially on multiple-use or private land. The Sisters lie totally within a designated wilderness area.

Second, the Sisters are the only Cascadian volcanoes found in a cluster. Each of the other major peaks is 40 to 80 miles away from its closest neighbor and accordingly reigns in solitary splendor over the surrounding landscape. In contrast, this dynasty is a family affair.

Early settlers traveling on wagon trains to the Willamette Valley used the Sisters as landmarks, calling them Faith, Hope, and Charity. More recently they've been rather unimaginatively identified by position: North, South, and Middle. Such prosaic names belie a dysfunctional family of volcanic temperament. A look at the names of adjacent peaks reveals that there are three sisters but only one husband; also a little brother and a wife (presumably his, but with this bunch who knows?) and a bachelor. We're talking a hotheaded group that has spent thousands of years throwing fire at each other and generally misbehaving until the entire lava-littered landscape is a record of family violence. This temperamental trio has displayed a greater number and variety of eruptions than any of the other volcanoes of Oregon.

Each of the three major peaks has a distinct character.

South Sister, the first on our route, is the tallest, at 10,358 feet. She is also the best preserved, crowned by the traditional circular summit crater, which in summer holds snowmelt and becomes the highest body of water in Oregon.

At 10,047 feet, Middle Sister is the smallest and least distinctive of the siblings, with neither a summit crater (due to erosion) nor a pronounced and dramatic pinnacle. Her shape is generally symmetrical, with the exception of a large amphitheater excavated by glaciers on her east side.

North Sister, 10,085 feet, is the oldest, eroded to the point where no crater remains, and she has been stripped of a third of her original bulk. North Sister appears to have had a cycle of construction and demolition much like that of Oregon's Matterhorn spires. It is possible that the only reason she doesn't have the same jutting vertical profile is because of her considerably larger size. She is considered the most difficult of the three to climb.

Belknap and Yapoah Lava Flows

Just north of North Sister, Highway 242 at McKenzie Pass cuts through a landscape so stark and severe you might think you have somehow been beamed up to the moon. McKenzie Pass is a gap through a massive lava flow that stretches for miles along the PCT, from just north of North Sister to just south of Three Fingered Jack. In this area, at least 125 separate eruptions have occurred in the post–Ice Age period. Along the PCT, you'll see a collection of cinder cones, each several hundred feet high, and a lava landscape unlike anything to be seen elsewhere on the trail—or, for that matter, anywhere else on any of America's national scenic trails.

You might assume that the dark jagged basalt, which covers an area of some 85 square miles, comes from the big volcanoes that dominate the region. But in fact, the lava can be traced to the much more modest craters and cinder cones. The eruptions that created these lava flows took place between 2,900 and 1,500 years ago. On the north side of McKenzie Pass, the Belknap Crater and the Little Belknap and South Belknap Cinder Cones are responsible. South of the pass, the Yapoah and Collier Cinder Cones did much of the damage. The latter, on the flanks of North Sister, may be the most recent of the cones to erupt in the area, producing a mile-square cinder field and lava flows that spread over more than 12 miles. All of these cones and craters are close to the PCT.

McKenzie Pass

The pass is named for Donald McKenzie, an employee of John Jacob Astor's Pacific Fur Company, who first explored Oregon's McKenzie River in 1811. A route through the pass was first opened in 1862 by Felix Scott, who with a party of 250 men and 90 women chopped their way up and over the pass to get their 106 wagons through. The location of their route was a bit to the south of the present-day road, which was built in 1872 as a toll road, replaced by a gravel road in 1925, and finally paved in the 1930s.

Mount Washington

Mount Washington (7,802 feet) is a Matterhorn-style peak, much like Mount Thielsen to the south. Probably about 2 million years old, Mount Washington was created in three separate stages. First, a wide shield volcano was built of very liquid lava. Second, a summit cone was constructed

Yapoah Lava Flow south of McKenzie Pass

of fragmented ejected material on top of the original shield. And third, a plug made of more viscous basalt was injected into the summit dome as a result of pressure from inside the earth.

The viscous basalt plug eventually caused pressure to build up inside. This pressure was released by vents on the side of the mountain, further weakening the structure of the volcano and making it susceptible to erosion. After the volcano became extinct, glaciers had plenty of time to sculpt the mountain into its current obelisk-like shape. Today, Mount Washington is a classic dissected volcano in which only the most durable matter has survived.

Mount Washington may have a relatively modest elevation, but climbing it requires technical skills and climbing gear. Because of its difficulty, it was not summited until 1923.

🚶 HIKING INFORMATION

Seasonal Information and Gear Tips
Most of this section is generally snow-free by mid-July, although some snow can stick around a little longer at the higher elevations. After unusually severe winters, snow deep enough to block (or at least, slow down) foot travel can linger into mid-August. August is peak hiking season, so expect company at popular campsites, especially in the mountainous heart of the Three Sisters Wilderness. September can be quite pleasant. If you don't mind a little cold at the higher elevations, you might well consider it the best month for hiking here. In October, the possibility of snow and storms increases with every day.

- As soon as the snow begins to melt, bug season commences, so you'll want a tent and DEET, especially in the southern lake-dotted part of the Three Sisters Wilderness.
- A map and compass are necessary early in the season when snow often blocks the PCT. In addition to strip maps of the PCT (found in the guidebooks) it's helpful to have Forest Service or wilderness maps (see the appendix for addresses) to determine bail-out trails and alternate routes.

Thru-hikers' Corner

This section continues to offer thru-hikers the opportunity to travel fast and light. If you're at the head of the stream of northbound thru-hikers, you might arrive here in late July, in which case you might encounter leftover snow at the higher elevations and/or mosquitoes. At such times, a tent instead of a tarp offers more comfort. Southbound thru-hikers are almost guaranteed to arrive here when there is still plenty of snow and mosquitoes. *Note:* In years of unusually high snow accumulations, the trail in the Three Sisters Wilderness can be snow-choked even in August, especially in the area around Obsidian Falls. Map and compass skills are handy, and boots and gaiters will keep feet dry.

Best Short Hikes

- This section offers day hikers and backpackers alike one of the most unusual walks to be found anywhere in North America. On either side of McKenzie Pass (see page 218), the trail goes through a rocky wonderland of lava. Views of snowcapped peaks only add to the drama. A 2.5-mile walk north of the pass will take you to the Belknap Crater and a half-mile scramble off-trail brings you to the crater rim.
- For a longer backpack, you can't go wrong by heading south from McKenzie Pass into the Three Sisters Wilderness (see pages 216–217). A hike of about 50 miles (depending on which trail you choose to use as an exit) will take you past the lava fields and all three of the sisters. To leave the wilderness, several side trails of between 2 and 3 miles lead out to Elk Lake, Devils Lake, or the Cascade Lakes Highway.

Resupplies and Trailheads

Shelter Cove and Elk Lake are the most commonly used.

Shelter Cove Resort (mile 0) is 1.4 miles east of the PCT from Pengia Pass. It has cabins (reservations recommended), campsites, groceries, and a laundry. Packages must be sent UPS. Contact: Shelter Cove Resort, West Odell Lake, Access Highway 58, Crescent Lake, OR 97425.

Elk Lake Resort (mile 44.5) is 1.1 miles from the PCT via the Island Meadow Trail, which goes to Highway 46. The entrance to the lodge is across the highway. Ship yourself everything (UPS only): The store has virtually empty shelves. Cabins and meals are available. Contact: Elk Lake Resort, Century Drive, Bend, OR 97709.

Sisters (mile 75.5), a full-service tourist town, is 15 miles east on Highway 242. Post office: General Delivery, Sisters, OR 97759

14

Santiam Pass to Cascade Locks

148.7 miles

On this section of trail, hikers walk on the shoulders of Oregon's two high-est peaks, then descend to the lowest point on the entire Pacific Crest Trail. Mounts Jefferson and Hood are the highlights, the first featuring beautiful subalpine parks covered with wildflowers, the second boasting excellent views of both volcanic ash and glaciers. Snow patches that linger well into the summer present an occasional obstacle on Mount Jefferson, as do fierce glacier-fed streams flowing from both mountains. The PCT passes right by the doors of historic Timberline Lodge on Mount Hood before winding its way around the mountain, past pretty (and popular) Ramona Falls, and then down into the Columbia River Gorge. For the final miles, the Eagle Creek Trail, which runs through a gorge filled with water-falls and swimming holes, is a popular alternative to the PCT.

THE ROUTE

Leaving Santiam Pass, the PCT climbs until it is just beneath the steep wall that holds the pinnacles of Three Fingered Jack. As the trail rounds the mountain, it offers the kind of views that will have you stopping every two minutes to take yet another picture.

Descending, the route returns to forest, where there are some pleasant lakeside campsites. For the next several miles, the trail stays relatively high, often on the Cascade Divide, with good views. Entering the Mount Jefferson Wilderness, it remains high on the watershed divide.

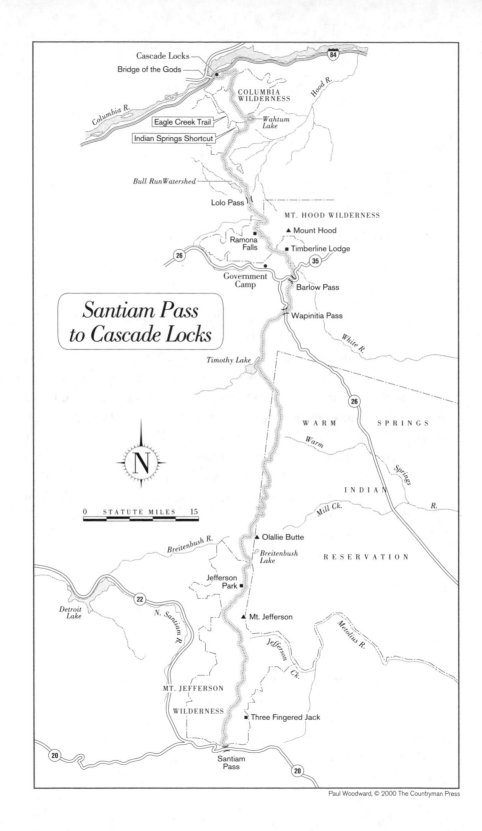

Cascade Locks
Bridge of the Gods

84

COLUMBIA
WILDERNESS

Hood R.

Columbia R.

Eagle Creek Trail

Wahtum
Lake

Indian Springs Shortcut

Bull RunWatershed

Lolo Pass

MT. HOOD WILDERNESS

▲ Mount Hood

Ramona
Falls

■ Timberline Lodge

26

35

Government
Camp

Barlow Pass

Wapinitia Pass

White R.

Timothy Lake

26

W A R M   S P R I N G S

Warm

N

I N D I A N

Springs

R.

0   STATUTE MILES   15

Mill Ck.

R E S E R V A T I O N

Breitenbush R.

▲ Olallie Butte

Breitenbush
Lake

Jefferson
Park ■

22

▲ Mt. Jefferson

Detroit
Lake

N. Santiam R.

Jefferson

Ck.

Metolius R.

MT. JEFFERSON

WILDERNESS

■ Three Fingered Jack

20

Santiam
Pass

20

Santiam Pass
to Cascade Locks

Soon, views of Mount Jefferson dominate the northern skyline. The power of the glaciers that continue to erode Mount Jefferson can clearly be seen as you cross Milk Creek, named after the amount of glacial sediment, or rock flour, it carries off the mountain. The trail crosses fast-flowing Russell Creek 4.4 miles later. This creek is unbridged, for good reason— a bridge would never survive the spring floods in this debris-studded canyon. In early season, hikers should try to cross Russell Creek as early in the day as possible, because low nighttime temperatures slow the melting of the glaciers and reduce the volume of water.

The trail then winds through the lovely upland meadows of unfortunately overused Jefferson Park. Although the campsites are picturesque, two things might chase you away: too much company of the two-footed kind—and too much company of the six-footed kind. The latter are ubiquitous right after the snowmelt, sometime in mid to late July.

North of Jefferson Park, late-lying snowfields can complicate travel because snow often lingers well into August. Some patches survive the entire summer.

The trail then enters the Mount Hood National Forest, where it makes its way through lake-dotted country to Olallie Lake, at the base of the symmetrical cone of Olallie Butte. North of the butte, the land becomes abruptly dry and the trail enters the backcountry of the Warm Springs Indian Reservation. For the next 20 miles, the trail is fairly flat, forested, and easy. It leaves the reservation near Clackamas Lake. There's a temporary surplus of water as the trail circles around Timothy Lake. But then it climbs a ridge and becomes dry again.

Mount Hood is only occasionally visible from the PCT. The first unrestricted close-up views are just north of the PCT's crossing of U.S. Highway 26 at Wapinitia Pass, a few miles past Timothy Lake. Then the views almost entirely disappear, blocked by thick forest. A few miles farther, the trail crosses Oregon Highway 35 at Barlow Pass, an important gateway for 19th-century immigrants. Now the trail climbs steadily until it is above treeline on the shoulder of Mount Hood.

And suddenly, you rise above the forest, and the views to the summit are breathtaking. Look closely at the tiny moving dots high up on the mountain slopes. You aren't seeing things: Those really are skiers, who take to the slopes almost year-round.

From Mount Hood, the trail circumambulates the west side of Mount Hood. (*Note:* There is an around-the-mountain trail that makes a loop encircling the whole peak.) It crosses a series of glacier-fed streams. Some of these can be tricky to negotiate during the snowmelt. Views up to Mount Hood's summit more than compensate for any difficulties.

The trail passes a turnoff for Paradise Park shelter. The dramatic views of scoured canyons and shimmering glaciers continue. Shortly after crossing the Sandy River (which has been recently bridged) the trail passes lovely Ramona Falls, a popular destination for day hikers who access it using a series of Forest Service back roads and trails. There's no camping within 500 feet of the falls, but it's a great place for a lunch stop.

Continuing on, the trail crosses Lolo Pass and climbs to a ridgeline. Seven and a half miles north of the pass, hikers can take a 0.5-mile side trail to the summit of Buck Peak, where unrestricted views extend south to Mounts Hood and Jefferson and north to Mounts Adams, St. Helens, and Rainier—the first time PCT hikers can see all five of these peaks at once.

After Buck Peak, the trail continues on a ridge to the Indian Springs campsite. A few miles later, it reaches Wahtum Lake, from which it begins a long gentle descent to the Columbia River Gorge.

Alternate Route

Most hikers do not take the Pacific Crest Trail into Cascade Locks, the last town in Oregon. Instead, they detour to the Eagle Creek Trail. The Eagle Creek Trail was not chosen to be part of the PCT's official route because it is impassable for horses. But the majority of thru-hikers reach the sensible conclusion that they are not horses, and therefore there is no reason to miss one of Oregon's most deservedly popular trails.

The Eagle Creek Trail can be accessed from one of two points. The shortest way (a 2-mile descent) is to take Indian Springs Trail 445 from the Indian Springs Campground. Steep and muddy, on a wet day this trail is almost slick enough to just sit and slide. A gentler but longer option is to continue on the PCT until the junction with the Eagle Creek Trail at Wahtum Lake. This choice is more pleasant and definitely easier—but it's also 3 miles longer than the Indian Springs shortcut.

Eagle Creek is a deep-cut gorge that feeds into the Columbia River. The Eagle Creek Trail parallels it, passing numerous campsites dotted along

Along the Eagle Creek Trail

the river edge. It's a very popular trail with day hikers and weekenders, but the campsites farther upstream are out-of-reach for most casual weekenders, so they tend to be less used, cleaner, and more attractive. Continuing downstream, the trail passes pools and cascades, and even goes behind a waterfall on trail that was blasted into the rock. Once at the Eagle Creek trailhead, hikers must follow Gorge Trail 400 for 2.6 miles to reconnect with the PCT at Moody Avenue on the outskirts of Cascade Locks. If you're going to the campground at Cascade Locks City Park, you should leave the Gorge Trail after 0.7 miles and take the bike path instead—it's quicker and more direct.

WHAT YOU'LL SEE

Three Fingered Jack

Three Fingered Jack is the last of Oregon's Matterhorn peaks. Like the others, it too was once a shield volcano that has been severely eroded by glaciers. Its central plug has survived, surrounded by spires—or fingers. The mountain has a different profile when viewed from different directions; all of the fingers are visible only from the southeast.

If you're a rock climber, you might enjoy spending a day here. Three Fingered Jack is very steep—even the snowfields at its base are at 50-degree angles—and it attracts hordes of climbers. The easiest route is up the South Ridge from Square Lake, which involves an ascent of 5 to 7 hours to the 7,841-foot summit.

Mount Jefferson

Lewis and Clark were the first European Americans to see Mount Jefferson when they stood near the mouth of the Willamette River on March 30, 1806. They promptly named the mountain for their benefactor. In later years there would be an attempt to name or rename the major peaks of the Cascadian chain after other American presidents, but only Mount Washington (a paltry 7,802 feet, which the PCT passed in chapter 13) and Mount Adams (in Washington, north of the Columbia River Gorge) were so named.

At 10,495 feet, Mount Jefferson starts to dominate the landscape about 5 miles north of Three Fingered Jack. Sitting on a ridge that averages

Mount Jefferson

5,500 to 6,500 feet above sea level, it rises more than a mile above the surrounding landscape. Oregon's second-highest peak is also one of its most photogenic, with five glaciers, including one—the Whitewater Glacier on its eastern side—that actually dips below tree line. Geologists estimate that Mount Jefferson's original elevation might have been as high as 12,000 feet, but that it has been cut down by glaciation, and its summit has been sharpened to a point. Like most of the other major Cascadian peaks, Mount Jefferson is a stratovolcano. It may be extinct.

The summit of Mount Jefferson is surrounded by wilderness on one side and the Warm Springs Indian Reservation on the other, so it is not readily accessible to climbers. The best route to the summit is via the Whitewater Glacier from the lakes in Jefferson Park. The climb is considered the most difficult of Oregon's volcanoes; the round trip takes about 8 to 10 hours.

Jefferson Park

Clinton Clarke described Jefferson Park as "unexcelled in the Pacific Northwest as a natural alpine garden sprinkled with lakes and streams, above which rises graceful, glacier-hung Mount Jefferson. The alpine region is a fascinating land of picturesque and friendly beauty. A paradise for camper and nature lover."

Jefferson Park is the first of the many alpine parks —natural alpine gardens—that are found along the PCT from here to Canada. Alpine gardens are ecotones between subalpine forest and alpine meadow. Here in Oregon, they occupy elevations ranging from 5,500 to 6,000 feet. The higher the elevation, the fewer the trees. These parks are in the Hudsonian zone, which thru-hikers first encountered 1,839 trail-miles south, when the trail briefly topped 9,000 feet in the San Jacinto Mountains. If you're a thru-hiker—or if you've previously hiked in southern California's mountains—you'll notice some significant differences in the character of the two Hudsonian zones. In southern California, the Hudsonian zone occupied the very pinnacles of only the highest mountains on steep slopes exposed to high winds. Here, the Hudsonian zone is found far lower on the mountain; the rock, ice, and glaciers of Mount Jefferson tower almost a vertical mile above. Instead of windswept ridges, the alpine parks occupy relatively flat meadows on which water from a deep, late-lying snowpack promotes the growth of grasses and flowers. In the weeks just after snowmelt, Mount Jefferson's alpine garden is a riot of color, made even more beautiful by the many lakes and ponds that reflect the snowy profile of the peak above.

Warm Springs Indian Reservation

After leaving the Mount Jefferson Wilderness and passing the Olallie Lake Ranger Station, the trail enters the Warm Springs Indian Reservation for 22 miles between Jude Lake and Clackamas Lake. This section was the subject of a long-standing land ownership debate between the Warm Springs Indian Confederation and the Forest Service. The disagreement dates back to two conflicting 19th-century surveys. The disputed area, called the McQuinn Strip after one of the surveyors, was also the corridor for the Pacific Crest Trail. In 1972 the matter was settled by Congress, which agreed with the Indians and transferred the strip from the Forest Service to the Confederated Tribes of Warm Springs. Special wording in the federal legislation provides for use of the strip by the Pacific Crest National Scenic Trail.

Barlow Pass and Road

As beneficiaries of cut trails and engineered Forest Service roads, hikers do not usually perceive Oregon's terrain to be unduly difficult—quite the contrary. But a century and a half ago, pioneers crossing the Cascades to the Willamette Valley would have had quite a different tale to tell. In the 1840s, crossing the Cascades meant attempting to following the Columbia River—a difficult task because of the many cataracts. Or it meant hoisting wagons up and down steep slopes by ropes and cables. Even today, scars from the cables and bits and pieces of old cable can still be found on the trees south of Mount Hood. A route over the Cascades was desperately needed.

Samuel K. Barlow was a wagonmaster looking for ways to get wagon trains to the Willamette Valley. In 1845, a partner of Barlow's named Joel Palmer climbed the upper slopes of Mount Hood and spotted the pass. In 1846, a road through the pass was opened.

Mount Hood

At 11,235 feet, Mount Hood is the highest peak in Oregon. Because it is located on one of the lowest points on the Cascade Crest, it looks even taller, and dominates the Portland region much as Mount Rainier to the north dominates Puget Sound. Planes flying into Portland from the east pass right by the north side of Mount Hood; try to get a seat on the left to see one of the best airborne views to be had from any plane going anywhere. Earlier travelers to the Portland area also appreciated their view of the mountain, which told them that their long and arduous journey was almost over.

Unlike Mount Jefferson, 50 miles to the south, nobody thinks Mount Hood is extinct. Mount Hood was active in the 19th century, and in 1973 shot a plume of vapor 1,500 feet into the air. The mountain frequently discharges vapors and smoke, sulfur odors, fumaroles, gas vents, and steam jets, and on its flanks a literally boiling-hot spring furiously bubbles. It is not unusual for steam and sulfurous fumes to escape from Crater Rock and form ominous-looking clouds above the summit.

Because the PCT's route just south of Mount Hood is forested, you don't get a good look at the mountain until you are very close to it. John Muir was (not uncharacteristically) moved by his first sighting. In *Steep Trails* he wrote,

> *There stood Mount Hood in all the Glory of the Alpenglow, looming immensely high, beaming with intelligence, and so impressive that one was overawed as if suddenly brought before some superior being newly arrived from the sky. The whole mountain appeared as one glorious manifestation of divine power, enthusiastic and benevolent, glowing like a countenance with ineffable repose and beauty, before which we could only gaze in devout and lowly admiration.*

Mount Hood's construction is unusual for a major volcanic peak because it is made mostly of pyroclastic material with very little solidified lava (unlike other major stratovolcanoes, which have more lava and infrequent layers of pyroclastic matter). The PCT crosses one of Mount Hood's dominant features: a huge debris fan on the southwest slope, which was produced some 1,700 to 2,000 years ago by the eruption of a single plug dome. The explosion melted ice fields and produced mudflows, which created the debris fan. The prominent crater rock above the fan is what is left of the plug dome, and the pools of boiling water around the rock are evidence of the mountain's ongoing geothermal activity. Other volcanic features include a 500-foot-thick, 8-mile-long lava flow, and piles of ash that PCT hikers must struggle to walk through. The mountain boasts 11 glaciers, which are responsible for eroding the peak from its original height of around 12,000 feet.

Indian Myths

Not having taken Geology 101, the Indians who lived in the area had other explanations for the behavior of Mount Hood, which they called Wy'east.

Wy'east was once so tall that when the sun shone on its south side it produced a shadow that was "a day's journey long." Evil spirits lived inside the mountain, and they routinely threw fire down on Indian homes. One day a brave decided to challenge the spirits and stop their persecution of his people. So he climbed up and threw rocks into the holes where the spirits lived. The spirits threw back hot rocks that rained on the village below and destroyed it. In grief the brave sank into the earth and was buried by lava. You can see his profile today, at the Chief's Face rock formation on the north side of the mountain.

Recreation on Hood

After Japan's Fujiyama, Mount Hood is the most often climbed snow-capped mountain in the world, and is regarded as an easy climb. As on so many other accessible peaks, you may hear the apocryphal story of a woman tottering to the summit in high-heeled shoes. The high-heeled lady may be merely a myth, but in 1867, the first woman to stand atop Mount Hood did reach the summit wearing a skirt. And in 1894, 193 people (including 38 women) climbed Mount Hood and founded the Mazamas, the first mountaineering club in the Pacific Northwest. *Warning:* Despite its popularity (and notwithstanding the business about skirts and high heels), Mount Hood is a serious climb. Don't attempt it without a guide unless you have mountaineering experience. Crampons, ice axes, rope, and an avalanche beacon are required, along with serious cold-weather gear. You must have a climbing permit. Most climbers start at midnight in order to climb on firm snow and reach the summit before sunrise—warm daytime temperatures create serious avalanche hazards. Prime climbing season is May through mid-July. The southern slopes are especially prone to rock-fall after the snow starts to melt in the beginning of July.

If skiing is your passion, you can also take a day off at Timberline Lodge. The ski area is open an average of 345 days a year. Lifts operate throughout the summer, whenever there is snow.

Timberline Lodge

Perched on Mount Hood near timberline at an elevation of 6,000 feet, Timberline Lodge is one of the finest example of so-called parkitechture, a rustic building design that makes use of natural materials and Indian and Western decorative themes. A Works Progress Administration (WPA) project, the structure was built during the heart of the Great Depression by unemployed craftspeople, who were given a chance not only to work, but to create something beautiful with their skills. The lodge was built entirely by hand of timber and stone, sometimes under difficult conditions. The site was surveyed in spring of 1936 when 14 feet of snow remained on the ground. Workers lived in tent cities, were trucked up the mountain, and sometimes had to warm their hands on portable stoves in order to keep going. The lodge was named a National Historic Landmark in 1978. Carefully restored and maintained, it has become a center for craftsmanship in the Pacific Northwest.

Bull Run Watershed

North of Lolo Pass, more land-use litigation briefly impacted the Pacific Crest Trail. The PCT runs along the boundary of the Bull Run management area, which is the watershed for the Portland region. As in the case of the land on the Warm Springs Indian Reservation, the initial dispute had nothing to do with the PCT.

In 1973 an environmental coalition sued the Mount Hood National Forest to prevent logging in the Bull Run preserve. The law they relied on was the 1904 Bull Run Trespass Act. In 1976 a federal judge agreed with the environmentalists—but in a narrow reading of the law, he closed all the trails in the area, saying that the law precluded recreational use as well. In 1977 Congress passed the Bull Run Watershed Management Act, which changed the area boundaries so that the trail is now outside the official watershed. You'll see the property boundary signs as you hike along, warning you to stay out.

HIKING INFORMATION

Seasonal Information and Gear Tips

Like the rest of Oregon, the best hiking season is August and September; August is more crowded. Parts of this section can be impassable well into July, especially in Jefferson Park, where snowfields typically don't melt until late summer. The ford of Russell Creek can also be dangerous in early season. In most years, the hiking season extends into October, although the weather is less predictable and both snow and freezing temperatures are possible at the higher elevations.

- Early-season hikers should take an ice ax, compass, and topo maps.

- July hikers need a tent and plenty of mosquito repellent.
- All hikers need rain gear.

Thru-hikers' Corner

Most northbound thru-hikers will come through this section of Oregon in peak season, usually sometime in August. There are no especial considerations: The hiking is easy and fast, the views superb. Enjoy it!

Southbounders may arrive in mid to late July, depending on their starting date. If you arrive early, or if the snowpack is especially high, you should carry an ice ax through the Mount Jefferson Wilderness. But what lies ahead is not as difficult as what lies behind: If you've had a relatively easy run through Washington, you can probably send home your ice ax.

Best Short Hikes

- From Santiam Pass on Highway 20, head north to Three Fingered Jack. This 14-mile (round trip) day hike takes you to fabulous views just below the jutting pinnacles. Unless you're a technical climber, though, you'll have to be content with admiring the summit from afar. The climb is for rock climbers only.
- Hike into Mount Jefferson Wilderness and Jefferson Park. The most direct entry is to park on Skyline Road 42 and hike south on the PCT; 7.6 miles (and a 1,500-foot elevation gain) takes you into the heart of Jefferson Park, where there are many side trails to lakes.
- From Timberline Lodge to Paradise Park is 4.5 miles (one way). There is an old, poorly maintained shelter at Paradise Park. This makes for a good out-and-back day hike, but if you've got a little extra time, you might want to bring your backpacking gear. Leave off your load at the shelter and take some time to explore a little farther before returning to camp for the night. The views in and out of Mount Hood's many canyons are spectacular.
- If you are more ambitious, a full loop of Mount Hood (16.2

miles on the PCT plus 22.7 miles on Timberline Trail 600) typically takes 3 to 4 days.

• Santiam Pass Loop, approximately 50 miles long, takes advantage of the old Oregon Skyline Trail. Start at Santiam Pass. After hiking 2.4 miles north, take Trail 3491 (Santiam Lakes Trail) 4 miles to Santiam Lake. Go 0.6 miles farther, then take Trail 3494 north for 2.5 miles. At Jorn Lake, take Trail 3492 east for 3.4 miles. Then take Trail 3437 for 2 miles to Marion Lake. Next up is Trail 3493 for 5.3 miles. After teeny Papoose Lake, the trail reaches a juntion. Going south shortens the hike by about 10 miles—you'll hit the PCT in 2 miles, from which it is about 20 miles back to Santiam Pass. If you continue north, past Pamela Lake, you'll also rejoin the PCT, but your hike will be 50 miles long instead of 40. This old Skyline Trail segment passes many lakes and campsites. *Note:* If there is heavy snow, this route offers a lower and less snowy alternate for early-season hikers (or for hikers struggling through the white stuff in midsummer after an especially snowy winter).

Resupplies and Trailheads

Timberline Lodge is the most commonly used.

Olallie Lake Resort (mile 46.2) is an unreliable resupply. Rangers are doing their best to help hikers, but the fact is that many packages sent here never get to the hikers—even those who use guaranteed mail delivery services. Here's the deal: You mail your package to the address listed below, and the rangers bring it to the resort, which holds it for hikers. Send your package several weeks in advance, because the rangers sometimes don't come around for a while. Also understand that after a severe winter, the roads may not be open—even in late July or early August. If your package doesn't get there, the resort store does sell enough food to get you to Timberline Lodge. They also offer cabins, showers, and tent sites. Send packages to: Olallie Lake Resort, c/o Clackamas Ranger District, 595 NW Industrial Way, Estacada, OR 97023.

Timberline Lodge (mile 100.4) on the shoulder of Mount Hood is an attractive rest stop, and it's right on the trail. Facilities include laundry (for lodge guests only) and a fine restaurant. There's also cheaper grub in the main ski building where you'll find the Wy'east Store, which holds hiker boxes. Don't expect to be able to buy provisions here: The store caters to the tourist crowd. You can't eat a T-shirt, so mail yourself everything you'll need to get to Cascade Locks. The lodge has several bunk rooms available for groups of different sizes. To send a resupply box, contact: Wy'east Store, Timberline Lodge, OR 97028.

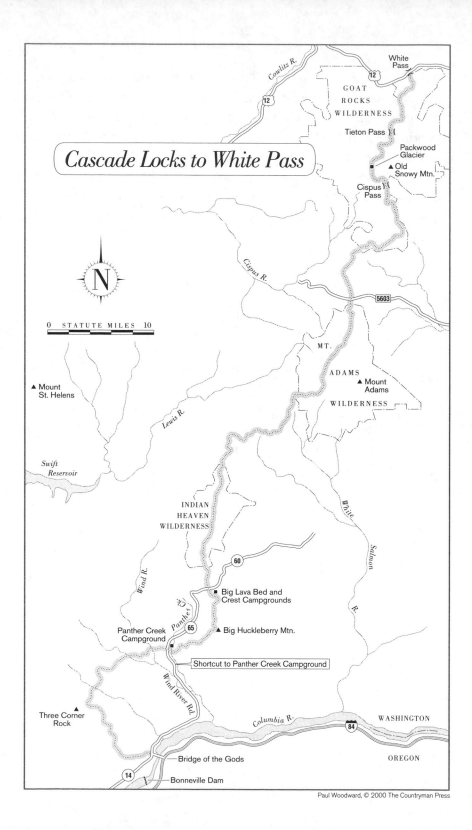

Cascade Locks to White Pass

15

Cascade Locks to White Pass

147.7 miles

The PCT's route in Washington follows much of the original route of the Cascade Crest Trail, built by the Forest Service in the period 1935–39. The 531-mile Cascade Crest Trail (today's Washington PCT is 558 miles) was built to connect with the Oregon Skyline Trail. Since most of the original Oregon Sky-line Trail is now abandoned, those parts of the Cascade Crest Trail that are still in use are the oldest miles on the PCT. Occasionally you'll see a weather-beaten sign that tells you you're on the Cascade Crest.

Formed by volcanic activity, glaciation, and plate tectonics, this section contains a great deal of variety. As in Oregon, southern Washington's PCT follows the line of great stratovolcanoes—Mount Adams, Mount St. Helens, and Mount Rainier—that, each in turn, rise a vertical mile or more above the surrounding mountains.

In the far south, the trail follows a series of ridges separated by steep, deep valleys. Between the ridges, the trail passes through lake-dotted woodlands. The views become more and more dramatic as the trail approaches Mount Adams, where you'll see extensive regions of lava flows, volcanic ash, pumice fields, and enormous mudflows. The section ends with a glorious traverse of the rock-and-ice landscape of the Goat Rocks Wilderness, one of the PCT's finest high-country rambles.

THE ROUTE

This section begins at the town of Cascade Locks on the Oregon side of the Columbia River. The trail crosses the river on the Bridge of the Gods, then, on the Washington side, reaches the lowest point (140 feet) on the entire PCT.

The first 35 miles of the section are often criticized, mostly because they involve an indirect route that gains then loses some 5,000 feet of elevation. For thru-hikers in a hurry, there's a direct option—a road walk up Washington Highway 14 and the Wind River Road—that is only 14.7 miles long with only a few hundred feet of elevation gain.

The official PCT route is a little on the bland side, although it does offer some good views of Mounts Hood, Adams, St. Helens, and even Rainier. Its meandering path from the Columbia River to Panther Creek Campground was largely dictated by private land considerations, so it doesn't especially make good foot-sense. Because water can be in scarce supply, you should carry extra. Similarly, there aren't many good campsites, so you may need to use a little ingenuity when deciding where to make your home for the night. Some short-term hikers with limited time in Washington might want to maximize the scenic quality of their hike by skipping these first 35 miles and starting instead at Panther Creek Campground.

From Panther Creek Campground, the trail follows a series of ridges. In good weather, be sure to take the 0.2-mile side trip up Big Huckleberry Mountain. The trail is usually overgrown with huckleberry bushes, but the views from the summit of all the major volcanoes is unparalleled. *Warning:* Until recently, the 15 miles between Panther Creek and Crest Campgrounds had few reliable water sources (and Crest Campground itself has no water source). But several new side trails to springs have recently been built, along with a water catchment just before Crest Campground. The guidebook does not include information about some of these sources of water, so check with the PCTA for up-to-date seasonal information.

Continuing north, the trail winds through the lake-dotted Indian Heaven Wilderness, then goes through the Sawtooth Huckleberry Fields where in August and September you're likely to be delayed by the tempting purple berries. The trail then undulates a bit before climbing for real into the Mount Adams Wilderness for a perambulation around the western flank of Mount Adams. The trail stays at about the 6,000-foot level, below the summer snow-line on the mountain's shoulder but high enough to offer excellent views in good weather. This area is especially popular with horse riders. Expect crowds on weekends, especially at popular campsites like Killen Creek, from which there is an excellent view of Mount Adams. *Warning:* Some of the stream crossings of glacier-fed creeks that drain Mount Adams can be tricky in early season.

While there's no shortage of water on this stretch, plan a rest stop at Lava Spring, about 5 miles north of Killen Creek on the north side of Mount Adams. Some hikers claim that this trailside spring has the best-tasting water on the entire PCT. It's worth a stop, even if your water bottles are full.

Between the Mount Adams Wilderness and the Goat Rocks Wilderness the trail stays below the tree line, passing a series of stagnant ponds that, even in August, provide breeding grounds for an unimaginable number of mosquitoes. If you're here in bug season, be prepared for plenty of buzzing, biting company, which you finally escape by climbing into the high country of the Goat Rocks Wilderness, the only true stretch of trail in southern Washington that is above tree line. Because of unpredictable weather, high winds, and long exposed stretches of trail, hikers need to use caution here. Be sure you have extra layers of clothes, and keep an eye on the weather.

Note: Both the guidebook and the data book make reference to the Dana May Yelverton Shelter, which was built after a hiker by that name died of exposure in the Goat Rocks. The shelter is gone. All that is left is a pile of rocks that might provide a slight windbreak in an emergency, if that. There are, however, excellent high-country campsites in the area if the weather is good.

North of the shelter site, the trail splits, and you have a choice of going across the upper slopes of the Packwood Glacier or taking an even higher route that leads up over the shoulder of Old Snowy Mountain. The glacier slopes are not steep, but they can be slick, especially after freezing rain. If you don't have an ice ax and you don't like the feel of the snow underfoot, taking the high route is an option, especially in good weather. The trail is boulder strewn, with a jumble of cairns pointing the way—and sometimes, confusingly, they point several ways, but they all lead to the same place. Once you reach the high shoulder of Old Snowy, you reconnect with the

PCT by simply continuing along the ridge over Packwood Glacier, then climbing back down on slippery scree to rejoin the PCT. On a blue-sky day, take the 300-foot detour from the trail's high point on the shoulder of Old Snowy to its 7,930-foot summit. The views are worth the effort, not to mention that, unless you go in for some serious peak-bagging, this will probably be your highest point in Washington. Be sure to sign the summit register.

Whichever way you go, the trails merge just south of a formation called Egg Butte, on a ridge that William O. Douglas described in his book *Man and Wilderness:* "This trail is only a few feet wide, the drop-off on each side is so great that some people get vertigo. It is indeed a bit like walking the cornice of the Empire State Building." Keep an eye out for mountain goats here. This is exactly the kind of precipitous terrain they consider ideal for a casual stroll.

Warning: From the Yelverton Shelter site, there is no water and no opportunity to camp for about 6 miles. The first obvious campsite, in a basin just north of the junction with Coyote Trail 79, is very exposed. In bad weather, you'll want to try to plan your day so that you have enough time to descend another few miles to tree cover and water. Many hikers familiar with this section are convinced that the mileage cited in the guidebook and data book for the distance between Yelverton Shelter and White Pass is too short: These 18 miles seem more like 20. So plan conservatively.

The trail climbs once more to traverse two wide, exposed bowls, where there's another good chance of seeing mountain goats. There are a couple of campsites up here, but you'll need to carry water. Leaving the Goat Rocks Wilderness, you'll pass some side trails leading to ski slopes. From here, it's all downhill. The trail makes an easy switchbacking descent to White Pass (where long-distance hikers resupply). Going straight down the ski slopes is more direct—and a sensible choice in mosquito season, as there are fewer mosquitoes in the ski-slope clear-cuts than in the forest.

WHAT YOU'LL SEE

Washington Weather

They say you can predict the weather by Mount Rainier. When you can see the mountain, it is going to rain. When you cannot see it, it is raining.

Washington weather is infamous for good reason. Heavy precipitation is one of the dominant characteristics of the Cascade Crest in Washington. It's one reason why the old-growth forests are so rich. Running parallel to the Pacific Ocean on a north-south axis, the Cascades act very much like the mountains of southern California: They wring rain and snow out of the moisture-laden air as it moves east. As the air rises, it turns to rain or snow. The difference here is the *amount* of rain and snow. The Pacific air in the Northwest contains much more moisture than the air in southern California, and the mountains are much higher. In some years, more than 700 inches of snow can fall on Mount Rainier!

Fortunately for hikers, the dry season falls during the summer (usually August and early September). However, if you're caught in four or more days of needle-sharp rain, you might wonder about the definition of dry season. Nonetheless, Washington's PCT offers some of the best hiking to be found anywhere. Bring rain gear—and a smile.

Columbia River

The Columbia River is the only major drainage that cuts through the entire 700-mile-long Cascade Range. The river is actually older than the mountains. As the mountains were uplifted as a result of tectonic activity, the river was able to hold its own because its rate of erosion was greater than the mountain range's rate of growth.

As the only natural waterway through the Cascade Mountains, the Columbia has always been an important transportation artery. It was first seen by Europeans when British explorer Robert Gray sailed by its mouth in 1792. In 1805, Lewis and Clark used it to make their way to the Pacific. They named the nearby mountains the Mountains by the Cascades because of the many cascades they passed. Later settlers—who also used the Columbia to reach the Pacific Coast—shortened the name, and the entire mountain range became simply (and appropriately) the Cascades.

Bridge of the Gods

Just after crossing into Washington on the Bridge of the Gods, the PCT reaches the lowest point on its entire three-state journey, 140 feet above sea level.

There are a number of Indian myths associated with this area, most of

Bridge of the Gods

which concern the behavior and relationships of the giant volcanoes. The stories differ in the details, but follow the same common plot, usually involving some combination of combative suitors, flirtatious maidens, and conflicts with cataclysmic results.

According to one version of the legend, the Bridge of the Gods was a stone bridge built by the great spirit Manitou. Manitou made the wise old woman Loo-wit the guardian of the bridge, and sent his sons Wy'east (Mount Hood) and Klickitat (Mount Adams) to help her. But the two sons soon began fighting over the attention of lovely Squaw Mountain, who also lived in the neighborhood. Squaw loved Wy'east, but couldn't resist flirting with Klickitat. The two suitors responded predictably: They hurled stones at each other across the river until they managed to destroy the bridge. Klickitat, the bigger mountain, won the battle and the lovely Squaw. But his affections went unrequited, and Squaw Mountain fell asleep forever. The old woman was rewarded for her efforts by Manitou and was turned into Mount St. Helens, the most beautiful mountain in the world.

The legend of the Bridge of the Gods has its origins in landslides along the Columbia River. Scientists say that 29,000 years ago there was indeed a land bridge across the Columbia. The bridge was created when a mountain on the Oregon side collapsed and blocked the river, damming it and creating an inland sea as far east as Idaho. Eventually, soft matter beneath the dam eroded, allowing water to pass underneath the rocks and ultimately wash away the dam.

You'll see evidence of landslides in the first 10 miles of Washington's PCT, which climbs 2,000 feet onto a ridge of Table Mountain. The footway is uncharacteristically steep and rubbly because of the debris from periodic earth slides that occur along the Columbia. These landslides are simply the result of gravity. The lower layer of the earth is clay, which is prone to collapse and slide. On top of this clay is more durable matter. When the clay finally succumbs to gravity and crumbles under the weight resting on it, it slides down into the Columbia River Gorge.

The actual bridge hikers walk across was built in 1926 and raised in 1933. The stones that figure in the Indian legend are underwater just upstream.

Big Lava Bed

About a mile before reaching Crest Campground on Forest Road 60, the PCT goes through the so-called Big Lava Bed, a 20-square-mile lava flow that erupted 8,200 years ago. The rocks here are very dark, made of basalt (a dark and fine-grained igneous rock that originated as molten magma in the earth's mantle, was spewed out of a vent, and then solidified). You will see dramatic jumbles of fractured lava, broken into blocks, chunks, and weird-shaped formations. The source of all this is a vent near Goose Lake, several miles east of the PCT. Except for a short stretch of PCT, no trails (let alone roads) cross the lava bed. The presence of this porous volcanic rock explains the paucity of water in this section. A few hardy pine trees are slowly attempting to colonize the area.

Indian Heaven Wilderness

The Indian Heaven Wilderness begins on the north side of Forest Road 60 just past Crest Campground. This area, geologically related to the Big Lava Bed as part of the Indian Heaven Rift, shows evidence of extensive volcanic activity that lasted for hundreds of thousands of years. It contains 45 volcanic vents similar to the vent that produced the Big Lava Bed, several extinct volcanoes, and numerous craters—some of which have become lakes. The trail passes several prominent volcanic features, including

Gifford Peak, the oldest volcano in the Indian Heaven Wilderness, which you'll see rising above Blue Lake. Gifford Peak was created some 730,000 years ago when several vents exploded, laying down a strata of lava. Continuing eruptions ended up building the cinder cones now known as Gifford Peak and Berry Mountain, which the PCT climbs. Farther north and just off the PCT is 5,323-foot Sawtooth Mountain, a shield volcano that erupted and spread basalt over the surrounding area some 300,000 years ago. It is the most conspicuous feature on the north end of the Indian Heaven Wilderness.

A rich land of abundant wildlife, berries, and fish, the Indian Heaven Wilderness has been used by Indian tribes for more than 10,000 years. One of its intriguing features is the Race Track, which lies about half a mile off the PCT on Trail 171A. During the annual berry harvest, Indians would race horses on this level meadow. More than 100 years later, the indentations they left behind are still clearly visible.

You might see evidence of other traditional Native American activity if you look closely at western red cedars for scars of peeled bark. These so-called basket trees were used by Indians to make baskets. On one tree, the scars can be dated to 1769.

Another more recent crop is beargrass, which is sold to florists for use in flower arrangements. Beargrass-picking is hard work, requiring tough gloves and a strong back. But the demand for the decorative greenery is high, and you may well run into beargrass pickers along the trail. In recent years, Asian immigrants have joined Native Americans in this occupation. Permits are required.

Beargrass

Sawtooth Huckleberry Fields

The Indians may not be racing horses in the Indian Heaven Wilderness anymore but they still harvest huckleberries.

There's no shortage of huckleberries anywhere along Washington's PCT, but the Sawtooth Huckleberry Fields just north of the Indian Heaven Wilderness are especially rich. Native Americans cyclically used fire to

clear vegetation and maintain the
vigor of the berry fields. For miles,
the huckleberry bushes tempt late-
August and September hikers to
slow down and snack.

For generations many Pacific
Northwest tribes, some from as far
away as what is now Montana,
gathered here in late summer for
an annual huckleberry feast. They
would harvest and dry berries,

Huckleberries

have horse races and competitive games, dry meat, tan hides, and fish.

In 1932, ownership of the Sawtooth Huckleberry Fields became an
issue when non-Natives began to harvest the berries. The Yakima Tribe
and the Forest Service signed an agreement that reserved the berry fields
east of Forest Road 24 for the Indians. The western side of the road
(through which the PCT passes) is open to all pickers, although commercial pickers must have a permit.

Mount Adams

William O. Douglas wrote:

> *I may not see it for hours on end as I travel this mountain area,
> for the trail is usually beneath a ridge. Yet when I travel there I
> almost feel the presence of the mountain. I am filled with the
> expectancy of seeing it from every height of land, at every open-
> ing of a canyon. And the sight of its black basalt cliffs crowned
> with white snow, both set against a blue sky, is enough to make
> a man stop in wonderment.*

Douglas's experience notwithstanding, PCT hikers usually have excellent views of Mount Adams, which dominates most of the trail in southern
Oregon. From about the Sawtooth berry fields northward, the PCT offers so
many good views of Mount Adams that you may well return home with several rolls of film showing the same white-topped peak.

At 12,276 feet, Mount Adams is the second-tallest mountain in

Mount Adams

Washington, a massive stratovolcano covering an area of 48 square miles. A squat-shaped mountain with a flat summit, Mount Adams is actually composed of several superimposed cones leaning on top of each other.

Geologist Stephen Harris describes Adams as "old, weather beaten and asymmetrical," and perhaps this is what led to the Indian legends portraying Adams (or Klickitat) as a beaten-down, tired old warrior (see page 254).

Certainly, it is ancient. The first eruptions in the area can be dated to almost a million years ago. Major eruptions that occurred about a half-million years ago formed a volcano about 3 miles south of the present summit; later eruptions moved the focus of activity north to the present summit, which began building about 460,000 years ago. The last eruptions on the summit are thought to have taken place about 10,000 years ago (although some geologists place the date at between 1,000 and 2,000 years ago). But the entire area is geothermally active, and certainly many younger parasitic cinder cones around the mountain's base have erupted as recently as 2,000 to 4,000 years ago.

You'll see lava from one of the more recent explosions above Lava Spring, just off the trail, where a 7-mile-long lava flow cut into the Muddy Fork drainage between 3,500 and 6,800 years ago. Two miles farther, the PCT passes a much older volcanic feature, 5,387-foot Potato Hill, a cinder cone that was created after a vent erupted 120,000 years ago. A cross-country ascent of 600 feet brings you to the summit, where you can see the shallow remains of the crater that once ejected so much lava that it filled the valley to the north to a depth of 90 feet.

Mount Adams is heavily eroded by glaciation, especially on the east side of the mountain, where the Klickitat Glacier has carved the second-largest cirque and amphitheater in the Cascades (the largest is on Mount Rainier). However, since Mount Adams lies much farther to the dry eastern side of the range than the other major Cascadian peaks, all of its glaciers occur above 6,500 feet. The PCT circles it at a reasonably level elevation of about 6,000 feet, well below the summer snow-line.

Mount Adams was first climbed in 1845 by three members of a work party that was building a military road through Naches Pass to connect the

Columbia River with Puget Sound. In 1918 and 1921, the Forest Service built a firetower on the summit, but soon abandoned it because of the difficulty of supplying it—and because views from the summit were too often blocked by fog.

In 1929 a local entrepreneur named Wade Dean filed a claim to the summit, built mule and horse trails, hauled up mining equipment, and started to extract sulfur. Active mining continued until 1959. Trains of pack stock were used to supply the miners. Their route, up the south side via Morrison Creek and Cold Springs, is today the easiest and most popular climbing route up the mountain. The ascent crosses a long snowfield and then follows a pumice ridge to the summit. While there are no technical difficulties, Mount Adams is a major mountain—the second-highest in Washington and the third-highest in the Cascades. If you attempt the climb, you should have an ice ax, crampons, and plenty of warm clothes.

From the PCT, you can access the summit route from Round the Mountain Trail 9, which joins the PCT in the Mount Adams Wilderness.

Mount St. Helens

Mount St. Helens is not on the PCT, but lies about 30 miles to the west of Mount Adams on almost an identical line of latitude. Early pioneers, using the mountains as points of reference, would often confuse the two. In those days, Mount St. Helens was 9,677 feet tall, a beautifully symmetrical peak, sometimes called the Fujiyama of America. Interestingly, it was the first Cascadian peak to be climbed strictly for pleasure, or recreation, rather than for economic, scientific, or military reasons. The first ascent was made by Thomas J. Dryer, founder of *The Oregonian*, on August 27, 1853.

Mount St. Helens is the youngest of the stratovolcanoes, its origins dating back about 40,000 years. But the pre-1980 summit was only about 15,000 years old, and the visible part of the present-day volcano took shape only about 2,200 years ago, well after the Ice Age. The mountain's relative youthfulness explains the symmetry it had before the 1980 eruption: It was too young to have suffered from significant erosion.

Even before its 1980 eruption, Mount St. Helens was more active and violent than any other volcano in the contiguous 48 states. Klickitat Indians called it Tah-one-la-clah—Fire Mountain—because of its history of eruptions.

Its eruption on May 18, 1980, was cataclysmic. An explosion equivalent to 30 million tons of TNT blew the top 1,300 feet of the mountain into the stratosphere, produced the largest avalanche in recorded history, killed 57 people, destroyed 150 square miles of forest, created a 4-mile-long lava flow with temperatures between 600 and 1400 degrees Fahrenheit, melted the upper 45 feet of St. Helens Glacier, clogged channels in the Columbia River with sediment for months, and blew 2 to 5 inches of ash as far away as Montana. The mountain, now 8,364 feet tall, is managed by Mount St. Helens National Volcanic Monument.

Goat Rocks Wilderness

William O. Douglas wrote, "The Goat Rocks seem holy to me—of this earth and yet apart from it. They are sanctuaries built on such a vast scale that he who approaches them from the south is certain to feel humble and reverent."

The region was sacred to the Yakima, who believed that is was the home of La-con-nie, God of the Goats. And although no PCT hikers have encountered the goat god, there are plenty of his charges to be seen.

The dramatic main ridge of the Goat Rocks is the remains of an ancient stratovolcano that was once as high as Mount Hood or pre-eruption St. Helens. The oldest rocks in the area—some 120 million to 140 million years old—originated from volcanic flows beneath the sea that were brought to the surface by the collision of the tectonic plates. About 3.8 million years ago, volcanic activity began to build the Goat Rocks, and between 1 million and 3 million years ago, the stratovolcano was formed. Over time, its explosion and erosions combined to sculpt the craggy terrain that is at the heart of this stark and dramatic landscape.

Mountain goat

The landscape is hands-down the most beautiful on southern Washington's PCT. It is also the southernmost range of mountain goats, and one of the places where you have the best chance of seeing these agile high-country ani-

Goat Rocks Wilderness

mals. Standing still, they sometimes look like big yellowish-white rocks. If you see one move, look closely, because mountain goats usually travel in herds. You may be lucky enough to see 20 or 30 at a time.

Mountain goats live above the tree line in territory so rugged that they are largely free of predators (if only because no predator can catch them as they leap and gallop over precipices and cliffs). Somehow they manage to find enough to eat—twigs, grasses, flowers, herbs, kinnikinnick (berries that grow in the high country), and lichen. They are superbly adapted for their chosen lifestyle. A shaggy outercoat and a soft woolly undercoat protect them from bitter winds and frigid cold. Their feet are equipped with cushioned skid-proof pads that work better on the slick rock and slippery ice than any Vibram sole yet invented by humans.

Toponyms

Mount St. Helens was given its name by George Vancouver to honor a British diplomat by that name. Mount Rainier commemorates a British admiral, and Mount Hood was named for another British naval officer. Mount Baker is named for one of Vancouver's lieutenants. In 1839, Hall Jackson Kelly, an early advocate of the colonization of Oregon, tried to turn the Cascades into a presidential range. Hood was to be renamed Mount Adams, St. Helens would become Mount Washington, The Sisters were to be renamed Madison, and Shasta would become Jackson. At the time, cartographers had only rudimentary maps, which didn't even show the presence of the mountain today known as Adams. In any event, the names were never changed. Only the name Adams stuck: It was mistakenly written in on a cartographer's map on a spot 40 miles distant from where it was supposed to be—and coincidentally there was an unnamed mountain there in need of a name (at least so far as European Americans were concerned; Indians in the region had long since been able to identify the mountain as Klickitat, a son of Manitou).

Indian Legends

Native American legends reflect the fact that each of the mountains has a very different character—some more explosive, others more beautiful. There are parallels with Old World mythology. Like the Greek gods who once inhabited Mount Olympus, the Native American gods inhabited the

Mount Rainier from Goat Rocks

great volcanoes. Like their Greek counterparts, they periodically erupted to express anger at each other or at humans. And Native American legends include a tale similar to the story of Noah's Ark, in which Mounts Jefferson, Shasta, and Baker offered refuge from the floods.

In one story, Klickitat (also known as Pahto, or Mount Adams) and his brother Wy'east (Mount Hood) are at it again, fighting over La-Wa-La-Clough (Mount St. Helens). (You may remember her as the beautiful incarnation of the old crone who had been turned into a lovely maiden by the god Manitou when she tried to protect the Bridge of the Gods.) La-Wa-La-Clough preferred Pahto. In a rage, Wy'east struck Pahto and flattened his head. Pahto, in defeat, stopped smoking, and never again lifted his head.

⚇ HIKING INFORMATION

Seasonal Information and Gear Tips

The elevations of the trail in southern Washington are, with the exception of the Goat Rocks Wilderness, considerably lower than the elevations in northern Washington. Generally, the trail is snow-free by mid-July. (Of course, winter snow accumulations vary, so you'll have to check with the PCTA. Or call the particular national forest in which you plan to hike.) August is usually a good month, and in years of lower-than-average snowpack, you may not have much of a bug problem. The later in the month you hike, the fewer bugs you'll have to swat. Hiking just after the snowmelt does have its reward: the beautiful alpine wildflower bloom.

September is bug-free, but weather-wise it's a crapshoot. This is a great time of year for locals to be on the trails. After Labor Day, the crowds are gone, the mosquitoes are gone, and if you live nearby, you have the flexibility to respond to changing weather conditions. In some years, September offers sunshine and Indian summer; in other years, you'll get weeks of nonstop rain, cold, and even snow at the higher elevations. From late August on, huckleberries are plentiful, feeding not only your taste buds, but also your eyes with their brilliant russet foliage. In most years, the hiking season in this section ends sometime in October.

- Bring bug protection. July is mosquito season, which can last well into August. They grow 'em fierce and hungry here. Especially buggy sections vary from year to year (and even from day to day), but wherever there's a lot of standing water and slushy snowmelt, you can expect buzzing company, especially in the Indian Heaven Wilderness (known locally as Mosquito Heaven) and in the lowland pond-filled section between Mount Adams and the Goat Rocks.
- Good rain gear is necessary, particularly at the beginning and end of the hiking season.

Thru-hikers' Corner

Northbound thru-hikers should concentrate on making mileage here: The trail is easy, and time is at a premium. In late September, you'll probably need to pick up an extra layer of clothes, because the nights can be cold, there can be long periods of cold rain, and you might even get a little snow.

Southbounders who have made it this far can rest assured that they've been through the bulk of the tough stuff. However, don't get rid of your ice ax just yet. It'll come in handy on the Packwood Glacier, and you may need it for the higher elevations around Mount Adams.

Best Short Hikes

- You can day-hike into the Big Lava Bed from Crest Campground, located on Forest Road 60.
- Mount Adams Wilderness offers a 25-mile hike that features superb scenery, excellent campsites—and one cardiac-challenging climb. Enter the wilderness at the trailhead at the junction of Forest Roads 23 and 8810 (it's 82.3 miles into this section). Your first miles are all uphill as you climb to just beneath the summer snow-line. After walking halfway around the mountain, you end the hike at Road 5603. You should plan to have a car at this end; there isn't much traffic on the road.
- From U.S. Highway 12 at White Pass, it's a 21-mile hike south across the Goat Rocks. It's an easy 2-day hike—but you could certainly spend 3 days exploring side trails and the high country. Take Trail 96 to Road 405—it's the shortest route in and out. For a longer hike (42.9 miles), continue on the PCT until the junction with Road 5603.

Resupplies and Trailheads

Cascade Locks is the most commonly used.

Cascade Locks (Oregon) (mile 0). This on-trail resupply just off Interstate 84 near the Bridge of the Gods offers everything you are likely to need: motels, restaurants, supermarket, a post office, public campground by the river. For gear, nearby Hood River has several outfitters. (Thru-hikers taking the road rather than the trail between Cascade Locks and Panther Creek Campground can also resupply 3.2 miles up the road in Stevenson or 4.4 miles farther, in Carson; both Washington towns have stores, motels, and restaurants.) Stock up: The next convenient resupply is at White Pass, 147.5 miles from Cascade Locks (only 126.7 miles if you take the shortcut road walk; see page 240). Post office: General Delivery, Cascade Locks, OR 97014

Panther Creek Campground (Washington) (mile 35.5) on Forest Road 65. No convenient resupply, but this is a good place to start a hike.

Crest Campground (mile 51.0) on Forest Road 60. No convenient resupply, but this is a good place to start a hike south into the Big Lava Bed or north into the Indian Heaven Wilderness.

Road 5603 (mile 94.3). No convenient resupply, but this is an excellent place to start a hike either south into the Mount Adams Wilderness or north into the Goat Rocks.

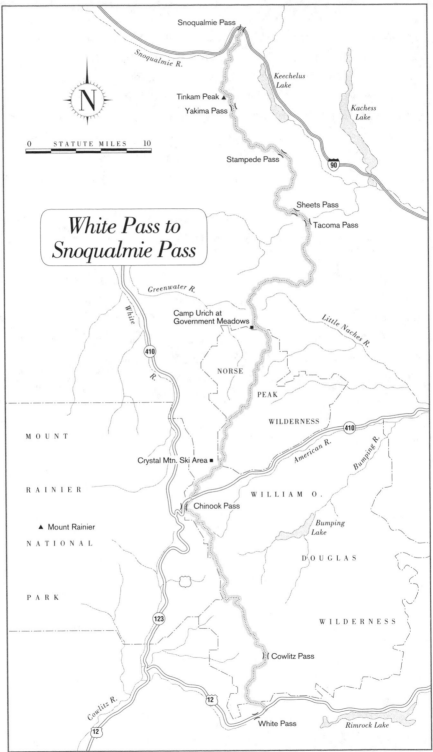

Snoqualmie Pass

Snoqualmie R.

Keechelus Lake

Kachess Lake

Tinkam Peak ▲

Yakima Pass

Stampede Pass

90

Sheets Pass

Tacoma Pass

White Pass to
Snoqualmie Pass

Greenwater R.

White

Camp Urich at
Government Meadows ■

Little Naches R.

410

R.

NORSE

PEAK

WILDERNESS

410

MOUNT

American R.

Bumping R.

Crystal Mtn. Ski Area ■

WILLIAM O.

RAINIER

Chinook Pass

Bumping Lake

▲ Mount Rainier

NATIONAL

DOUGLAS

PARK

WILDERNESS

123

Cowlitz Pass

Cowlitz R.

12

12

White Pass

Rimrock Lake

16

White Pass to Snoqualmie Pass

98.6 miles

This section can be divided in two. The first half includes the beautiful
William O. Douglas and Norse Peak Wildernesses and a brief foray into the
eastern part of Mount Rainier National Park. The terrain ranges from lakes
and forests to high windswept ridges, with ever-closer views of the undis-
puted lord of the Northwest, mighty Mount Rainier.

But the second half of this section includes the ugliest miles on the
entire Pacific Crest Trail: the 40 miles just south of Snoqualmie Pass,
which are an unrelenting series of checkerboard clear-cuts. Writer Chris

Urich Cabin is one of the PCT's few shelters.

A serene landscape in William O. Douglas Wilderness

Townsend, who hiked the PCT in 1983, said that "The walk to Snoqualmie is one of, if not the worst, of the whole trail. Virtually all the forest has been cleared out, and the trail is a total muddy snagged mess. The sound of chainsaws and bulldozers echoed all around." Nothing has changed since then—except that even more acres have been clear-cut.

Short-distance hikers are advised to hike the first 52 miles of this section and then bail out at the first possible opportunity after Government Meadow. (There are lots of logging roads to choose from; the larger roads have enough traffic for reliable hitchhiking.) If you have to walk through the clear-cuts, you can console yourself with the endless acres of huckleberries, which grow well in the disturbed soil.

THE ROUTE

North of White Pass, the trail rambles through the William O. Douglas Wilderness, named after the Supreme Court justice, environmentalist, hiker, and writer who was one of the 20th century's most articulate and passionate voices on behalf of wilderness.

The first miles are flat and easy, followed by a climb to higher country. *Note:* Until August, especially after a wet winter, this section's lakes can house swarms of mosquitoes.

Now Mount Rainier dominates the view, growing larger and larger with every mile. The trail briefly enters Mount Rainier National Park, then descends into Chinook Pass, where it crosses Washington Highway 410 near a popular trailhead and viewpoint for park visitors. It then climbs again, passing lovely Sheep Lake, which, because it is only 2 miles from the trailhead at Chinook Pass, inevitably suffers from overuse. From Sheep Lake, the trail continues to rise and enters the Norse Peak Wilderness, one ridge away from the Crystal Mountain ski area. Here, the toponyms— Placer Lake, Pickhandle Basin, Gold Hill, Bullion Pass, Silver Creek— give clues to the area's history as a mining center.

For about 12 miles, the trail traverses the high slopes of sweeping open cirques with wide views. This is a windswept, exposed section, so make note that a half-mile off the trail in Big Crow Basin is a deteriorating shelter that provides welcome, if mediocre, protection from the elements in bad

The PCT passing through William O. Douglas Wilderness

weather. When the trail returns to forest a few miles later, it passes the turnoff for what used to be Arch Rock Shelter. Although that shelter is mentioned in trail literature, it no longer exists. You will, however, find water and a campsite. About 5 miles later, the trail leaves the wilderness at Government Meadow and reaches the PCT's best shelter. Camp Urich is a cozy, well-maintained cabin that has a sleeping loft and a wood-burning stove.

North of Government Meadow, everything changes. Not only is much of the trail between Government Meadow and Snoqualmie Pass a nonstop sequence of clear-cuts and logging roads, but to make things worse, the trail is frequently in bad repair, with blowdowns, logging snags, and uneven footway. No wonder: What volunteer would gain satisfaction from spending weekends cleaning up after the logging trucks? Many of the clear-cuts are covered by huckleberry bushes that overgrow the trail. In wet weather, the bushes will soak you from the neck down. This is hands-down the worst section of the entire PCT. There's no point in doing it unless you're trying to hike the entire trail. *Note:* Even if you are trying to hike the entire trail, it's possible to detour here and walk on roads from Tacoma Pass to Snoqualmie Pass. The Forest Service map (see appendix A for contact information) shows several ways to do this.

If you do stay on the trail, watch your water, because there aren't many water sources, and some have been destroyed by logging activity. One place to look is on the western side of Tacoma Pass, where the PCT crosses a road. Go down the road about a quarter-mile to half-a-mile west and you should see some water flowing.

At the end of this section the trail descends into Snoqualmie Pass via a ski slope. From here, you can look ahead with relief to the craggy, white-capped peaks of the North Cascades.

WHAT YOU'LL SEE

William O. Douglas Wilderness

William O. Douglas served on America's highest court from 1939 to 1975. But his eponymous wilderness pays tribute not to Douglas the jurist, but to Douglas the environmentalist, a native of Washington who grew up roaming the wild country around the Goat Rocks Wilderness. Thru-hikers will be interested to know that Douglas is one of us: He hiked the entire Appalachian Trail (and wrote about it in a book titled *East to Katahdin*). But his heart was always in Washington's wild country. Several of his books describe this area and make a case for its preservation:

> *The thrill of tramping alone and unafraid through a wilderness of lakes, creeks, alpine meadows, and glaciers is not known to many. A civilization can be built around the machine, but it is doubtful that a meaningful life can be produced by it . . . When man worships at the feet of avalanche lilies or discovers the delicacies of the pasque flower or finds the faint perfume of phlox on rocky ridges, he will come to know that the real glories are God's creations. When he feels the wind blowing through him on a high peak or sleeps under a closely matted white bark pine in an exposed basin, he is apt to find his relationship to the universe.*

Mount Rainier

The PCT enters Mount Rainier National Park near Chinook Pass. At 14,410 feet, Mount Rainier is perhaps the most identifiable landmark on the entire PCT. It's also the most famous natural feature in the Pacific Northwest. From the PCT, it is visible for more than 300 miles, from just before the Columbia River Gorge in northern Oregon to Red Pass in the North Cascades. The mountain's lofty heights seem even more so because none of its neighboring peaks are more than 7,000 feet tall.

Some facts: Established on March 2, 1899, Mount Rainier National Park was the fifth national park to be designated. It is the only national park that has a glaciated volcano. The mountain has 26 named glaciers, which cover 37 square miles—the largest glacier system in the contiguous states. One of them, the Emmons Glacier, is the largest in the lower 48. Mount Rainier is 1 million years old and is showing its age. Once 16,000 feet tall, it has been eroded by glaciation and looks very different when viewed from different angles.

Rainier is one of the most closely studied volcanoes in the world. In the past, its eruptions have been cataclysmic: One major eruption 2,500 years

Mount Rainier

ago deposited 392 million cubic yards of debris, which extended the Puget Sound shoreline as much as 31 miles. Rainier erupted frequently between 1841 and 1870. Today, on the summit, steam vents and fumaroles attest to the forces that still churn beneath the mountain's icy surface.

Mount Rainier was first seen by Europeans during the George Vancouver expedition of 1792 and was named, in typical European fashion, after a British admiral. The name is controversial, and lawsuits—so far unsuccessful—have been filed to have the mountain's name changed to Tacoma. The Indians called it "the mountain that is god."

The first reported ascent was in 1870 by appropriately named Hazard Stevens and Phillmon Van Trump, who reached the top at 5 PM. The climbers were forced to spend the night on the mountain. They survived, warming themselves by huddling next to the steam vents in the summit crater.

Climbing Mount Rainier

PCT hikers taking time off to peak-bag along the way will find Mount Rainier the biggest challenge so far. Only highly experienced mountaineers with advanced glacier-travel skills should tackle this peak without a guide. Others will need to take a 1-day ice-ax and crampon class with Rainier Mountaineering, Inc. (RMI), the concessionaire that runs Mount Rainier's guide service.

After you've successfully completed your basic skills class, you can join a climb, which is an exhausting 2-day affair. On the first (easy) day, you climb 5,000 feet from Paradise to Camp Muir. On the second day, you awaken between midnight and 2 AM to climb the remaining 4,000 feet to the summit. Then you turn around and go all the way back down to Paradise. Give yourself a day off to recover before resuming your thru-hike. Sign up in advance, especially in August, and if you intend to stay at Paradise Lodge, be sure you have reservations. (Less-expensive lodgings are available outside the park at the base of the mountain. RMI can give you information when you sign up for a climb. Call 360-569-2227.)

Passes and Pioneers

This section has several passes that have been important in Washington history—many of which, like the mountains, have been named for 19th-century explorers and settlers.

White Pass. White Pass is named for engineer Charles W. White of the Northern Pacific Railway Company, who discovered it. The pass, just north of the stupendously beautiful Goat Rocks Wilderness, is geologically complex. The exposed rock at the pass is 145 million years old. Back then, North America's Pacific Coast was somewhere in Idaho; Washington was underwater—and the rocks of White Pass were mud and sand on the bottom of an offshore shelf. Plate tectonics uplifted the land and formed the mountains we see today.

If you have the opportunity to take some time off at White Pass, be sure to stop at the Palisades viewpoint a few miles west of White Pass just off U.S. Highway 12. Like the High Sierra's Devils Postpile (chapter 7), this is a jointed columnar lava flow. As in Devils Postpile, erosion (in this case, caused by the Clear Fork of the Cowlitz River) removed volcanic debris, exposing the harder 200-foot-thick lava flow beneath.

Government Meadow and Naches Pass. Although Joseph Hazard calls it The Pass of the Pioneers, the pioneers were latecomers to Naches Pass, which had been used for centuries by Indian tribes traveling between their winter residences near Puget Sound and their summer home in the mountains.

European Americans discovered the pass in 1841. In 1853, Theodore Winthrop led the first successful wagon train crossing of the Cascades in the Puget Sound area by following the Naches River headwaters to Naches Pass. One member of the party was nine-year old David Longmire, who later homesteaded at the base of Rainier. Longmire deeded his land to the national park (and is remembered via the toponym of one of the park's most-visited areas). The pioneers used the flat open field at what is now called Government Meadow to hunt and graze. Today you're still likely to see elk in the meadow.

In 1855 the Naches Wagon Road was built through Naches Pass as an extension of the Oregon Trail. But although the intention was to provide a path to bring settlers from the eastern Cascades to the Puget Sound region, the road was soon abandoned because of its difficulties, which included some 40 crossings of the Naches River, steep grades, and a difficult descent down the western slope, which required lowering wagons one at a time with ropes. In 1857 the route through the pass was used as a military road to connect forts on both sides of the Cascades.

Stampede Pass. Between Chinook Pass and Snoqualmie Pass, the Cascades narrow to a single ridge, which is cut by eight major passes. Land scandals and inefficiencies delayed the selection and construction of a railway route until someone realized that there were 44 million acres of land at stake. In order to encourage railroads to build lines through difficult terrain, the government had promised huge land grants—but the deadline was 1884.

In 1880, Virgil Bogue, an employee of the Northern Pacific Railway Company, was sent to find a temporary railroad route that could be quickly built over the Cascades to Tacoma. In 1881 he discovered and recommended Stampede Pass.

The line was constructed hurriedly in order to meet the deadline. The "temporary" line still operates, although you won't see it. Today's trains go under the pass through a tunnel.

The land grants that spurred construction of a railway line here were to have an enormous effect on land-use patterns in the West. The railroads received every other section of land, which began the checkerboard pattern of land ownership that still affects logging patterns today. Sometimes the railroads made as much money from the land and its timber as they did on transporting people and goods. Today, most of these parcels of land have been sold to big logging companies, which manage it strictly for timber. The

EVENDEN '00

Yellow monkeyflower

Pacific Crest Trail has easements and permission to cross this land, but hikers should understand that recreation is distinctly a low-priority item.

Wildflowers

One of the most rewarding features of this section is its wildflower bloom, which occurs in the short period after snowmelt and before the arrival of frost. In *Of Man and Mountains*, William O. Douglas writes:

The sight of 10 or 20 acres of avalanche lilies in bloom is breathtaking. There may be a whole hillside of deer's tongue, paintbrush, or cinquefoil. An entire basin may be covered with the shooting star or the speedwell. The stream that feeds it may be lined with the yellow monkeyflower as far as the eye can see. These flowers are all fragile, and their colors are delicate. No matter how often I see them I am amazed at their capacity to thrive in this rigorous environment, for the altitude ranges from 4,500 to 7,000 feet.

Horses

This section (along with the Mount Adams Wilderness) is the one in which you are most likely to see horse-packers. In recent years, conflicts between horses and hikers have escalated on the PCT, largely due to an anti-equestrian sentiment that has become increasingly voiced. This book is not going to take sides on that issue. In our years of hiking on the PCT, most of the horsemen we've met have been courteous, friendly, and helpful. But a few haven't been. (The greeting from one surly fellow was, "Get off the trail to the downhill side.")

Regardless of how you feel about horses (or, if you use horses, about hikers), both hikers and horses are here to stay. Horses have the right-of-way, mostly because many of the people who ride on commercial trips haven't the slightest control over their mounts. Also, there's less impact on the land if a hiker steps aside than if a horse steps aside. And it's usually easier and safer for a hiker to step aside than it is for a horse.

In general, when encountering horses:

- Talk to the horse. Horses are easily frightened by things they can't identify, and that includes people wearing backpacks. If you're stopping to chat with an equestrian and the horse is acting up, try taking off your pack.
- On average terrain, simply stand to the side. Where the trail cuts across a hillside, step off the trail to the downhill side; you will appear smaller to the horse and be less likely to spook it. Also, if you go off-trail uphill, bits of rock and dirt can slip away underfoot and fall into the horse's path, giving it yet one more thing to be scared of. However, it's not always the easiest thing for a hiker to scramble down and then back up a friable slope. If you don't think you can safely leave the trail to the downhill side, or if you don't feel safe having the horse to your uphill side, climb uphill from the trail, preferably several yards. Stand still so that you don't knock any rocks around. And talk to the horse so it knows you're there.
- Stay away from the horse's back legs. If a horse is frightened, it's more likely to kick than to bite.

HIKING INFORMATION

Seasonal Information and Gear Tips

Seasonal information here is much the same as in chapter 15: August is the best season, September can be nice. In July, you'll still have some snow and lots of mosquitoes.

Mosquitoes can be a major problem well into August, especially in the lower regions of the William O. Douglas Wilderness. DEET, tents, and bug clothes or a head net are recommended if you're traveling during bug season.

Thru-hikers' Corner

Assuming you have good weather, there's nothing especially difficult about this section for either northbound or southbound hikers. Southbounders will hit some mosquitoes, but in a normal year should be out of most of the snow. Northbounders are simply racing winter.

Best Short Hikes

- White Pass (Highway 12) to Chinook Pass (Highway 410): A 2- to 3-day, 29.5-mile backpack through the William O. Douglas Wilderness, with views of Mount Rainier.
- Chinook Pass (Highway 410) to Government Meadow (access via logging roads): This 2-day high-country traverse through the Norse Peak Wilderness offers spectacular views of Mount Rainier.
- Day hiking: Chinook Pass is the best day-hiker's trailhead because the views come almost immediately. You can go either south or north from Chinook Pass. Both require climbing, but the views are worth the work.

Resupplies and Trailheads

White Pass is the most commonly used.

White Pass (mile 0). The trail crosses Highway 12 a half-mile east of the White Pass ski area. White Pass has a Forest Service campground, a convenience store offering extremely limited supplies, and a motel. You can receive mail, but cannot send packages out. Showers and laundry are available at the store. If you need more services or a better variety of food, it's an easy hitch down to Packwood, 15 miles west. Post office: White Pass Rural Branch Post Office, Kracker Barrel Store, 48851 U.S. Highway 12, Naches, WA 98927

Chinook Pass (mile 29.5). The PCT crosses Highway 410 near a big parking lot and trailhead near the eastern boundary of Mount Rainier National Park. No convenient resupply, but this is a popular trailhead for day hikers.

Logging roads in the Mount Baker–Snoqualmie National Forest. Swear you might at the clear-cuts, but the logging roads make the Norse Peak Wilderness accessible from the north, and they give you lots of chances to bail out. You can get a map of the forest by writing to the address listed in appendix A.

17

Snoqualmie Pass to Stevens Pass

75 miles

From the ridges of central Washington just before Snoqualmie Pass, you get a glimpse ahead into the North Cascades, which block the horizon like an impenetrable wall. Isolated and rugged, serrated and snaggle-toothed, the North Cascades rival California's High Sierra for scenic mountain vistas, yet are completely different in character.

By comparison to the southern Cascades, a profile map of the North Cascades looks positively terrifying. Ascents and descents of more than 3,000 feet are common, and are sometimes lined up like a series of hurdles. Plan conservative mileage here. Even though most of the climbs are extremely gentle and well-graded, going up and down 3,000 feet at a time can wear out even strong hikers.

Alpine Lakes Wilderness near Waptus Creek

This 75-mile section traverses the exorbitantly scenic Alpine Lakes Wilderness, the southernmost section of the North Cascades. Because of both its wild rugged beauty and its proximity to Seattle, the Alpine Lakes Wilderness is one of the most popular hiking destinations in Washington. The trailhead at Snoqualmie is only an hour from downtown Seattle— and reachable by Greyhound bus (there's a regularly scheduled stop at the Time Wise Deli at the pass).

Most of this section is in wilderness, making it one of the longest roadless stretches on the entire PCT. Thru-hikers motivated by the fear of winter weather can do this section is 4 long days. Others would be better advised to take 5, 6, or even 7 days to savor the views—and recover from the climbs.

THE ROUTE

In the first 11 miles of this section, the trail gains more than 3,000 feet as it ascends from Snoqualmie Pass to the high ridges of the Alpine Lakes Wilderness. You'll be amply rewarded for your effort with views of Mount Rainier, Glacier Peak, Mount Thompson, Mount Stuart, and later of Alta Mountain, Three Queens, and Mount Daniel.

Note: In a dry year, or late in the season, watch your water, because some of the climbs can be quite dry. On a sunny day, the exposed slopes can be surprisingly hot. If you miscalculate, you may be able to slake your thirst in the occasional stagnant pool or late-lingering snowfield.

Throughout this section, you will spend much of your time going up or down steep sidewalls, formed when glaciers scoured out the valleys. On these long, alder-choked switchbacks, there are very few places to camp. So when planning your day, consider that if you start up (or down) a 3,000-foot slope in the late afternoon, you're probably going to have to make it all the way to the top (or bottom) before you'll be able to find even the most basic bivouac site.

The trail is actively maintained, but the crews sometimes can't keep up with deterioration caused by erosion on the steep slopes. You can also expect some tedious miles on the steep sidewalls where alder can quickly overrun the trail.

The PCT leaves the Alpine Lakes Wilderness 4.5 miles short of Stevens Pass. These last miles are less dramatic than those in the heart of the wilderness, and they can be tedious, with some stiff ups and downs. You pass several dirt roads and a ski resort before finally reaching the section's end at U.S. Highway 2. Short-term hikers not intent on doing the entire PCT might better enjoy a shortcut that descends on Trail 1060 past beautiful Surprise Lake, getting to Highway 2 in 4 miles. At that point, you are 6 miles west of Stevens Pass and 8 miles from Skykomish. *Note:* If you reverse direction and take this alternate route southbound, be prepared to for a long, steep climb!

WHAT YOU'LL SEE

The North Cascades

Geology confirms what common sense infers: The North Cascades are very different mountains than their cousins to the south.

The Cascades of Oregon and southern Washington are dominated by the line of volcanic giants—The Sisters, Jefferson, Hood, Adams, St. Helens, Rainier. With the exception of the Goat Rocks, the mountains and ridges on the PCT's route through Oregon and southern Washington are rounded and gentle.

In contrast, the North Cascades have only two major volcanoes, Mount Baker and Glacier Peak (both visible from the PCT in the section covered in chapter 18). But while these big volcanoes (along with Mount Rainier to the south) might dominate the skyline, it is the lower mountains that give the North Cascades their fierce, wild character: This is a landscape of steep peaks, narrow gorges, and sharp angles cut by ice and snow. The North Cascades boast more than half of the glaciers in the contiguous 48 states.

Clinton Clarke described the terrain of the North Cascades as "the most primitive and roughest in the [contiguous] United States."

The trail described in chapters 17 and 18 is thus steeper, wilder, more rugged, and higher than the trail to the south. In the Alpine Lakes Wilderness, the trail several times climbs to nearly 6,000 feet. (And in chapter 18, it goes even higher: Just south of the Canadian border, the trail

Paul Woodward, © 2000 The Countryman Press

stays largely above 6,000 feet for 33 miles, and reaches the highest point on Washington's PCT at 7,126 feet.) Because tree line drops about 300 feet for every 100 miles of latitude, elevations of 6,000 and 7,000 feet this far north mean exposed and windswept trails. The difference is noticeable. While the timber on Mount Hood grew up to elevations of about 6,000 feet, in the North Cascades the trees start to thin out at around 5,000 feet; only a few hundred feet higher, there's nothing left but shrubs. For hikers this means fine views in good weather, but potentially dangerous exposure in bad.

The differences between the southern Cascades and the North Cascades are grounded in their different geological histories. The North Cascades are an old range, formed about 10 million years ago. Unlike the Cascades of Oregon and southern Washington, they are not made of igneous rock (products of volcanic activity), but rather of metamorphic and sedimentary rock that has been uplifted and eroded. Both the southern and North Cascades are the product of tectonic activity—the result of collisions that occurred when the earth's plates shifted. But in the southern subrange, this tectonic activity led to subduction, and volcanism shaped the landscape. In the North Cascades, the collision of plates uplifted the mountains, which were then given their current shape by the sculpting action of ice, water, and wind.

During the Ice Age the North Cascades were further uplifted. As a result, the peaks grew higher while at the same time ice was cutting into the valleys, making them lower. The result is a maze of sharp peaks and narrow gorges, of cirques, moraines, and vertical headwalls. The few valleys that exist are deeply cut, with flat floors and steep sides. For hikers, this means a vertical landscape of major elevation changes. William O. Douglas quotes a hiking partner thus: "This is a country where one looks either up or down."

Access into the North Cascades has always been difficult. Unlike the southern Cascades, which are traversed by the Columbia River, the North Cascades are unbroken, not crossed by any rivers. Water that drains to the west finds its way fairly directly to the Pacific Ocean. But water that drains to the east has a longer journey. It is forced by the mountains to first flow southward, where it runs into the Columbia River and thence to the Pacific.

Nor is there convenient access by land. Indians who crossed the mountains to trade, hunt, fish, and gather food in the rich old-growth forests used several trails over the high passes, including Suiattle Pass, Cloudy Pass, and White Pass. Later, these trails were used by early European American trappers and traders. But as European settlement began for real, these passes failed to provide a feasible route through the mountains for wagon roads and railroads—although not for lack of trying.

Alexander Ross, an explorer for the American Company based at Fort Okanogan, crossed over Cascade Pass in 1814 and reported that, "A more difficult route of travel never fell to man's lot." As a result of reports like this, the first railroads crossed the Cascades farther to the south, through Stampede Pass and then through Snoqualmie Pass. The railroad through Stevens Pass was not built until 1893.

In the period between 1880 and 1900, prospectors located some gold, copper, silver, lead, and zinc in the North Cascades. But the hard rock surfaces were difficult to prospect and roads were almost impossible to build.

Snoqualmie Pass

With its relatively low elevation and gentle grades, Snoqualmie Pass is the best railroad and highway pass in Washington, and indeed it is the only pass in Washington that has both a railroad and an interstate highway.

The first survey to try to identify a route through the Cascades took place in 1853, when George R. McClellan (later a Union general in the Civil War) was commissioned for the job by the governor of Washington Territory. His report was full of errors. Of the 11 passes he considered possibilities for a railroad route, he did not include Snoqualmie—the widest and gentlest pass with the fewest engineering obstacles.

The survey was completed by someone else in 1854, but scandals and land schemes delayed selection of Snoqualmie as a railroad route until 1880. The route through Stampede Pass (which the PCT crosses just to the south, in the section covered in chapter 16) was actually completed first.

In 1865 the first wagon road crossed the pass. In 1914 it became a highway that was the precursor of Interstate 90, now the busiest crossing of the Cascades in Washington.

Stevens Pass

At the northern end of this section, Stevens Pass is also crossed by a railroad. The pass is named for John F. Stevens, the engineer for the Great Northern Railway who in 1890 surveyed and recommended the route.

At 4,062 feet in elevation, Stevens Pass was a much more difficult proposition than Snoqualmie Pass, elevation 3,030 feet. The first rail route over Stevens Pass, which opened in 1893, used switchbacks to climb the steep grades. (Just north of Stevens Pass, the PCT follows some of this old railway grade.) Between 1897 and 1900, a 3-mile tunnel was added, eliminating the need for some of the switchbacks. In 1929 the route used today was constructed, which uses an 8-mile-long tunnel. Skykomish, on the western side of the tunnel, became a railroad town—a major hub of activity on the western slope. (The name is that of a local Indian tribe; it translates as *inland people*.)

Ascending into Alpine Lakes Wilderness

Alpine Lakes Wilderness

Aptly called the "backyard wilderness," the Alpine Lakes Wilderness is easily accessible from metropolitan Seattle. Nestled between Interstate 90 and Highway 2, the 393,000-acre wilderness has become one of the most popular hiking destinations in Washington. It was also the site of a long and protracted battle between timber companies, the Forest Service, recreation groups, and conservation organizations.

The battle dates back almost 70 years. In the 1930s, conservation and recreation groups became concerned about the long-term prospects for this beautiful but threatened area. The Forest Service was traditionally sympathetic to the timber companies; its efforts at protection had been limited to identifying parts of the region that might be considered suitable for potential wilderness status. Meanwhile, the conservation groups—The Mountaineers, the North Cascades Conservation Council, the Sierra Club, and the Mazamas—made the mistake of trying to deal as separate entities, with similar but independent agendas, with the Forest Service. The waters became further muddied when recreation groups started lobbying for and against each other's ideas.

The passage of the Wilderness Act of 1964 gave conservation groups some leverage by taking away the right to designate wilderness from the Forest Service and giving it to Congress, but still no resolution was reached. Then, in 1968, the North Cascades National Park was created, putting some land that had been under Forest Service management under the control of the National Park Service. With the Cascades National Park lost to them, timber interests now turned their attention back to the Alpine Lakes area. This new threat motivated the four conservation-oriented organizations to mobilize and unite. In 1968 they agreed to act together by forming ALPS (Alpine Lakes Protection Society) and briefing members of Congress on the details of the situation—including maneuvering by the Forest Service, timber interests, and developers, all of whom wanted to prevent wilderness designation. Finally, in 1976, Congress established the Alpine Lakes Wilderness Area.

Today, overuse of the area is still a problem. Now, however, users come armed not with chain saws but with trekking poles. Because of its accessibility, Alpine Lakes Wilderness on a sunny August weekend can be jam-packed with hikers, which has led to a permit system and strict camping and fire regulations. The last chapter of the story of the protection of this magnificent area remains to be written.

🚶🚶 HIKING INFORMATION

Seasonal Information and Gear Tips
Here again, the hiking season is July through early October.

- Typical summer gear. for this section is three-season alpine: shorts and T-shirts for walking during the day and a light layer of polypro for night. Bring a lightweight fleece layer, a hat, and rain gear just in case.
- In early or late season (early and mid-July or September and October), you'll want another layer.
- If you have a choice, go with a fiber-fill rather than a down sleeping bag. Fiber-fill bags retain their heat insulating capacity better if they get wet.
- In July and early August, consider taking a tent rather than a tarp for mosquito protection.

Thru-hikers' Corner
This section is generally a good one for northbound thru-hikers, if the weather holds. Northbounders arrive in late August or September, which is Washington's prime hiking season.

For southbounders, passage is still touch-and-go because of the possibility of lingering snow. Early in the season, you may find the high country still impassable. However, one thing that is true of southbound thru-hiking is this: If you've made it through the Glacier Peaks Wilderness to the north, everything to the south is easier (until, that is, you face new and different challenges in the Sierra and southern California). How much snow you'll face in the Alpine Lakes Wilderness depends on how early you start your hike and what the snow accumulation has been that year. Hang onto your ice ax.

Best Short Hikes

This roadless 75-mile section can't be conveniently divided into shorter hikes. However, day hiking north of Snoqualmie Pass offers strong hikers a chance to get a good uphill workout with a scenic reward—6.4 miles takes you 2,400 feet to the Cascade Crest. Going back is a lot easier! (*Note:* In the Alpine Lakes Wilderness, even day hikers need permits. See appendix A.)

Resupplies and Trailheads

Snoqualmie Pass (mile 0) at Interstate 90 is approximately 50 miles east of Seattle and is accessible via Greyhound Bus. The pass is right on the trail. It offers a motel, a post office, and a couple of basic stores and restaurants. Post office: General Delivery, Snoqualmie Pass, WA 98068

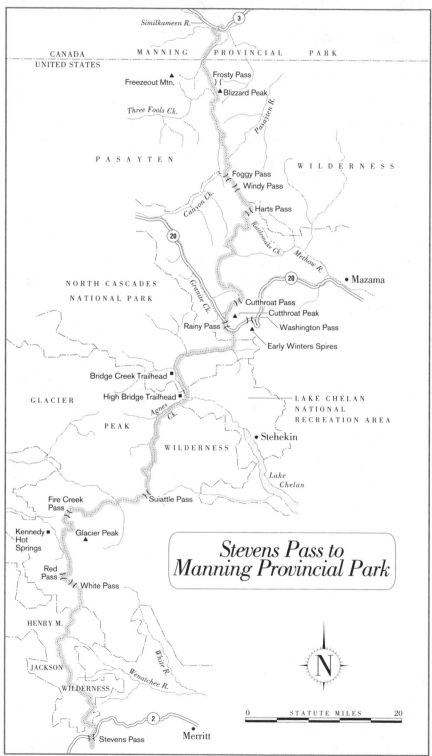

Similkameen R.

③

CANADA
UNITED STATES

MANNING   PROVINCIAL   PARK

Freezeout Mtn. ▲

Frosty Pass
▲ Blizzard Peak

Three Fools Ck.

Pasayten R.

P A S A Y T E N   W I L D E R N E S S

Foggy Pass
Windy Pass

Canyon Ck.

Harts Pass

Rattlesnake Ck.

Methow R.

②⓪

NORTH CASCADES
NATIONAL PARK

Granite Ck.

②⓪

• Mazama

Cutthroat Pass
▲   Cutthroat Peak

Rainy Pass   ▲   Washington Pass

Early Winters Spires

Bridge Creek Trailhead ■

High Bridge Trailhead ■

Agnes Ck.

G L A C I E R

LAKE CHELAN
NATIONAL
RECREATION AREA

P E A K

W I L D E R N E S S

• Stehekin

Lake
Chelan

Fire Creek
Pass

Suiattle Pass

Kennedy ■
Hot
Springs

Glacier Peak ▲

Red
Pass

White Pass

*Stevens Pass to
Manning Provincial Park*

HENRY M.

White R.

JACKSON

Wenatchee R.

WILDERNESS

②

N

0   STATUTE MILES   20

Stevens Pass

Merritt

Paul Woodward, © 2000 The Countryman Press

18

Stevens Pass to Manning Provincial Park, Canada

187.1 miles

"The mountains of the Pacific Northwest are tangled, wild, remote and high," writes William O. Douglas,

> *They have the roar of torrents and avalanches in their throats.*
> *There are no slow moving, sluggish rivers in these mountains.*
> *The streams run clear, cold, and fast. There are remote valleys*
> *and canyons where man has never been. The meadows and lakes*
> *are not placid, idyllic spots. The sternness of the mountains has*
> *been imparted to them . . . Trails may climb 4,000 feet or more*
> *in two miles. In twenty miles of travel one may gain, then lose,*
> *then gain and lose once more, several thousand feet of elevation.*
> *The blights of forest fires, overgrazing, avalanches, and excessive*
> *lumbering have touched parts of this vast domain. But civiliza-*
> *tion has left the total scene in strange degree alone.*

The first part of this section, from Stevens Pass to Stehekin River Road, runs through the Henry M. Jackson and Glacier Peak Wildernesses. With a combination of rugged terrain, many climbs, isolation, and potentially stormy weather, this stretch of trail is often considered one of the most difficult on the entire PCT. It's also one of the most varied and beautiful. The landscape ranges from glacier-scoured bowls to old-growth forests; elevations range from 1,550 to 7,126, and the weather can challenge hikers with four seasons' worth of conditions, sometimes in a single day.

The second section of this hike begins at Stehekin River Road, from which it climbs to 6,820 feet at Cutthroat Pass and pretty much stays high from there to Canada. Frequently above tree line, and almost always with sweeping views, this northernmost section is, in fact, the highest stretch on the Washington PCT. It rises above 7,000 feet only a few miles from the Canadian border. The toponyms—Cloudy Pass, Early Winters Pass, and Foggy Pass—give fair warning and something to think about when planning a hike early or late in the season. Nonetheless, this last, northernmost section of the Pacific Crest Trail is a fittingly dramatic finale, as well as a fine 187-mile hike. (Figure two weeks if you're in decent shape, 10 days if you're in tip-top thru-hiking shape.)

THE ROUTE

This section begins in forest, following an old railroad grade just north of Stevens Pass. Several lakes, including Valhalla, Janus, and pretty little Sally Ann (really a tarn), offer beautiful, if popular, campsites in the first 2 days.

Having gained elevation, the trail stays high and scenic. The traverse between White Pass (yes, another White Pass) and Red Pass is especially rewarding, with views of the Monte Cristo Peaks to the west, as well as Grizzly, Glacier, and Kodiak Peaks to the north and a peek back to Mount Rainier, still floating above the clouds on the southern skyline.

After Red Pass, the trail descends into a rocky, windswept basin as it approaches Glacier Peak. A few miles below Red Pass, hikers can detour to Kennedy Hot Springs (see page 289). Continuing north, the PCT begins 30 miles of climbing and descending the ridges of Glacier Peak, a forbidding, raw, ice-scoured monster of a mountain. Construction of a level, contouring trail—such as the one that circles Mount Adams—was considered impossible here because Glacier Peak was simply too steep and too prone to avalanches. So instead, the PCT continuously ascends and descends the mountain's many sidewalls and ridges.

Even this route cannot avoid the peak's occasional wrath. Campsites can be snow-covered until the middle of summer, and bridges are frequently washed out by flooding. If you are lucky enough to have a clear

White Pass to Red Pass traverse

day, expect unforgettable, magnificent, awe-inspiring views of Glacier Peak each time you climb to another vantage point and see it from a different angle. As in the Alpine Lakes Wilderness, most of the trail here is well-maintained, but the Forest Service and volunteer crews sometimes fall behind the alders and erosion, especially on the steep sidewalls. In wet weather, especially, this can make for tedious going.

At the lower elevations, this section introduces hikers to a completely unique ecosystem: the old-growth forests of the Pacific Northwest. Especially noteworthy are Vista and Agnes Creeks, where thousand-year-old western red cedars and Douglas firs loom over the forests you've thus far seen, like Mount Rainier looms above the Cascadian landscape—overwhelmingly out of proportion.

Just after Suiattle Pass, hikers can take a shortcut on the old PCT route, which makes a quick descent down to the Agnes Creek drainage and rejoins the new route at Hemlock Camp. This saves several miles, so it might be a good option if you're racing bad weather. However, the longer, official PCT circles around the base of two glacially scoured bowls, the first of which is cluttered with rocks the size of houses—an unforgettable spectacle that is well worth the extra effort.

Agnes Creek

Once in the Agnes Creek drainage, the trail meanders through several more miles of majestic old-growth forest before entering the Lake Chelan National Recreation Area. Shortly after, it arrives at High Bridge Trailhead at the Stehekin River Road, where there is a shelter, and where hikers can hop on a National Park Service shuttle that makes regularly scheduled runs several times a day between the trailheads and the village of Stehekin. The trail then parallels the Stehekin River Road for 5 miles before reaching the Bridge Creek trailhead, which also has a shelter and a shuttle stop. Confirm the schedule in advance, however. In early and late season, the shuttles run less frequently than in midsummer.

Leaving Stehekin River Road, the trail gently climbs 3,255 feet to well-named Rainy Pass, where it intersects Washington Highway 20, the main thoroughfare through North Cascades National Park. From Rainy Pass, the trail continues upward another 1,965 feet to Cutthroat Pass (named not after criminals, but after the trout that inhabit nearby streams). Highlights of the upcoming high-country traverse include the alpine ridge-walks from Cutthroat Pass to Methow Pass, from Glacier Pass to Harts Pass, and from Windy Pass to Hopkins Lake.

The PCT ends at the clear-cut that marks the U.S.-Canadian border. On the Canadian side, you'll find plenty of obviously oft-used campsites. From there, it's a 7-mile walk to Manning Provincial Park headquarters and Canadian Highway 3.

WHAT YOU'LL SEE

Glaciers

The North Cascades have been described as being in a contemporary ice age. The range contains more than half of all the active glaciers in the 48 contiguous states, with 318 glaciers alone in North Cascades National Park (and even more outside the park's boundaries). But the glaciers that patiently carve the mountains even today are only small remnants of a much more extensive set of ice sheets.

Evidence of this extensive past glaciation includes the rubble left behind when the glaciers retreated (terminal and lateral moraines, the mixture of stone types on the valley floors, and the huge boulder fields just north of Suiattle Pass), the classical glaciated formations of cirques and headwalls in the high country, the steep-walled valleys, and 50-mile-long Lake Chelan, which was carved and filled by a glacier.

Glacial debris

View of Glacier Peak from the ascent to Fire Creek Pass

Glacier Peak

At 10,541 feet, Glacier Peak is the dominant mountain on the PCT in the North Cascades, and its glaciers are among the PCT's most dramatic. Glacier Peak is one of the North Cascades' two volcanic peaks, a mountain created by both fire and ice. It is also the most glacially eroded peak in the North Cascades. Indians called it Da Kobad—Great White Mother Mountain.

"Glacier Peak is not visible from any major highway," noted Douglas in *Man and Wilderness.* "Foothills hide the alpine area. The peaks are locked in a remote area that is a true recluse. This inner realm is remote and exquisite."

"Surrounded by deep valleys, cliffs, and forbidding ramparts of ice, Glacier Peak bestows familiarity only to those willing to strive for it," says geologist Stephen Harris.

As a result of its isolation and difficulty, Glacier Peak is one of the Cascades' least-visited major peaks.

Glacier Peak's most recent major eruptions occurred between 12,000 and 13,500 years ago, with an explosion second only to Mount Mazama's. It laid down a layer of pumice 12 feet thick as far away as 12 miles, and chunks of the mountain ended up in Idaho and Oregon. The same explosion deposited a layer of ash that covered most of eastern Washington, northeast Oregon, the Idaho Panhandle, western Montana, and parts of southern Canada.

Glacier Peak is extremely steep. One of the reasons is that its summit cone was built on an already existing high ridge. As a result, it has a high, narrow, and erosion-prone summit cone. Frequent rockslides have often altered the Suiattle River drainage.

Not studied until recently because of its remoteness, Glacier Peak is now considered extinct by most geologists.

Hoary marmot

Kennedy Hot Springs

Geologists might consider Glacier Peak extinct, but the underlying land is far from quiet. A few miles north of Red Pass, hikers can detour to visit Kennedy Hot Springs, where Glacier Peak's magma bubbles close beneath the surface. Don't expect solitude—this hot spring is accessible to day hikers from a side trail.

To reach the hot springs from Sitkum Creek, you can opt to take Trail 643 down to Kennedy Hot Springs, with adjacent camping. From there, follow Trail 643 a quarter-mile more to a junction with 643A, which climbs back to the PCT. This 3.25-mile alternate route is 1.6 miles longer than the PCT and involves 1,025 feet of lost (and regained) elevation.

North Cascades Ecology

Hikers doing even a small part of this section can't help but be impressed with the ecological variety to be found here. There are four distinct ecological areas in the North Cascades. Hikers walk through three of them, and have ample views of the fourth.

Valley Bottoms. The classical U-shaped valleys are covered with dense, lush, coniferous forests of red cedar, spruce, hemlock, and fir. This is the realm of the old-growth forest. Higher up, cottonwood and willow also thrive on deep soils that hold ample amounts of water.

Sidewalls. The scouring action of the glaciers left behind steep walls:

Alpine gardens of hardy high-country plants

cliffs and exposed rocky outcrops. Because they are higher than the valleys, the sidewalls attract more precipitation. Because they are subject to erosion, they have thin soils that cannot hold moisture. As a result, most precipitation runs off quickly and produces deep gullies, often covered in alder. (It also erodes the trail.)

Vegetation that grows on the sidewalls has to deal with the evaporative effects of strong wind and exposure to sun. Trees are smaller, and woody plants like huckleberry thrive—making climbs up and down the side a slow but tasty process during September's peak berry season.

Alpine and subalpine zones. Long harsh winters, thin sandy soil, minimal summer moisture, and high evaporation are only some of the challenges plants and animals face in the alpine and subalpine zones. The plants that do manage to adapt grow low to the ground, to escape the wind, and have most of their mass underground, where it can be to somewhat insulated from the elements. Because of the dry summer growing season, these alpine plants must, like cacti, be able to hold any moisture that comes their way. To reduce water loss, they have only a few small leaves. Many of the leaves are covered in a layer of fuzz, which helps them to catch and hold water.

Rock and ice. Above the alpine meadows, even the hardy high-country vegetation surrenders to the elements. The ground cover is chunks of rock, which might occasionally support a colony of lichen and not much else. At its highest elevations in Washington, the PCT just barely skirts the edge of the rock-and-ice zone. Hikers wanting more can challenge themselves on Glacier Peak—but only if they have mountaineering equipment and the necessary skills.

Old-growth Forests

By this point in time, thru-hikers might be excused for thinking they've seen everything the Pacific Crest Trail has to offer, from deserts to lava fields to glaciers to gorges. But now, the trail introduces something entirely new—and utterly unforgettable. As the trail wends its way up and down the ridges of Glacier Peak, it descends into a magical, misty forest—the realm of the giant trees of the old-growth forests. The most stunning examples are found along Vista and Agnes Creeks.

Spotted owl

Old-growth forests are defined as forest systems which have not been catastrophically impacted either by human activities or by natural and geologic processes. At the minimum, an old-growth forest is 200 years old. But the ancient forests of the Pacific Northwest are more commonly 350 to 750 years of age, with some stands of 1,000 years or more. Some individual trees can reach ages of up to 3,500 years (making them some of the oldest trees on earth).

The numbers are impressive: the height of the trees, the length of time they can live. Walking along the trail, you'll come face to face with some of the other marvels. The base of the western red cedars, for one: The circumference of these magnificent trees can reach an astonishing 30 or more feet. Even the mushrooms are big here, some species measuring almost a foot in diameter.

Another thing you'll undoubtedly notice are the vast number of fallen and rotting trees that lie cluttered all over each other, as though God himself (a mere giant wouldn't be big enough) had been playing a game of pickup sticks. Sometimes the logs are piled so high that it is impossible to imagine how someone could walk though the forest without the aid of a trail. Dead these trees may be, but they play a vital role in the forest ecosystem, providing nesting sites for small animals and birds, a food source for plants, protection from predators, and shelter from weather. It can take more than 500 years for a log to decay (even though the forest is almost continually moist), during which time it performs all those functions. You'll often see one of these so-called nurse logs supporting a virtual garden of smaller plants that are growing right on it. Think of them as incubators for a new generation of great trees—as well as shrubs, ferns, lichens, and fungi.

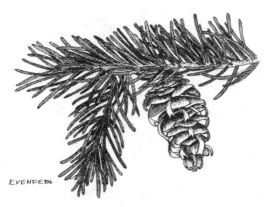

EVENPEDI

Douglas fir

The diversity of plant life, from seedlings to thousand-year giants, creates habitat for a wide variety of species, and indeed, old-growth forests are richer in wildlife than their second-growth counterparts. Some species, like the endangered spotted owl, are found nowhere else.

Adapted for life in a difficult environment, old-growth forests can survive long winters, low temperatures, high snowfall, and a dry summer growing season. But they may not be able to survive human economics. The trees have enormous commercial value. Red cedars, for example, are easily split, and their long-lasting, rot-resistant wood is ideal for shingles. Douglas firs are the most valuable timber species in the world. Their strong wood is highly sought for framing houses and making plywood. Logging has, in fact, eliminated almost all old-growth forests on private land, and on much public land as well. More than 90 percent of the Pacific Northwest's ancient forests have been cut down. Realistically speaking, considering their thousand-year life cycles, they can never be replaced.

Lake Chelan and Stehekin

Fifty miles long and one mile wide, Lake Chelan was originally a depression cut by stream erosion. During the Ice Age, the depression filled with ice; the pressure of the ice sculpted the valley and the lake into their present shapes. The thickest ice produced what is now the deepest part of the lake, which is 1,149 feet deep—actually 340 feet below sea level. (The name of the lake derives from the Native American words *Tsill-Anne*, or *deep water.*)

The lake itself was formed when the Columbia River Glacier retreated and left behind a moraine that dammed the water so that it became a lake rather than a free-flowing river. Later a dam was built because the moraine was in danger of collapsing from erosion. The dam raised the water level 21 feet.

Today's settlement of Stehekin is an isolated community on the lake's western shore. You can get there by boat, ferry, floatplane, or foot—but you can't get there by car. No roads go to this small lakefront town, although if you're a permanent or seasonal resident, you can have your car shipped in. (Once you do, you can drive it along the community's single 10.6-mile-long road, which leads to the PCT trailheads.) It's ironic, then, that the name for such an inaccessible place translates from the local Indian dialect as *the pass* or *the way through*. Sauk Indians entered the Cascades here to cross the Cascade Crest over Suiattle Pass to trade with the Wenatchee people to the west.

Stehekin was settled in the 1880s as a mining and trapping community, but neither activity was successful. Today there are still a few small ranches, but the town is mostly supported by the recreation industry and second homes. Much of the land is owned and managed by the National Park Service as part of the Lake Chelan National Recreation Area.

North Cascades National Park

North Cascades National Park is really a complex of four areas: North Cascades National Park (split into two sections—north and south), Ross Lake National Recreation Area (which separates the two units of the park), and Lake Chelan National Recreation Area.

The PCT passes through the Lake Chelan National Recreation Area and, for about 15 miles between Stehekin and Rainy Pass, through the southern section of North Cascades National Park. Ninety-three percent of North Cascades National Park is managed as wilderness.

Harts Pass

This northernmost section of the Pacific Crest Trail is one of its most remote. In this section, there is only one paved road, the North Cascades Highway (Highway 20), which crosses the PCT at Rainy Pass. The only other road that the PCT crosses is Forest Road 5400 at Harts Pass, which offers one of the last chances for hikers to bail out in bad weather.

The road opened in 1895 to access mines that scoured the earth for copper, silver, zinc, and lead. The pass was named after Captain Del Hart, owner of the Bonita Mine, one of the more successful mining operations in the Slate Creek area. In 1895, Hart commissioned Charles H. Ballard to survey a road connecting the mining areas to the town of Mazama. Most miners abandoned this area when the Klondike boom began. Detritus of mining operations still remains in the Benson Creek Camp area below Windy Pass.

Mount Baker

Mount Baker is not on the route of the PCT, but it is the other major volcanic peak in the North Cascades, and it dominates the view to the west from the ridges just north of Harts Pass. It rises to 10,778 feet, and its size is emphasized by the fact that it stands some 5,000 feet above the ridges that surround it. There is no proof of any major eruption for several thousand years, but in the 1840s (and again in 1975) it sporadically emitted steam and ash. It is now being carefully studied for the first time.

HIKING INFORMATION

Seasonal Information and Gear Tips

You might not believe it when confronted with a snowstorm in July, but there is actually a slight rain shadow in effect as you go north in this section. The Cascades are shaped somewhat like a wedge. While they are only 30 miles wide in the south, in the north they can be as much as 80 miles wide. As the PCT goes north, it veers toward the eastern side of the range. After Rainy Pass, most of the Cascades are to the west of the trail. Since the storms here are fed by eastward-moving Pacific ocean moisture, the western side of the range collects most of the precipitation. Most, but not all—there's plenty of rain to go around. For a real rain shadow, you have to drop into the flatlands a few miles to the east.

The best time to hike this section is in August and early September. In June, the high country is snow-covered; in July, mosquitoes rule the forests. In August, the mosquitoes begin to abate and the weather is generally good. September can be pleasant, or it can engulf you in the Northwest's version of a monsoon. The later in the month, the colder the rain and the higher the possibility of early winter storms. By

October, the wet season starts in earnest and winter is usually blowing its frosty breath. Although in some years it is possible to hike through part of October, snow is always on the horizon.

- Gear you'll need depends on the season in which you'll be hiking. In mosquito season take a tent, and if you're especially sensitive, a head net and plenty of DEET.
- In midsummer, your clothing bag should contain a layer of polypro or the equivalent for nights, plus an additional light weight layer (maybe a fleece or microfleece jacket and a hat).
- Good raingear is essential.

Thru-hikers' Corner

This section's high elevations and unpredictable weather offer some potentially severe challenges to thru-hikers, no matter which way you're going. Southbound thru-hikers attempting to start their hikes in June will almost invariably be mired in snow at least some of the time—and frequently, the snow lasts well into July. In a high snow year, southbounders who start in June usually have tales to tell of miles of deep snow above tree line, snow-choked passes, and navigating for miles on end with map and compass. Most also admit to taking lower, alternate routes because of dangerous or impassable conditions. Do not underestimate this traverse—even if the rumor mill tells you it's been a light snow year. The definition of light snow in the North Cascades has its own idiosyncratic meaning.

Northbound thru-hikers have it a little easier—if, that is, they get here soon enough. Most northbound thru-hikers arrive in Washington in September. Although it is possible to complete a thru-hike until the middle of October, after October 1 you're rolling the dice. It is not uncommon for early-season snows to shut the high country in the first week of October. There is no easy way to bail out if you're stuck here in the snow. Keep one eye on the weather—and keep moving. Because thru-hikers hit the North Cascades either at the very beginning or the very end of the hiking season, this is not a good place to try out ultralight hiking techniques. Even if ultralight hiking has served you well in the previous miles, you'd be well-advised to bite the bul-

Taking notes at Red Pass

let and pack some extra equipment in this section. Late-season northbounders should have boots and enough warm clothes to handle snow and potentially many continuous days of cold rain. Southbounders starting in June or early July should additionally have an ice ax and good map and compass skills.

In addition to its environmental challenges, the PCT in the North Cascades throws one more at hikers traveling ultra-light: In the North Cascades, the PCT traverses some of the most remote wilderness in the contiguous United States. For many miles, there is not so much as a dirt Forest Service Road. Once you're in the middle of this wilderness, it can take several days to find a way out if conditions get bad. If you're hiking on the edges of the season, be sure to bring along a good comprehensive map of the area so you can find alternate routes. (*Warning:* There aren't many of them.) It is not at all unusual for early- and late-season hikers to be surprised by suddenly impassable conditions that force long detours. Early-season hikers, in particular, often have difficulty in the area of Fire Creek Pass in the Glacier Peaks Wilderness.

When you get to the Canadian border, take a moment to add your name to the register that is kept inside the border monument, which you'll recognize from the Mexican border such a long time ago. There's a hinge on this monument, which allows you to lift the top from the base. Inside the base, there's usually a register. Plan to spend a few minutes absorbing the entirety of what you've just achieved—a thru-hike of one of the greatest footpaths in the world!

Best Short Hikes

This section can be conveniently divided into two shorter sections, each of which makes for a good long backpack. The midpoint is Stehekin River Road (or, if you prefer, Highway 20 at Rainy Pass; your decision will depend on both mileage and transportation logistics.) To get to Stehekin (or to leave from Stehekin) requires taking a trip on the Lady of the Lake ferry up Lake Chelan; the town of Stehekin is not accessible by car. For information, call 509-682-4584.

- From Stevens Pass on Highway 2, it's a 98-mile hike to the Agnes Creek trailhead on Stehekin River Road (or 118 miles to Rainy Pass). This section is the most varied and dramatic because of its proximity to Glacier Peak and because it spends time in the old-growth forests.
- From the Bridge Creek trailhead on Stehekin River Road to Manning Provincial Park in Canada, it's 85 miles (if you start at Rainy Pass, it's 70 miles). This section is one of the highest in Washington, with mile after mile of high-country views. If you're an alpine addict, this is your hike.
- Day hikers can spend a pleasant day going north from Stevens Pass (Highway 2). Lake Valhalla, a lovely destination, is 5.5 miles.
- Another good day hike is to start at the Agnes Creek trailhead on the Stehekin River Road and go south into the old-growth forests.
- From Rainy Pass on Highway 20, day hikers can climb north to Cutthroat Pass for classic high Cascades scenery.
- The section between Harts Pass (Forest Road 5400) and Windy Pass offers a 5.2-mile high traverse, plus a look at what's left of some of the old mining operations.

Resupplies and Trailheads

Stevens Pass, Stehekin River Road, and Manning Park are the most commonly used.

Stevens Pass (mile 0). The PCT crosses Highway 2 at Stevens Pass, 15 miles east of Skykomish, which has motels, a convenience store, and a post office. Post office: General Delivery, Skykomish, WA 98288

Stehekin River Road (mile 97.8 and 102.7). The PCT crosses Stehekin River Road twice, at Bridge Creek and at High Bridge. A park shuttle runs several times a day between both trailheads and Stehekin, which has a campground, hotel, restaurant, laundry, post office, and a poorly stocked store. Post office: General Delivery, Stehekin, WA 98852

Rainy Pass (mile 117.5). The PCT crosses the North Cascades Highway (Highway 20) at Rainy Pass, 20 miles west of Mazama, which has more supplies than Stehekin. Most hikers choose Stehekin because you don't have to hitchhike.

Harts Pass (mile 148.0). Emergency bail-out to Mazama is possible via a gravel road, but it's not well-traveled.

Manning Provincial Park (British Columbia, Canada) (mile 187.1). The end (or beginning) of your journey. The park has a hotel and restaurant and there is Greyhound bus service to Vancouver or Osoyoos (from which you can connect on the Empire bus line to Ellensburg, Washington). Canadian Greyhound goes to Vancouver twice a day, late morning and early evening. Call 1-800-661-8747 for the schedule; the trip takes about 5 hours. From Vancouver to Seattle, you can take Greyhound (1-800-231-2222) or Amtrak (1-800-972-7245).

Appendix A: Agencies and Permits

Wilderness permits are increasingly being required to camp along much of the PCT. Permits for overnight trips are required in most national park lands along the PCT and in many wildernesses. Some areas also require day hikers to have permits. In addition, fees have been implemented in many national forests, especially for parking at or near a trailhead.

In some wildernesses, backcountry permits are self-issuing (you fill out the form when you enter the wilderness, drop one copy in a locked box, and carry the other). In others, you need to call or write to make arrangements in advance. If you will be hiking for more than 500 miles, you can ask the Pacific Crest Trail Association for a thru-hiker's permit, which is good for your entire hike: PCTA, 5324 Elkhorn Boulevard, #256, Sacramento, CA 95842; 1-888-PCTRAIL; www.pcta.org.

If you are hiking less than 500 miles, you do not need a separate permit for each forest, park, and wilderness on your route. Instead, contact the agency that manages the land where you will be *starting* your hike. Give them a rough itinerary and ask for a joint use permit.

You will also need a California campfire permit—even if you are only planning to use a stove! (The permit is available from any national forest office.)

Both permit and fee regulations are constantly changing. Following are the agencies to contact for up-to-date rules. The list is in geographical order, from south to north.

Bureau of Land Management
333 S. Waterman Avenue
El Centro, CA 92243
760-337-4400
No permit required for any BLM area

Bureau of Land Management
1695 Spruce Street
Riverside, CA 92507
909-337-4400
No permit required

Cleveland National Forest (including Hauser Wilderness)
10845 Rancho Bernardo Road, Suite 200
San Diego, CA 92127-2127
858-674-2901
Wilderness permit required

San Bernardino National Forest
1824 S. Commercenter Circle
San Bernardino, CA 92408
909-383-5588
Wilderness permit required

San Jacinto Wilderness
Idyllwild Ranger Station
P.O. Box 518
Idyllwild, CA 92408
909-659-2117
Wilderness permit required

Angeles National Forest and Sheep Mountain Wilderness
701 N. Santa Anita Avenue
Arcadia, CA 91006
626-574-5200
No permit required

Bureau of Land Management
Kiavah, Owens Peak, Dome Land Wildernesses
3801 Pegasus Drive
Bakersfield, CA 93308-6837
661-391-6000
No permit required

Sequoia and Kings Canyon National Parks
   and Dome Land West, South Sierra and Golden Trout Wildernesses
Backcountry Permits Office
Three Rivers, CA 93271
559-784-1500
Wilderness permit required, $10 fee

Inyo National Forest and John Muir Wilderness
873 N. Main Street
Bishop, CA 93514
760-873-2400
No permit required

Sierra National Forest (including John Muir Wilderness)
1600 Tollhouse Road
Clovis, CA 93612
209-297-0706
Wilderness permit required; self-issuing

Ansel Adams Wilderness
Mammoth Ranger District
P.O. Box 148
Mammoth Lakes, CA 93546
760-924-5500
Wilderness permit required

Yosemite National Park, Wilderness Office
P.O. Box 577
Yosemite, CA 95389
Main number: 209-372-0200; Wilderness permit number: 209-372-0740
Wilderness permit required

Stanislaus National Forest
19777 Greenley Road
Sonora, CA 95370
209-532-3434
Wilderness permit required

Emigrant Wilderness and Carson-Iceberg Wilderness,
   Mokelumne Wilderness
Calaveras Ranger Station for information: 209-795-1381
Wilderness permit required

Eldorado National Forest
Information Center
3070 Camino Heights Drive
Camino, CA 95709
530-644-6048
Wilderness permit required, $5 fee

Desolation Wilderness
Lake Tahoe Basin Management
870 Emerald Bay Road
S. Lake Tahoe, CA 95731
530-573-2600
Wilderness permit required

Tahoe National Forest
631 Coyote Street
Nevada City, CA 95959
530-265-4531
No permit required

Granite Chief Wilderness and Bucks Lake Wilderness
Plumas National Forest
P.O. Box 11500
Quincy, CA 95971
530-283-2050
No permit required

Lassen National Forest
55 S. Sacramento Street
Susanville, CA 96130
530-257-2151
No permit required

Lassen National Park
P.O. Box 100
Mineral, CA 96063
530-595-4444
No permit required

Shasta-Trinity National Forest (including Castle Crags and
   Trinity Alps Wildernesses)
2400 Washington Avenue
Redding, CA 96001
530-926-5411
Wilderness permit required

Klamath National Forest (including Russian and
   Marble Mountain Wildernesses)
1312 Fairlane Road
Yreka, CA 96097
530-842-6131
No permit required

Rogue River National Forest (including Red Buttes Wilderness)
P.O. Box 520
Medford, OR 97501
541-858-2200
No permit required

Winema National Forest
2819 Dahlia Street
Klamath Falls, OR 97601
541-883-6714
No permit required

Crater Lake National Forest
P.O. Box 7
Crater Lake, OR 97604
541-594-2211
No permit required

Umpqua National Forest
P.O. Box 1008
Pineburg, OR 97470
541-672-6601
No permit required

Deschutes National Forest
1645 Highway 20 East
Bend, OR 97701
541-388-2715
Wilderness permit required; self-issuing

Willamette National Forest
P.O. Box 10607
Eugene, OR 97440-2607
541-465-6521
Wilderness permit required; self-issuing

Mount Hood National Forest
2955 N.W. Division Street
Gresham, OR 97030
503-622-7674
*Wilderness permit required; subject to change due to environmental
  policy changes*

Gifford Pinchot National Forest
6926 E. Fourth Plain Boulevard
Vancouver, WA 98668-8944
360-891-5000
Wilderness permit required; self-issuing

Mount Baker-Snoqualmie National Forest
1022 First Avenue
Seattle, WA 98104
425-775-9702
No permit required

Tahoma Woods
Star Route
Ashford, WA 98304
360-569-2211
Wilderness permit required two months in advance

Wenatchee National Forest
P.O. Box 811
Wenatchee, WA 98807
509-548-6977
Wilderness permit required

North Cascades National Park
2105 Highway 20
Sedro Woolley, WA 98284
360-856-5700
Wilderness permit for overnight

Okanogan National Forest
P.O. Box 950
Okanogan, WA 98840
509-826-3275
No permit required

Appendix B: Suggested Reading

Guides and Reference Works

Berger, Karen. *Advanced Backpacking: A Trailside Guide*. New York: W.W. Norton & Company, 1998.
Covers all of the essential elements needed to plan and prepare for a long-distance hike.

Croot, Leslie C. *Pacific Crest Trail Town Guide*. Sacramento, CA: Pacific Crest Trail Association, 1999.

Darvill, Fred T. *Mountaineering Medicine*. Berkeley, CA: Wilderness Press, 1992.
The classic reference work for backcountry health and safety.

Fleming, June. *Staying Found: The Complete Map and Compass Handbook*. Seattle, WA: The Mountaineers, 1994.
A step-by-step guide to map reading and land navigation skills.

Fletcher, Colin. *The Complete Walker III*. New York: Knopf, 1984.
The how-to bible, written by one of the world's premier long-distance walkers.

Go, Benedict. *Pacific Crest Trail Data Book*. Sacramento, CA: Pacific Crest Trail Association, 1997.

Jardine, Ray. *Beyond Backpacking*. LaPine, OR: Adventurelore Press, 1999.
Ultra-light backpacking strategies.

———. *The Pacific Crest Trail Handbook*. LaPine, OR: Adventurelore Press, 1997.
A guide to super-lightweight backpacking combined with an orientation to Jardine's philosophy of outdoor travel.

Schaffer, Jeffrey P. et al. *The Pacific Crest Trail, Vol. I: California*. Berkeley, CA: Wilderness Press, 1996

———. *The Pacific Crest Trail, Vol. II: Oregon and Washington.*
Berkeley, CA: Wilderness Press, 1990.
The essential guidebooks for any long-distance journey on the Pacific Crest Trail.

Hikers' Journeys: The Early Days

Clarke, Clinton C. *The Pacific Crest Trailway.* Pasadena, CA: The Pacific Crest Trail System Conference, 1945.
The dream of establishing a crest trail told by the visionary who was one of the first to conceive the idea of a border-to-border trail.
Douglas, William O. *Of Men and Mountains.* New York: Harper and Brothers Publishers, 1950.
Supreme Court Justice Douglas writes of his love for the Pacific Northwest.
———. *My Wilderness: The Pacific West.* Garden City, NY: Doubleday and Company, Inc., 1960.
Writing decades ago, Douglas foresaw many of the present-day challenges of the preservation of the wild areas of the Pacific Northwest.
Fletcher, Colin. *The Thousand-Mile Summer: In the Desert and High Sierra.* Berkeley, CA: Howell-North Books, 1965.
The story of Fletcher's journey through Southern and Central California.
Hazard, Joseph T. *Pacific Crest Trails.* Seattle, WA: Superior Publishing Company, 1946.
The writing of one of the earliest activists involved in the creation of a Pacific Crest Trail.
King, Clarence. *Mountaineers in the Sierra Nevada.* Philadelphia, PA: J. B. Lippincott Company, 1963.
A reprint of the 1872 work by one of the early explorers of the High Sierra.
Knibbs, David. *Backyard Wilderness: The Alpine Lakes Story.* Seattle, WA: The Mountaineers, 1982.
The story of the battle to protect one of the premier wilderness areas of Washington.
Muir, John. *Nature Writings.* William Cronon, ed. New York: Library of America, 1997.

A comprehensive compilation of Muir's writings on virtually all aspects of the environment.

Hikers' Journeys: The Present Day

Berger, Karen, and Daniel Smith. *Along the Pacific Crest Trail.* Englewood, CO: Westcliffe, 1998.
With photographs by Bart Smith, the authors' account of a 1997 thru-hike.
Green, David. *A Pacific Crest Odyssey.* Berkeley, CA: Wilderness Press, 1974.
Hotel, Bob. *Soul, Sweat, and Survival on the Pacific Crest Trail.* Livermore, CA: Bittersweet, 1994.
Chronicles an endurance runner's journey along the Pacific Crest Trail.
Ross, Cindy. *Journey on the Crest: Walking 2,600 Miles from Mexico to Canada.* Seattle, WA: The Mountaineers, 1987.
A woman's tale of her two long-distance hikes.

Historical

Dowdell, Dorothy and Joseph. *Sierra Nevada: The Golden Barrier.* Indianapolis, IN: Bobbs-Merrill, 1968.
A social and economic history of the range.
Farquhar, Francis P. *A History of the Sierra Nevada.* Berkeley, CA: University of California Press, 1966.
A comprehensive and beautifully written story of the inhabitants, explorers, and pioneers of the region.

Geology and Natural History: California

Bakker, Elna. *An Island Called California.* Berkeley, CA: University of California Press, 1971.
An introduction to the environmental regions of the state.
Barbour, Michael et al. *California's Changing Landscapes: Diversity and Conservation of California's Vegetation.* Sacramento, CA: California Native Plant Society, 1993.
A guide to the biogeography of the state.

Hill, Mary. *California Landscape: Origin and Evolution.* Berkeley, CA: University of California Press, 1984.
An explanation, in lay terms, of the geologic forces that have created California's dominant physical features.

Jaeger, Edmund C. *The California Deserts.* Palo Alto, CA: Stanford University Press, 1965.
An introduction to the physical landscape, flowers, and plant life of California's desert communities.

McPhee, John. *Assembling California.* New York: Farrar, Straus, and Giroux, 1995.
A modern explanation of California's physical evolution aimed at novices in the field of geology.

Storer, Tracy I. and Robert L. Usinger. *Sierra Nevada Natural History.* Berkeley, CA: University of California Press, 1969.
A survey of the natural plant and animal communities of the range.

Geology and Natural History: Oregon and Washington

Baldwin, Ewart M. *Geology of Oregon.* Dubuque, IA: Kendall/Hunt, 1981.
A comprehensive analysis of the state's geologic regions.

Franklin, Jerry F. and C. J. Dyrnes. *Natural Vegetation of Oregon and Washington.* Portland, OR: United States Department of Agriculture, 1973.
A study of the plant communities of the Pacific Northwest.

Harris, Stephen L. *Fire and Ice: The Geology of the Pacific Northwest.* New York: McGraw-Hill, 1972.
An exhaustive analysis of the earth-forming processes that produced the Cascade Range.

Muellar, Marge and Ted. *Washington's South Cascades Volcanic Peaks.* Seattle, WA: The Mountaineers, 1995.
An examination of the evolution of the major peaks coupled with information about hiking and climbing opportunities.

Index